The Mathematical Theory of the Dynamics of Biological Populations II

Based on the proceedings of a conference on
The Mathematical Theory of the Dynamics of Biological Populations
organised by The Institute of Mathematics and its Applications
and held in Oxford, 1st-3rd July, 1980

Edited by

R. W. HIORNS

Department of Biomathematics
University of Oxford
Oxford, England

D. COOKE

School of Mathematical and Physical Sciences
University of Sussex
Brighton, England

1981

ACADEMIC PRESS

A Subsidiary of Harcourt Brace Jovanovich, Publishers

London New York Toronto Sydney San Francisco

ACADEMIC PRESS INC. (LONDON) LTD.
24/28 Oval Road,
London NW1

United States Edition published by
ACADEMIC PRESS INC.
111 Fifth Avenue
New York, New York 10003

British Library Cataloguing in Publication Data
The Mathematical Theory of the Dynamics of
  Biological Populations II
  1. Biology — Mathematical models — Congresses
  I. Hiorns, R. W.   II. Cooke, D.
  574.007'2   QH323.5

  ISBN 0-12-348780-3

  LCCCN 73-1468

Printed in Great Britain by
Whitstable Litho Ltd., Whitstable, Kent

CONTRIBUTORS

R.M. ANDERSON; *Imperial College Field Station, Silwood Park, Ascot, Berkshire SL5 7PY.*

M.S. BARTLETT, FRS; *Priory Orchard, Priory Avenue, Totnes, Devon TQ9 5HR.*

P. CLIFFORD; *University of Oxford, Mathematical Institute, 24-29 St. Giles, Oxford OX1 3LB.*

D. COOKE; *Department of Mathematics, University of Sussex, Falmer, Brighton BN1 9RH.*

R.M. CORMACK; *University of St. Andrews, Department of Statistics, The Mathematical Institute, North Haugh, St. Andrews KY16 9SS.*

R.N. CURNOW; *Department of Applied Statistics, University of Reading, Reading.*

K. DIETZ; *Institut Für Medizinische Biometrie, University Tubingen, 7400 Tubingen 1, Hallstattstrasse 6, Germany.*

J. GANI, FIMA; *CSIRO, Division of Mathematics and Statistics, P.O. Box 1965, Canberra City, ACT 2601, Australia.*

W.D. HAMILTON, FRS; *Museum of Zoology, The University of Michigan, Ann Arbor, Michigan, USA 48109.*

G.A. HARRISON; *Department of Biological Anthropology, University of Oxford, Pusey Street, Oxford OX1 2JZ.*

R.W. HIORNS, FIMA; *Department of Biomathematics, University of Oxford, Pusey Street, Oxford OX1 2JZ.*

R.A. KEMPTON; *Plant Breeding Institute, Maris Lane, Trumpington, Cambridge CB2 2LQ.*

S.A. LEVIN; *Section of Ecology and Systematics, Cornell University, Ithaca, NY 14850 USA.*

P.D.M. MACDONALD; *Department of Mathematical Sciences, McMaster University, 1280 Main Street West, Hamilton, Ontario L8S 4K1, USA.*

R.M. MAY, FRS; *Department of Biology, Princeton University, Princeton, New Jersey 08544 USA.*

D. MOLLISON; *Department of Mathematics, Heriot-Watt University, Edinburgh EH1 1EX.*

T.R.E. SOUTHWOOD, FRS; *Department of Zoology, South Parks Road, University of Oxford, Oxford.*

E.A. THOMPSON; *Statistics Laboratory, Department of Pure Mathematics and Mathematical Statistics, King's College, 16 Mill Lane, Cambridge CB2 1SB.*

PREFACE

This volume contains the papers read at a conference held in
Oxford in July 1980 on the Mathematical Theory of the Dynamics
of Biological Populations, arranged by the Institute of
Mathematics and its Applications. This meeting was envisaged
as a natural successor to the one held eight years previously
in Oxford under the same title, and the Organizing Committee on
this occasion consisted of Dr. R.W. Hiorns (Chairman) and
Professor P. Armitage (both of the Department of Biomathematics,
Oxford), Professor M.S. Bartlett, FRS (formerly of the
Department of Biomathematics, Oxford), Mr. R.J.H. Beverton,
CBE, FRS (NERC, Swindon) and Mr. D. Cooke (School of
Mathematical and Physical Sciences, Sussex).

The success of the previous conference in partly achieving
the main objective of developing an understanding between
biologists and mathematicians in certain key areas encouraged
the committee in planning the latest meeting. Some of the
emphasis in the approach of the mathematical models has changed
and some new key areas are covered. Although not all of the
desired topics and speakers could be included in the final
programme we were grateful for the very high rate of acceptance
by the invited speakers. The standard of presentation of the
papers was uniformly high and most of the contributions were
stimulating in the way we had hoped.

Recent advances have been made in the study of biological
populations from two key viewpoints: the stability and control
of populations, and the behaviour and structure of populations.
Although these aspects cannot be mutually exclusive in any study
of actual populations, they do serve as useful starting points
for mathematical analysis. Most of the contributions in the
present volume develop the discussion of a particular topic
from one or other of these viewpoints. Also included in some of
the papers are the biometrical aspects concerning the interpretation of population data relating to the phenomena found in
particular populations.

The conference proved to be of special interest to two types
of participant. On the one hand, the biologist who wishes to

explore the further contributions which mathematics and
statistics can make to his subject; and, on the other, the
mathematician who is interested in applying his talents outside
the traditional fields of applied mathematics. Likewise, we
trust that each of these two types of reader will be rewarded
in his search for knowledge and stimulation by the contents of
this volume.

As is inevitable from the conjunction of specialists from two
diverse fields such as mathematics and biology, which happened
at both meetings, new friendships and close links are formed
which are essential to the success and vitality of future work
on the interfaces between these fields. A concensus view of the
participants at the most recent meeting was that these meetings
should be held more frequently, perhaps every four years, and
this view has been noted. Other comments and suggestions on
this point or on the composition of future meetings will be
welcomed by the Institute of Mathematics and its Applications,
Maitland House, Warrior Square, Southend-on-Sea, Essex SS1 2JY.

Finally, acknowledgements must be made to the hard work and
commitment to this conference on the part of the contributors.
The Secretary of the IMA, Mr. Norman Clarke, and the Deputy
Secretary, Miss Catherine Richards, provided invaluable guidance
and support in the planning and execution of the arrangements
for the conference. The staff of the IMA were as usual magnifi-
cently professional and efficient: Mrs. Susan Hockett and Miss
Jayne Foster in turn took care of the delicate negotiations
between the Organizing Committee and the contributors whereas
Miss Denise Wright and Miss Michelle Wigmore dealt most ably
with the administrative details at the conference itself. Our
thanks are also due to Somerville College for providing
excellent hospitality and accommodation for participants and to
the Mathematical Institute of the University of Oxford for the
use of a splendid lecture theatre and its facilities.

April 1981   R.W. Hiorns
                                Department of Biomathematics
                                University of Oxford

                                and

                                D. Cooke
                                School of Mathematical and
                                Physical Sciences
                                University of Sussex

ACKNOWLEDGEMENTS

The Institute thanks the authors of the papers, the editors, Mr. D. Cooke (University of Sussex) and Dr. R.W. Hiorns (University of Oxford) and also Miss J. Fulkes, Mrs. S. Hockett and Miss D. Wright for typing the manuscripts.

CONTENTS

INTRODUCTORY REMARKS

It is a pleasure to welcome all the participants to this
conference, some of whom have travelled a considerable distance
to attend. Some of you were also present at the previous IMA
conference on population dynamics at Oxford in September 1972,
and will remember the pertinent introductory remarks on the
importance of mathematics in population biology by the late
Professor Charles Coulson, who was at the time President of the
Institute.

Looking back at that conference, I think one could claim,
broadly speaking, that it was well worthwhile, in spite of some
obvious difficulties of content and exposition. To recall these
difficulties, there was firstly the problem of adequately cover-
ing the subject matter in a short conference, this being tackled
by trying to combine a judicious mix of research and exposition
in the various papers. The resulting amalgam is of course still
in part a reflection of the interests and views of the organis-
ing committee; and even a broadly based committee, including
mathematicians and biologists, may not be able to ensure that all
relevant topics are included.

In the organisation of the present conference, the committee
was conscious of considerable progress in certain areas of
theoretical population biology in the last few years, and tried
to make sure by their selection of invited speakers that such
progress would be emphasised. There are, however, regrettably
always some extinction effects to be reckoned with, due to the
inability of a few invited speakers to attend, and the final
programme therefore includes a certain amount of random drift
from the original version; but I believe that we have been able
to retain sufficient of the relevant structure, and I personally,
and I trust the rest of you also, look forward to a most informative and stimulating meeting.

To go back for a moment to the second problem which a conference of this kind faces, referred to by Charles Coulson, but
perhaps not so successfully dealt with last time, this is the
problem of finding a satisfactory common meeting ground for both
mathematicians and biologists. To my mind this problem is in
some ways even more acute than ever, for the mathematics of population biology is admittedly difficult, and yet its relevance
in the light of the recent progress to which I have referred,
and to be aired by our speakers, even more undeniable. A little
while ago I was sitting in the audience at a symposium on popu-

lation genetics, and found myself chatting to a biologist sitting next to me. I was interested to have his reaction to the content of some of the symposium papers. He was a little wistful about the growing importance of mathematics in population biology, but at the same time he recognised its inevitability. Whether we shall succeed in coping with this problem any better than last time I cannot say, but at least we have become very conscious of it, and must do what we can to help solve it.

One thing to be quite clear about, and that is the purpose of theoretical models. They will not tell you what is, but what may be, and how what is may have arisen, or what it may become. In population biology the present situation is interesting, because, perhaps for the first time, we are beginning to have a superfluity of models, so that, as in all good science, we have to try to discriminate between them, not only against known facts, but against future observation or experiment actually suggested by the models.

M.S. Bartlett

PART I

STABILITY AND CONTROL

IN

BIOLOGICAL POPULATIONS

THE DYNAMICS OF NATURAL AND MANAGED POPULATIONS

R.M. May

(Princeton University, New Jersey, USA)

1. INTRODUCTION

It is eight years since the Institute of Mathematics and its
Applications held its earlier conference on the mathematical
theory of the dynamics of biological populations (Bartlett and
Hiorns, 1973). This chapter aims to outline some of the
advances in our understanding of the dynamics of single populations that have been achieved since then. Many people have con-
tributed to these advances, and much of the work is the subject
of recent specialized reviews. Accordingly, what follows is a
brief overview rather than a detailed account; a road map rather
than a Baedeker.

The review is largely confined to mathematical models that
are in the tradition of classical applied mathematics; that is,
the review deals mainly with relatively simple deterministic
differential and difference equations, giving little attention
to stochastic complications (which are discussed thoroughly in
Bartlett's chapter) and no attention to large "systems" models
with multitudes of parameters. Furthermore, population genetics
and the effects of spatial heterogeneity are both ignored (the
latter effects are reviewed by Levin, later in this volume).
This less-than-encyclopaedic, not to say capricious, coverage
simply reflects my own particular interests.

Section 2 comprises the bulk of the chapter, and surveys the
range of dynamical behaviour (stable points, stable cycles,
chaos) that can be exhibited by nonlinear first-order difference
and differential-delay equations that are simple and deterministic. This behaviour is by now well understood for first-order
difference equations; the even more complicated behaviour manifested by first-order differential-delay equations is less
understood, and it is discussed in detail. Section 2 concludes
with a survey of some general speculations about "turbulent"
behaviour in deterministic systems. Section 3 indicates some
applications of the mathematical results of Section 2, both to

understanding particular observations on laboratory or field
populations and to planning general strategies for the harvesting or control of natural populations. Stochastic effects enter
in Section 4, which discusses the way environmental unpredicta-
bility can influence population dynamics, and the implications
this has for harvesting natural populations.

Sections 5-8 sketch the further complexities that arise when
two or more interacting populations are considered. Section 5
deals with the simplest extension beyond a single population,
namely one species in which the dynamics of female and male populations are treated separately (as is necessary, for example,
in harvesting sperm whales). Section 6 gives signposts to the
extensive literature on two species interacting as competitors,
mutualists or as various forms of prey and predator. Section 7
hints at the messier things that can happen in systems of three
interacting species. Some of the variety of approaches to
understanding the structure and dynamical behaviour of systems
with many species are listed in Section 8.

2. DYNAMICS OF SINGLE POPULATIONS: STABLE POINTS, STABLE CYCLES, CHAOS

In nature, the dynamical behaviour of most populations is
likely to be influenced by their interaction with other species,
so that we are usually uncertain whether we are dealing with a
genuinely "single species" situation; these difficulties are
pursued further in the chapter by Southwood. Truly single
species studies can, however, be conducted in the laboratory.
In either event, elucidation of the properties of simple mathematical models for single populations is a basic first step
toward understanding what is going on.

2.1 Nonoverlapping Generations; Difference Equations

Many biological populations, including annual plants and many
temperate zone insect species, are effectively made up of a
single generation, with no overlap between successive generations. For these organisms, population growth occurs in discrete steps, and the appropriate mathematical models are difference equations relating the population in generation $t + 1$, N_{t+1},
to that in generation t, N_t:

$$N_{t+1} = F(N_t).   (2.1)$$

The biologist's task is to find this function or "mapping",
$F(N)$, in specific instances. Many such functions have been proposed, in various contexts; for a catalogue and review, see May
and Oster (1976). For most of these functions, the population

tends to increase from low densities and to decrease from high
densities, with one or more biological parameters controlling
the severity of this nonlinear propensity to "boom and bust".
In particular, the relation

$$N_{t+1} = N_t \exp\left[r(1-N_t/K)\right] \qquad (2.2)$$

(or other equivalent forms) has been studied as a model for fish
(Ricker, 1954) and insect (Moran, 1950) populations; here the
steepness of the nonlinear behaviour is determined by the parameter r. The simplest such mapping is the quadratic (sometimes
called the logistic difference equation),

$$N_{t+1} = N_t\left[1+r(1-N_t/K)\right]. \qquad (2.3)$$

By rescaling, this equation (2.3) can be rewritten as

$$X_{t+1} = aX_t(1-X_t). \qquad (2.4)$$

In this form it is the canonical example of a first order
difference equation with one critical point, and, as such, is
the form usually chosen for study by mathematicians.

Earlier work on nonlinear difference equations was confined
to linearized stability analysis, which showed the equilibrium
point was locally stable provided the mapping was not too steep
($0 < r < 2$ in equation (2.2); $1 < a < 3$ in equation (2.4)).
Numerical studies (e.g., Ricker, 1958) showed there were cycles
or apparently noisy dynamical behaviour once the fixed point
became unstable, but these phenomena were not pursued until
recently. It is now widely realized that, as nonlinearities
become increasingly severe, difference equations such as (2.2)
or (2.4) unfold the following panorama of behaviour:

(i) if the nonlinearity or hump in F(N) is not too steep,
there is a stable fixed point;
(ii) as the hump steepens, the fixed point becomes unstable,
giving rise by successive "pitchfork" bifurcations to a cascade
of stable cycles with periods $2,4,8,\ldots,2^n$;
(iii) beyond the point of accumulation of these stable cycles of
period 2^n lies a region often called "chaotic" in which the trajectories are, in many ways, effectively indistinguishable from
the sample function of a random process. A detailed understanding of the underlying processes can be attained in various ways
(using geometrical arguments, combinatorial theory, dynamical
systems theory, or other techniques); May (1976), Guckenheimer
(1979) and Guckenheimer, Oster and Ipaktchi (1976) give reviews
emphasising the mathematics, and May and Oster (1976) give a
review focused on the biological implications of this work.

   As discussed in these review articles, the detailed mathematical structure of the so-called chaotic region (r > 2.692.. in
equation (2.2); a > 3.570.. in equation (2.4)) is exquisitely
intricate, and is a beautiful example of a very complicated
sequence of bifurcation processes that can be understood in great
detail. From the biologist's point of view, however, it may be
observed that as the nonlinearities steepen (that is, as r and a
increase in equations (2.2) and (2.4), respectively) the dynamics
goes from a stable point, to cycles in which the population
alternates up and down in a regular manner, to more ragged oscillations in which the population still alternates high and low in
successive generations, and finally to apparently random population fluctuations. The relation between these broad patterns
("stable points, stable cycles, chaos"), and the kaleidoscopic
underlying mathematical structure, is discussed elsewhere (May,
1976).

2.2 Overlapping Generations; Differential-Delay Equations

   At the opposite extreme from the populations of Section 2.1
are species with continually overlapping generations, in which
population growth may be regarded as continuous. The dynamics
of these populations will be described by differential equations;
time is now a continuous variable (in contrast with Section 2.1,
where it was a discrete variable).

   The earliest studies of such populations involved nonlinear
first-order differential equations, of which the most commonly
used is the logistic

$$dN/dt = rN(1-N/K). \tag{2.5}$$

Following Hutchinson (1948), it has been increasingly realized
that the nonlinear or "density dependent" effects on the right
hand side of equations like equation (2.5) are unlikely to
operate instantaneously, and that time lags in the operation of
such effects are likely to have important dynamical consequences.
Hutchinson suggested that equation (2.5) be modified to

$$dN/dt = rN[1-N(t-T)/K], \tag{2.6}$$

to take some rough account of the effect of time lags in regulatory processes. As discussed in detail elsewhere (May, 1974,
1981b), equation (2.6) gives a stable point if $rT < \frac{1}{2}\pi$, and
stable cycles (of period approximately 4T) if $rT > \frac{1}{2}\pi$.

   Very recently, however, it has been realized that the comparative simplicity of the dynamical behaviour of equation (2.6),
with its stable point or stable cycle, obscures the analogy
between the first-order difference equations and the typical

first-order differential-delay equations that describe biological populations. Like the difference equations of Section 2.1,
these first-order differential-delay equations can have a stable
point or stable cycles (with cascades of period doubling), or
apparently chaotic dynamics; unlike the difference equations,
the dynamics tends to emerge from apparent chaos into a simple
and stable cycle when the nonlinearities become very severe.

I now give some examples of such differential-delay equations.
As their behaviour is less familiar to most people than is the
behaviour of the difference equations discussed in Section 2.1,
I also (in Section 2.3) summarize the linearized stability
analysis, and give a numerical exploration of the nonlinear
dynamics.

Population growth can be represented as the outcome of gains
from birth or recruitment processes (which often incorporate
time lags), offset by losses from natural mortality (or
harvesting):

$$dN/dt = - \mu N + R(N(t - T)).\qquad(2.7)$$

Here $N(t)$ is the population at time t, μ the per capita mortality rate, and the nonlinear recruitment function $R(N)$ is
assumed to have a time lag of exactly T. More generally, the
time delays will be distributed (rather than there being a specific fixed interval, T) leading to an integro-differential
equation:

$$dN/dt = -\mu N + \int^t R(N(t'))W(t-t')dt'.\qquad(2.8)$$

Here $W(t-t')$ weights the contributions to overall recruitment
at time t arising from a time t' in the past; equation (2.7) is
recovered if W is constituted of a single sharp spike,
$W(\tau) = \delta(\tau-T)$.

One specific example is the equation used by the International
Whaling Commission (IWC) to model populations of baleen whales.
In essentials, this equation is (2.7) with

$$R(N) = \tfrac{1}{2}(1-\mu)^T N[P+Q\{1-(N/K)^Z\}].\qquad(2.9)$$

Here N represents the population of sexually mature, adult
whales; T is effectively the time taken to achieve maturity; K
is the pristine, unharvested equilibrium density of the whale

population; P is the per capita fecundity of females at this
pristine equilibrium point N = K; Q is the maximum increase in
per capita fecundity of which the whales are capable as population densities fall to low levels; and z measures the severity
with which this density dependent response is manifested. This
recruitment relation is illustrated in Fig. 1. We see that
z = 1 corresponds to the conventional logistic assumption, in
which the density dependent increase in fecundity is manifested
linearly, with per capita fecundity rates rising linearly from
P to P + Q as N falls from K to O. For z > 1 the density dependent response is mainly concentrated around the equilibrium point
N = K (and for z >> 1, the per capita fecundity rises from P
essentially to P + Q for small decreases in population density
below K). Conversely, for z < 1 the density dependent response
is not manifested until the population falls to quite low levels.
The factor $(1-\mu)^T$ simply measures the fraction of the newly born
whales that survive, with probability $1-\mu$ for each of T years,
to adulthood. Finally, the factor $\frac{1}{2}$ arises because it is assumed
that exactly half the population is female, so that the per
capita fecundity of females is to be multiplied by $\frac{1}{2}N$, the total
number of females.

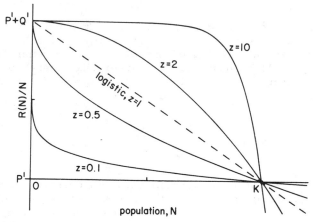

Fig. 1   The per capita recruitment, R(N)/N, is plotted as a func-
          tion of N, illustrating the IWC recruitment relation,
          equation (2.9), for various values of the density depen-
          dence parameter z. The per capita recruitment ranges
          from $P' = \frac{1}{2}(1-\mu)^T P$ to $P' + Q' = \frac{1}{2}(1-\mu)^T (P+Q)$ as N
          decreases from K to O; the detailed nature of the
          response, however, depends on z, as illustrated. For
          further discussion, see the text.

Notice that the parameters μ, T and P in equation (2.9) are not independent. The equilibrium population in the unexploited system is, by assumption, $N(t) = N(t-T) = K$; substituting this in equations (2.7) and (2.9) gives the identity, or "balance equation",

$$\mu = \tfrac{1}{2}(1-\mu)^T P. \qquad (2.10)$$

Using equation (2.10), and further defining $q = Q/P$, the baleen whale equation may be written

$$dN/dt = -\mu N + \mu N' [1+q\{1-(N'/K)^Z\}], \qquad (2.11)$$

with

$$N' \equiv N(t-T). \qquad (2.12)$$

Other interesting nonlinear differential-delay equations include the family

$$dN/dt = \frac{aN'}{1+b(N')^C} - eN. \qquad (2.13)$$

These and other differential-delay equations have been studied by Mackey and Glass (1977; see also Glass and Mackey, 1979, and Lasota and Wazewska, 1976) as models for specific physiological processes; these authors were (to my knowledge) the first to draw attention to the spectrum of dynamical behaviour exhibited by such equations. Frauenthal and Swick (1981; see also Swick, 1980) have shown that some integro-differential equations arising from studies of human demography (and having the general form of equation (2.8)) also display the range of dynamical behaviour outlined above and expounded in more detail below.

2.3 Dynamical Behaviour of Differential-Delay Equations

Equation (2.11) has an equilibrium point at $N^* = K$. More generally, equation (2.7) has one or more equilibrium points determined by the solutions of the algebraic equation $\mu N^* = R(N^*)$. The local stability of these equilibrium points is studied in the usual way by putting $N(t) = N^* + x(t)$, expanding the equation in a Taylor series (discarding terms of order x^2), and setting $x(t) = x(O) \exp(\lambda t)$ in the resulting linear equation. The local stability is then characterized by the eigenvalue(s) λ, determined from the transcendental equation

$$\lambda = -\mu - \mu b e^{-\lambda T}. \qquad (2.14)$$

Here b is defined in general as the (dimensionless) derivative of R(N) at the equilibrium point:

$$b \equiv -(1/\mu)(dR/dN)*. \qquad (2.15)$$

In the specific case of the IWC equation (2.11), $b = qz - 1$.

In the absence of time lags ($T = 0$), λ is necessarily negative ($\lambda = -\mu(1+b)$, and $b > 0$ for all reasonable R(N)), corresponding to local stability. As T increases, the eigenvalue(s) will move toward the imaginary axis, and the system undergoes a Hopf bifurcation from local stability to stable limit cycle behaviour as λ crosses the imaginary axis. The marginal stability condition is therefore found by substituting $\lambda = i\omega$ in equation (2.14); this criterion for local stability of the equilibrium point is

$$\mu T < \frac{\pi - \cos^{-1}(1/b)}{(b^2 - 1)^{\frac{1}{2}}}. \qquad (2.16)$$

This relation is illustrated in Fig. 2 (for the specific equation (2.11); more generally, the same figure applies with the y-axis labelled $b + 1$, rather than qz). Fig. 2 also shows the parameter combinations actually used in the IWC models for sei, minke and sperm whales; all these populations have relatively sluggish population growth parameters, and their dynamics is a stable equilibrium point.

The period T_0 of the stable limit cycle when it first arises by Hopf bifurcation is given by $T_0 = 2\pi/\omega$, whence it follows that

$$T_0 = \left(\frac{2\pi}{\pi - \cos^{-1}(1/b_0)} \right) T. \qquad (2.17)$$

Here b_0 is the critical value of b at which left and right hand sides of equation (2.16) are equal; that is, b_0 corresponds to the stability boundary line in Fig. 2.

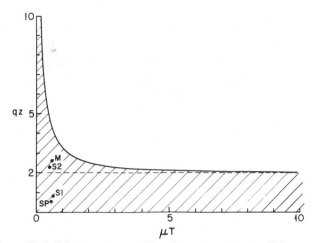

Fig. 2 The shaded area shows the domain of parameter space in which the differential-delay equation (2.11) has a locally stable equilibrium point. The IWC parameters μ, T, q and z are as defined in the text. The four points correspond to the parameter values actually used by the IWC for specific whale populations: the point labelled M is for minke whales; S1 is for sei whales (in a model with z = 2.4); S2 is also for sei whales (in an earlier model with z = 1); and SP is for female sperm whales. More generally, the stability boundary shown here applies to the general differential-delay equation (2.7), with qz replaced by the general expression b + 1 (b being defined by equation (2.15)); for further discussion, see the text.

Numerical studies show that, as the nonlinearities become more severe (that is, as b continues to increase), this stable limit cycle undergoes a cascade of period doublings, eventually entering a regime of apparently chaotic dynamical behaviour. Finally, as b becomes very large (zq >> 1, corresponding to the steeply nonlinear recruitment curve illustrated in Fig. 1), the dynamics suddenly condenses back into a single, relatively simple cycle.

This array of behaviour is illustrated in Figs. 3a-e, for the IWC equation (2.11) with the particular parameter choices T = 2, μ = 1, q = 1, and steepening nonlinearity as the density dependent exponent z takes the values z = 3.0, 3.5, 3.7, 3.8 and 4.0. The sequence of Figs. 3a-e are asymptotic phase space portraits, with N(t-T) plotted against N(t), after initial transients have died away. The simple cycle of Fig. 3a (with period given approximately by equation (2.17)) undergoes a period doubling to give Fig. 3b. A few further doublings, to about 4, 8 and 16

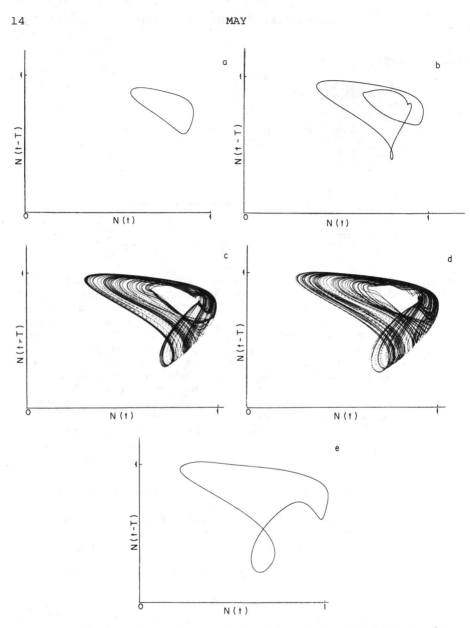

Fig. 3a-e   Phase-space plots of the asymptotic solutions to the
            differential-delay equation (2.11) are shown for the
            illustrative parameter choice μ = 1, T = 2, q = 1, and
            various z: (a) z = 3.0 (stable cycle); (b) z = 3.5
            (stable cycle after first "period doubling");
            (c) z = 3.7 and (d) z = 3.8 (apparently chaotic
            trajectories); (e) z = 4.0 (stable and relatively
            simple cycle).

times the initial period, can be distinguished, before the detail gets lost. In Figs. 3c and 3d, the orbit is apparently chaotic. The situation up to this point is strongly reminiscent of the by now well-known properties of simple first-order difference equations with steepening nonlinearities (Section 2.1).

The feature that is new, and perhaps surprising, for the differential-delay equation is that the orbit again becomes a simple cycle, as shown in Fig. 3e, for sufficiently steep nonlinearity (sufficiently large z, here z > 3.9). This simple orbit, which appears to persist for arbitrarily large z (corresponding to a step function R(N) in equation (2.11)), seems to condense out of the chaotic regime sharply as z increases beyond a critical value, but neither my numerical studies of this equation, nor any other studies of similar equations of which I am aware, have been sufficiently exhaustive to exclude the possibility of a very rapid "inverse cascade" leading to this simple cycle.

These general features of Fig. 3 are precisely as found for other functional forms of R(N), such as Mackey and Glass' equation (2.13) (where c plays a role analogous to z), and in Frauenthal and Swick's studies of related integro-differential equations. A more mathematically detailed account of these results is given by May (1980) and in the earlier work of Mackey and Glass (1977). Biologically oriented discussions of the properties of the IWC equation (2.11) are in Clark (1976) and May (1981a).

For the first-order difference equations of Section 2.1, we have analytic results that lay bare the intricate structure of the apparently chaotic regime. In contrast, for the first-order differential-delay equations of Section 2.2 we have mainly the results of extensive numerical studies. Some crude approximations that provide a degree of analytic understanding are presented elsewhere (May, 1980).

2.4 *"Turbulent" Behaviour in Deterministic Systems*

The extremes of populations with discrete, nonoverlapping generations (first-order difference equations; Section 2.1) and continuously overlapping generations (first-order differential equations; Section 2.2) represent two ends of a continuum. Many, if not most, organisms have well defined breeding seasons, and their populations occupy an intermediate position on this continuum, consisting of many distinct but overlapping age classes. We have seen, however, that these two extremes manifest very similar regimes of dynamical behaviour. It therefore seems likely that, quite generally, single populations can exhibit behaviour ranging from stable points, to stable cycles, to

apparent chaos, depending broadly on the steepness of the density
dependent regulatory mechanisms.

The difference and differential-delay equations considered
above had just one "hump" or critical point. Other kinds of
biological studies (for example, consideration of the population
genetics of frequency dependent selection) lead to mappings with
two or more critical points. Such systems have a bifurcation
structure even more complicated than those outlined above (for
an introductory account, see May, 1979). The mappings discussed
in Section 2.1 are technically described as having negative
Schwarzian derivative; essentially, this restriction is to ensure
that the map does not do tricky things in the neighbourhood of
the fixed point, and that it has the generic behaviour of the
quadratic equation (2.4) rather than being, for example, a
quartic disguised as a "one hump" map.

The phenomenon whereby simple and fully deterministic equations can give rise to dynamical behaviour having the superficial
appearance of random noise has disturbing implications. For
example, even if one could rely on a simple deterministic model,
long term predictions would be difficult if the dynamics were
chaotic. Similar problems have been noted for predictive metero-
logy by Lorenz (1963), and they are likely to arise in other contexts in biology. For a more full discussion of the implications
of deterministic chaos, in population biology and other contexts,
see May and Oster (1976).

On a less gloomy note, it has been observed that the phenomenon of deterministic chaos, which can be understood in analytic
detail for first-order difference equations, may help to advance
our understanding of turbulent behaviour in fluids. Focusing
on the process of "period doubling", in which a cascade of
successive bifurcations gives rise to a hierarchy of cycles each
with period approximately double that of its predecessor,
Feigenbaum has made the bold suggestion that certain invariant
properties of this process for first-order difference equations
may apply also to the Navier-Stokes equations (Feigenbaum, 1978,
1979; Collet, Eckmann and Lanford, 1980; May and Oster, 1980).
This leads to quantitative predictions about experimentally-
observable features of the onset spectrum of turbulence; some
recent experiments by Libchaper and Maurer (1980) on the onset
of turbulence in Raleigh-Bénard flow appear to accord with
Feigenbaum's predictions. To see theoretical biology informing
theoretical physics is to witness a pleasing role reversal. But
I digress.

3. APPLICATIONS TO NATURAL AND MANAGED POPULATIONS

3.1 Specific Experiments and Observations

There are several studies in which field or laboratory data have shown populations to have monotonic damping at one temperature, and oscillations (either damped or persistent) at other, higher temperatures. In other studies, different subspecies (or different species within a single genus) have been shown to exhibit a range of dynamical behaviour, from monotonic damping to sustained cycles. In addition, there are many examples in the laboratory (for example, Nicholson's blowflies) and in the field (the 4 year cycle of mice, voles and lemmings in boreal regions, and the 10-11 year cycle of snowshoe hares) of stable cycles in population density. A summary of these observations, and an explanation on the basis of the work outlined in Section 2, is given elsewhere (May, 1981b, ch. 2).

3.2 General Implications for Management and Control

A very general moral may be drawn from the results of Section 2. Since single populations are capable of exhibiting a great range of dynamical behaviour, depending on the details of the parameter values characterizing their life histories, policies for the management or control of natural populations must envision a wide range of different strategies.

These ideas have been developed and applied to the control of insect pest species by Conway (1976), Southwood (1977) and others. These authors show that populations of different kinds of crop and orchard pests have different kinds of dynamical behaviour, and that there is an appropriate spectrum of control techniques (including, inter alia, pesticides, natural enemies, release of sterile males or of pheromones), rather than any single best strategy. For a full discussion see Conway (1981).

Similarly, Bradley (1972) has indicated a classification of infectious diseases, according to the way the disease organism is transmitted between and maintained within individual hosts. Such classification of infectious diseases on the basis of their population biology is further discussed by Anderson and May (1979).

As mentioned in the next section, there is likewise no single scheme for the harvesting of fish and whale populations, but rather the management regime must be be keyed to the specifics of the recruitment curve (R(N) in equation (2.7)) and the consequent population dynamics.

4. ENVIRONMENTAL STOCHASTICITY IN SINGLE SPECIES SYSTEMS

The equations considered in Section 2 were deterministic, with
all the parameters assumed to have specified, constant values.
In reality, the unpredictable fluctuations in the environment,
to which all populations are subject to a greater or lesser
degree, will have the effect of causing some of the parameters
in the equations to exhibit stochastic variation. To take a
simple example, in the logistic differential equation (2.5) both
the intrinsic per capita growth rate r and the carrying capacity
K may be regarded as stochastic variables, specified by statistical distributions; equation (2.5) then becomes a stochastic differential equation, and in place of the deterministic population
trajectory N(t) we have a probability distribution P(n,t) (giving
the probability for the population to have the value n at time
t). Such "environmental stochasticity" is to be distinguished
from the "demographic stochasticity" which arises from the fact
that N is a discrete rather than a continuous variable (animals
come quantized in integer numbers) and which tends to be
relatively unimportant once N is very large.

A large and still-growing literature is devoted to combining
the kind of dynamical exploration outlined in Section 2 with the
effects of environmental stochasticity. A good recent review
is by Turelli (1978; see also May, 1974; Feldman and Roughgarden,
1975; Ludwig, 1975).

One sector of this recent literature which I find particularly
interesting deals with the interplay between environmental noise
and the effects of harvesting in natural populations. Consider,
for simplicity, a fish or other population which, in its pristine
state, obeys the logistic equation (2.5), with the carrying capacity K constant but with the intrinsic growth rate r fluctuating
randomly (as white noise) around a mean value r_o. Suppose the
population is harvested under "constant effort", at a rate E, so
that the net additional mortality due to fishing is EN. The
relevant equation is then

$$dN/dt = r(t)N[1-N/K]-EN. \qquad (4.1)$$

The equilibrium probability distribution for N can be obtained,
and the probability distribution for the net yield of fish
(Y = EN) plotted as a function of the designated harvesting
effort (E), to get results such as depicted in Fig. 4.

Various questions of relevance to fisheries management now
arise. Under the above assumptions, which lead to Fig. 4, it
can be seen that the relative magnitude of the fluctuations in
the yield (the coefficient of variation of the yield) increases

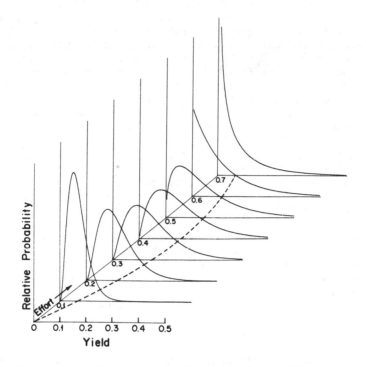

Fig. 4 The probability distributions of the yield are shown for
        various levels of harvesting effort E. The vertical
        axes depict the relative probability of attaining a given
        yield, and all the yield distributions are normalized to
        unit probability. The dashed line in the Y-E plane shows
        the average yield as a function of E. As discussed in
        the text, these calculations are based on the logistic
        equation with harvesting, equation (4.1); the environ-
        mental noise enters as "white noise" in r(t) (r has a
        mean value of unity, and variance $\sigma^2 = 0.4$). For
        details, see May et al (1978).

as harvesting effort increases, becoming very severe as one
exceeds what would, in the deterministic analysis, be the point
of maximum sustainable yield (MSY). It has been suggested that
management policies consequently should not seek simply to maxi-
mize sustainable average yield, but should also give weight to
keeping fluctuations relatively low (Doubleday, 1976; Sissenwine,
1977; Beddington and May, 1977).

   More extensive investigations (Shepherd and Horwood, 1979;
May et al, 1978) show that population dynamics and environmental
stochasticity work together in subtle ways in moulding the overall fluctuation spectrum; in discussing the effects of environmental noise we need to know both the shape of the recruitment
curve and the places in which the noise enters our equation. For
instance, if the pristine population corresponds to a stable
equilibrium point, then harvesting (which tends to slow the
characteristic time to recover from disturbance) tends to make
the system less stable and more prone to fluctuation; but if
the pristine state were stable cycles, or chaotic dynamics, then
the dynamical sluggishness induced by harvesting would actually
be a stabilising influence. Many of these questions turn on the
shape of the recruitment curve, which effectively has the form
of Fig. 1 with z > 1 for most marine mammals, and the form of
Fig. 1 with z << 1 for most fish.

   These questions concerning the harvesting of natural populations in an uncertain world are explored in more detail by
Shepherd and Horwood (1979) and May et al.(1978), and in the
special case of baleen whale populations by Horwood, Knights and
Overy (1979) and Beddington and Grenfell (1979). For a general
review, with particular emphasis on the role played by the shape
of R(N), and on the biological considerations influencing this
shape, see May (1981a).

5. BEYOND SINGLE POPULATIONS: ONE SPECIES, TWO SEXES

   Many qualitatively new complications arise when we move beyond
a single population. As an example, consider the simplest extension, namely, to models in which female and male populations
within a single species are described separately.

   This complication is necessary in describing sperm whales,
which have a relatively complex social structure: the females
attain sexual maturity at a significantly earlier age than do
males (typical IWC figures are 10 years for females and 25 years
for males); females aggregate in "pods" which typically comprise
around 10 sexually mature females; sexually mature males will
join the pods during the breeding season, but spend most of the
year apart, travelling much further south in the summer than do
females; and, as is typical in such socially structured species,
there is pronounced sexual dimorphism. Denoting all quantities
pertaining to the female and male populations by the subscripts
f and m respectively, the equations corresponding to equation
(2.11) become

$$dN_f/dt = -\mu N_f + \tfrac{1}{2}\exp(-\mu T_f)N'_f[P+Q\{1-(N'_f/K)^Z\}]p(N'_f,N'_m), \quad (5.1)$$

$$dN_m/dt = -\mu N_m + \tfrac{1}{2}\exp(-\mu T_m)N_f''[P+Q\{1-(N_f''/K)^z\}]p(N_f'',N_m''). \quad (5.2)$$

Here μ is the mortality rate (assumed the same for females and males), and T_f and T_m the times taken to attain sexual maturity. The recruitment terms for females and males are essentially as described before in equation (2.9), with P and Q as defined before (P is the per capita fecundity around the pristine equilibrium density, and P+Q is the per capita fecundity in the limit $N \to 0$). N_f' and N_f'' are the female populations at the appropriate earlier times:

$$N_f' = N_f(t-T_f), \quad (5.3)$$

$$N_f'' = N_f(t-T_m). \quad (5.4)$$

The factor $\tfrac{1}{2}$ arises from the assumption of a 1:1 sex ratio at birth, and the factors $\exp(-\mu T)$ describe the mortality occurring in the T years taken to reach reproductive age. Finally, the factor p represents the probability that a female in estrus will encounter (and be inseminated by) an adult male; this is an important biological consideration that is conventionally ignored in baleen whale models (where the social structure is simpler, and sex ratios probably remain around unity in unexploited populations). This probability p will in general depend on the population density of both females and males, but a very rough functional form may be assigned as follows. Let η denote the average number of adult females in a pod. Then the "effective sex ratio", ρ, may be defined as the number of males per pod of females, $\rho = \eta N_m/N_f$. If we assume that one adult male will take possession of a pod of females for the entire breeding season, and that males are essentially infinitely efficient in finding "unowned" pods, then the mating probability p takes the simple form:

$$\left.\begin{array}{l} p(\rho) = 1 \; ; \; \text{if } \rho > 1 \\[2mm] p(\rho) = \rho \; ; \; \text{if } \rho < 1 \end{array}\right\} \quad (5.5)$$

In the pristine equilibrium state we have $N_f = K$, $dN_f/dt = 0$ and $dN_m/dt = 0$, which for equation (5.1) leads to a relation among P, μ and T_f similar to that of equation (2.10), and for equation (5.2) gives the effective sex ratio at equilibrium as

$$\rho^*/\eta = \varepsilon \equiv \exp[-\mu(T_m - T_f)].\qquad(5.6)$$

If this system is now harvested, it will (if harvesting is not too severe) settle to a new equilibrium, in which the sustainable yields of females, Y_f, and of males, Y_m, are:

$$Y_f = qX_f(1-X_f^Z)p - X_f(1-p),\qquad(5.7)$$

$$Y_m = \varepsilon qX_f(1-X_f^Z)p + X_f(\rho^*p-\rho)/\eta.\qquad(5.8)$$

Here $X_f \equiv N_f/K$, $q = Q/P$, and the yields are expressed in units of μK. The sustainable yields thus possible for this system are illustrated in Fig. 5; in this figure, the unweighted sum of the yields,

$$Y = Y_f + Y_m,\qquad(5.9)$$

is depicted as a function of the female and male stock densities, $X_f = N_f/K$ and $X_m = N_m/K$.

Figure 5. illustrates several points. In the front region of the X_m - X_f plane, labelled A, the male population is too low to permit a sustainable harvest of females. Conversely, in the region labelled B, the female population is too low to permit a sustainable harvest of males. For combinations of X_f and X_m lying in the stippled region of the X_f - X_m plane, sustainable harvests are possible, as illustrated. For given X_f, or for given X_m, the maximum sustainable total yield lies along the curve corresponding to one male per pod, $\rho = 1$.

A much more biologically and mathematically detailed account of all this is given elsewhere (May, 1981a). The main purpose of the present exposition is, however, to draw attention to the way in which Fig. 5 is substantially more complicated than the simple MSY curve that would relate yield and stock density in the corresponding single population model. The "edges" one can fall off in Fig. 5 are absent in the single species analogue, and these edges clearly make management of the 2-population system a more delicate and complex affair.

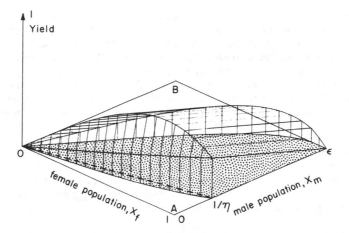

Fig. 5 This three-dimensional figure aims to show the sustainable yield of sperm whales as a function of the female
and male population densities, X_f and X_m. The yield
(vertical axis) is taken to be the unweighted sum of Y_f
and Y_m, equation (5.9). For combinations of X_f and X_m
lying in the region A in the X_f-X_m plane, the male population is too low to allow a sustainable harvest of
females; in region B, the female population is too low
to allow a sustainable harvest of males; in the pie-
shaped stippled region, however, sustainable harvests of
this effectively two-species system are possible. As
indicated clearly in the figure, the maximum sustainable
yield lies along the line $\rho = 1$ ($X_m = X_f/\eta$). The parameters in this illustration are close to the IWC ones:
$\varepsilon = 0.4$, $z = 2.4$, $q = 0.5$, $\eta = 10$. For further discussion, see the text.

6. BEYOND SINGLE POPULATIONS: TWO SPECIES

Two species can interact in various qualitatively distinguishable ways, as competitors, mutualists, or prey-predator. Earlier
work, begun in the 1920s and 1930s, clarified the basic dynamical
character of these interactions. Recent studies have become more
detailed in many different ways; in particular, there have been
advances in understanding the full array of nonlinear dynamical
behaviour possible in such systems. I think the best self-
contained survey is by Christiansen and Fenchel (1977). An up-
to-date guide to many of the primary sources is in May (1981b,
ch. 5).

The biological realities of two-species associations are usually too complicated to permit clear confrontation between observed facts and theoretical models. Among the wide range of interactions subsumed under "prey-predator" (which includes plant-herbivore, zebra and lion, and hosts and infectious diseases) are, however, some with simplifying features that enable such confrontation to take place. One class of examples comes from insect parasitoids and their hosts; here the predator's numerical response is relatively simple, and there has been progress in using mathematical models to understand field and laboratory observations (for a recent exposition, see Hassell, 1978). Another class of examples comes from the interaction between parasitic infections and their hosts; the chapter by Anderson shows how theory and observation can come together nicely for some such prey-predator associations.

In Section 2 it was observed that genuinely single species situations rarely exist in nature. But many prey-predator systems can be reduced to a single equation for the population dynamics of the prey species, in which the dynamics of the pre-dator does not appear explicitly, but rather implicitly as a time lag in the action of density dependent processes. Thus much of the discussion of differential-delay equations for single populations, in Section 2, is formally equivalent to discussion of a two-species prey-predator system. This idea is developed further elsewhere (May, 1981b, ch. 5 and references therein). More generally, techniques based on the recognition of different time scales for different dynamical processes can be used effec-tively to reduce the dimensionality of multispecies systems (see, for example, Anderson and May, 1979, 1981).

7. BEYOND SINGLE POPULATIONS: THREE SPECIES

The dynamical complexities get even worse as one moves from two to three interacting species. So long as the system is described by a pair of coupled first-order differential equa-tions, the trajectories must lie in a plane (and cannot cross), so that the possible behaviour is limited. In particular, it is usually possible to employ the Jordan closed curve theorem to show that a prey-predator model possesses either a fixed point or a stable limit cycle. But once the step to three dimensions has been taken, all manner of "strange attractors" are possible (Hirsch and Smale, 1974).

To cite one among many possible examples, consider the simple Lotka-Volterra model for three competitors. The corresponding model for two competitors is very tame, exhibiting at worst two alternative stable points. The three competitor model can, however, exhibit peculiar behaviour in which the dynamical tra-jectory spirals among the neighbourhood of three different states, taking an ever lengthening time to complete successive turns of the spiral. This strange attractor was first analyzed by May and Leonard (1975); the phenomenon appears also to occur in some physical contexts (Busse and Heikes, 1980; Schuster, Sigmund and Wolff, 1979), and its mathematical structure has been discussed more formally by Arneodo, Coullet and Tresser (1980).

8. BEYOND SINGLE POPULATIONS: MULTISPECIES SYSTEMS

In systems with many interacting species, any general understanding of the nonlinear dynamical behaviour is unlikely. It is therefore not surprising that most theoretical studies of the structure and dynamics of communities of interacting species of plants and animals deal either with empirically observed patterns (relative abundance of species; number of species in relation to area; patterns of energy flow) or with abstract mathematical models used as metaphors in the exploration of general questions (such as the relation between stability and complexity in communities that are assembled randomly or according to specified rules). Many interesting aspects of this subject are discussed in the chapter by Levin; another overview, and a guide to recent work, is by May (1981b, ch. 9).

9. CONCLUSIONS

As spelled out explicitly in the introduction, this review has concentrated narrowly on relatively simple models for the dynamical behaviour of populations (mainly single populations), ignoring dispersal and other spatial complications. Even within this restricted framework, however, we have seen that an astonishingly rich spectrum of behaviour is possible.

The understanding that emerges is useful in several ways. First, much of the work has intrinsic mathematical interest (even to the extent that some of the results are beginning to spill over into other disciplines, slightly countering a flow that has heretofore been wholly the other way). Second, the work helps explain the wide range of dynamical behaviour actually observed in biological populations, relating the dynamics to the life history parameters (and to the interactions among species). Third, increased knowledge about the dynamical properties of nonlinear equations with stochastic coefficients can provide helpful insights in the management or control of natural populations.

10. ACKNOWLEDGEMENTS

I am indebted to many people, and particularly to R.M. Anderson, J.R. Beddington, M.P. Hassell, G.F. Oster and T.R.E. Southwood, for helpful conversations. This work was supported in part by the National Science Foundation under Grant DEB77-01565.

10. REFERENCES

Anderson, R.M. and May, R.M. (1979) Population biology of infectious diseases: Part I, *Nature,* **280**, pp. 361-367, and Part II, *Nature,* **280**, pp. 455-461.

Anderson, R.M. and May, R.M. (1981) The population dynamics of micro-parasites and their invertebrate hosts, *Phil. Trans. Roy. Soc. B.*

Arneodo, A., Coullet, P. and Tresser, C. (1980) Occurrence of strange attractors in three-dimensional Volterra equations. (Preprint).

Bartlett, M.S. and Hiorns, R.W. (eds) (1973) The mathematical theory of the dynamics of biological populations, Academic Press, New York.

Beddington, J.R. and Grenfell, B. (1979) Risk and stability in whale harvesting, *Int. Comm. Whaling Rep.,* **29**, pp. 171-173.

Beddington, J.R. and May, R.M. (1977) Harvesting natural populations in a randomly fluctuating environment, *Science,* **197**, pp. 463-465.

Bradley, D.J. (1972) Regulation of parasite populations: a general theory of the epidemiology and control of parasitic infections, *Trans. Roy. Soc. Trop. Med. Hyg.,* **66**, pp. 697-708.

Busse, F.H. and Heikes, K.E. (1980) Convection in a rotating layer: a simple case of turbulence, *Science,* **208**, pp. 173-175.

Christiansen, F.B. and Fenchel, T.M. (1977) Theories of populations in biological communities, Springer Verlag, New York.

Clark, C.W. (1976) A delayed-recruitment model of population dynamics, with an application to baleen whale populations, *J. Math. Biol.,* **3**, pp. 381-391.

Collet, P., Eckmann, J.P. and Lanford, O.E. (1980) Universal properties of maps on an interval, *Commun. Math. Phys.,* **76**, pp. 211-254.

Conway, G.R. (1976) Man versus Pests, *In* "Theoretical Ecology: Principles and Applications", First edition, Ch. 14, Blackwell, Oxford and Saunders, Philadelphia, (R.M. May, ed.).

Conway, G.R. (1981) Man versus Pests, Ch. 15 in May, 1981b, *op. cit.*

Doubleday, W.G. (1976) Environmental fluctuations and fisheries management, *Int. Comm. Northw. Atlant. Fish. Sel. Pap. 1*, pp. 141-150.

Feigenbaum, M.J. (1978) Quantitative universality for a class of nonlinear transformations, *J. Stat. Phys.*, **19**, pp. 25-52.

Feigenbaum, M.J. (1979) The onset spectrum of turbulence, *Physics Letters*, **74A**, pp. 375-378.

Feldman, M.W. and Roughgarden, J. (1975) A population's stationary distribution and chance of extinction in a stochastic environment, *Theor. Pop. Biol.*, **7**, pp. 197-207.

Frauenthal, J.C. and Swick, K.E. (1981) Limit cycle oscillations in human population dynamics. In preparation.

Glass, L. and Mackey, M.C. (1979) Pathological conditions resulting from instabilities in physiological control systems, *Ann. N.Y. Acad. Sci.*, **316**, pp. 214-235.

Guckenheimer, J. (1979) The bifurcation of quadratic functions, *Ann. N.Y. Acad. Sci.*, **316**, pp. 78-85.

Guckenheimer, J., Oster, G.F. and Ipaktchi, A. (1976) The dynamics of density dependent population models, *J. Math. Biol.*, **4**, pp. 101-147.

Hassell, M.P. (1978) The dynamics of arthropod predator-prey associations, Princeton University Press, Princeton.

Hirsch, M.W. and Smale, S. (1974) Differential equations, dynamical systems, and linear algebra, Academic Press, New York.

Horwood, J.W., Knights, P.J. and Overy, R.W. (1979) Harvesting of whale populations subject to stochastic variability, *Int. Comm. Whaling Rep.* **29**, pp. 219-229.

Hutchinson, G.E. (1948) Circular casual systems in ecology, *Ann. N.Y. Acad. Sci.*, **50**, pp. 221-246.

Lasota, A. and Wazewska, M. (1976) Mathematical models of the red blood cell system, *Mat. Stosowana*, **6**, pp. 25-40.

Libchaper, A. and Maurer, J. (1980) Une expérience de Rayleigh-Bérnard de geometric réduite, Ecole Normale Supérieure, Preprint, 1979, in press.

Lorenz, E.N. (1963) Deterministic nonperiodic flow, *J. Atmos. Sci.*, **20**, pp. 130-141.

Ludwig, D. (1975) Persistence of dynamical systems under random perturbations, *SIAM Review,* 17, pp. 605-640.

Mackey, M.C. and Glass, L. (1977) Oscillation and chaos in physiological control systems, *Science,* 197, pp. 287-289.

May, R.M. (1974) Stability and complexity in model ecosystems, Second edition, Princeton University Press, Princeton.

May, R.M. (1976) Simple mathematical models with very complicated dynamics, *Nature,* 261, pp. 459-467.

May, R.M. (1979) Bifurcations and dynamic complexity in ecological systems, *Ann. N.Y. Acad. Sci.,* 316, pp. 517-529.

May, R.M. (1980) Nonlinear phenomena in ecology and epidemiology, *Ann. N.Y. Acad. Sci.,* in press.

May, R.M. (1981a) Mathematical models in whaling and fisheries management, *In* "Some Mathematical Questions in Biology", Vol. II, American Math. Soc., Providence, Rhode Island, (G.F. Oster, ed.).

May, R.M. (1981b) Theoretical ecology: principles and applications, Second edition, Blackwell, Oxford and Sinauer, Sunderland, Massachusetts.

May, R.M., Beddington, J.R., Horwood, J.W. and Shepherd, J.G. (1978) Exploiting natural populations in an uncertain world, *Math. Biosci.,* 42, pp. 219-252.

May, R.M. and Leonard, W.J. (1975) Nonlinear aspects of competition between three species, *SIAM J. Appl. Math.,* 29, pp. 243-253.

May, R.M. and Oster, G.F. (1976) Bifurcations and dynamic complexity in simple ecological models, *Amer. Natur.,* 110, pp. 573-599.

May, R.M. and Oster, G.F. (1980) Period doubling and the onset of turbulence: an analytical estimate of the Feigenbaum ratio, *Physics Letters,* 78A, pp. 1-3.

Moran, P.A.P. (1950) Some remarks on animal population dynamics, *Biometrics,* 6, pp. 250-258.

Ricker, W.E. (1954) Stock and recruitment, *J. Fish. Res. Bd. Canada II,* pp. 559-623.

Ricker, W.E. (1958) Maximum sustained yields from fluctuating environments and mixed stocks, *J. Fish. Res. Bd. Canada* 15, pp. 991-1006.

Schuster, P., Sigmund, K. and Wolff, R. (1979) On ω-limits for competition between three species, *SIAM J. Appl. Math.*, 37, pp. 49-54.

Shepherd, J.G. and Horwood, J.W. (1979) The sensitivity of exploited populations to environmental "noise", and the implications for management, *J. Cons. Int. Explor. Mer.*, 38, pp. 318-323.

Sissenwine, M.P. (1977) The effect of random fluctuations on a hypothetical fishery, *Int. Comm. Northw. Atlant. Fish. Sel. Pap.* 2, pp. 131-144.

Southwood, T.R.E. (1977) The relevance of population dynamics theory to pest control, *In* "The Origins of Pest, Parasite, Disease and Weed Problems", Blackwell, Oxford, (J.M. Cherrett and G.R. Sagave, eds).

Swick, K.E. (1981) Stability and bifurcation in age-dependent population dynamics, *Theor. Pop. Biol.*, in press.

Turelli, M. (1978) A re-examination of stability in randomly varying versus deterministic environments with comments on the stochastic theory of limiting similarity, *Theor. Pop. Biol.*, 13, pp. 244-267.

STABILITY IN FIELD POPULATIONS OF INSECTS

T.R.E. Southwood

*(Department of Zoology, University of Oxford,
Oxford, England)*

If it is permissible to generalise from a personal view,
ecologists seek to apply mathematics to their work for two
purposes: firstly to describe more precisely the phenomena they
observe and secondly to analyse them so that the underlying
mechanisms may be better interpreted and understood. Confusion
between aims and achievements under these two headings is not
uncommon and it is important for biologists to appreciate not
only that correlation is not causation, but that models may
simply be mimics and that several different mechanisms may, for
example, underlie a distribution as precise mathematically as
the negative binomial. It will be against this general background that I will attempt in this paper to describe some of
the types of evidence for stability or instability detected in
field populations and point out possible mechanistic models.
We will look to our mathematical colleagues for better ways of
describing what we observe and for testing the match of the
model, as well as for a greater understanding of the dynamic
implications of models.

At the Brookhaven Symposium, eleven years ago, Lewontin
(1969) and Watt (1969) pointed out and explored several interpre-
tations of stability. For the field worker and the purposes of
this paper there are two aspects:-

1. Stability in the size of population of a single species:
    following May (1973) stability is shown by those populations
    that have relatively small population fluctuations.

2. Stability in the composition of multispecies populations,
    which is essentially a measure of the persistence of species
    in time. Put another way the population of any given
    species contributes to instability at the multispecies or
    faunal level, only when it falls to zero. If extinction and
    colonisation rates are low the fauna will be stable, what-
    ever the single species fluctuations.

1. STABILITY IN POPULATIONS OF ONE SPECIES

Taking the definition of stability as being relatively
small population fluctuations, a useful description is the net
reproductive rate, or gradation coefficient (Benedek 1970):-

$$R = N_{t+1}/N_t$$

which is the ratio of the current population size against the
previous one, at the same stage, so that when plotted a point on
the diagonal represents a constant population. A series of such
ratios constitute a Moran or Ricker curve; they are often plotted on log/log axes, when exponential population growth will be
linear, and are an informative way of displaying data: the
greater the scatter of points the less the stability. Wolda
(1978a) has used the variance of log R to provide a measure of
annual variability (AV). This is of course sensitive to the
smallest population in the comparison, (i.e to the sample size),
and he shows that when this is 5 or less, high values of AV
are usually obtained. Thus AV's based on data containing some
very small samples must be discounted as evidence on population
stability. The value of AV gives no indications of mechanisms
involved, but the actual pattern of the Moran curve does.

The mechanisms of population change fall into two broad
categories; density dependent or regulating factors and density-
independent or disturbing factors. Whilst the former will move
the population in a manner related to, and normally towards the
equilibrium value, the latter is unrelated to the equilibrium
and will frequently be away from it. May (1974, 1975 and 1976)
and co-workers (Hassell et al, 1976; May et al, 1974; May and
Oster, 1976) have elucidated how the parameter values of models
containing a density dependent modifier, such as

$$N_{t+1} = [\lambda(1+aN_t)^{-b}]N_t$$

which is due to Hassell (1975), will determine the behaviour of
the population. This behaviour may range from monotonic damping
through limit cycles to chaos; in other words a regulated population may have a high value of AV and appear as if much influenced by disturbing factors, although in effect regulated.

This model and its analogues (May and Oster, 1976) are so
versatile, that there is a temptation to consider that they
describe all the processes in populations; this is not so, other
mechanisms are involved and the Moran plot helps us to recognise
this. Its general utility in the study of population dynamics
has been brought to our notice by Rogers (1979), who used it to

reanalyse data on the tsetse fly. The Moran curve for a species
may be calculated from the value for its average fecundity and
as suggested by Rogers (1979), it will inflect when density
dependence starts to operate; the departures (which will, unless
there is extensive immigration, be negative) from the line will
reflect net mortalities. Departures before the inflection of
the curve represent the action of density independent factors;
populations beyond that point will reflect the action of both
density dependent and density independent factors. The extent
of this zone of joint action in any model will depend on the
form of the density dependent model and the particular value of
the density dependent modifier. Hassell's (1975) curvilinear
model, for example, would lower the point at which density
dependence might be considered to act, compared with the model
used by Rogers (1979).

Now tsetse fly (<u>Glossina</u>) populations fluctuate widely and
it has often been thought that only density independent factors
operate. The life history is truncated, the female gives birth
to fully developed larvae; reproductive and mortality values
are, for an insect, relatively low, thus the Moran curve for
logistic growth 'wraps' fairly closely round the Moran plot of
the population data (Fig. 1). We can easily see the high level
of density independent mortality during the months of March to
June (except April of the second year); however later in the
year the operation of density dependent limitation can be recognised. Rogers (1979) shows how these are related to the rainfall pattern.

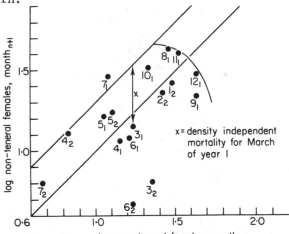

Fig. 1   Moran plot for tsetse-fly (<u>Glossina morsitans
submorsitans</u>) populations in the Yankori Game Reserve,
Nigeria (after Rogers, 1979) (The numbers represent the
month and the subscripts the year).

To return to populations where density dependence is operating: as May (this volume) has shown, many types of behaviour characteristic of natural populations may be generated from these simple equations. One such behaviour is limit cycling. It is shown in some of the finest, and oldest, data from field studies of insects: that for forest insects, especially that of Schwerdtweger (1935, 1941) for the abundance of moths in German forests over 80 years, Klomp's (1966) studies on the pine looper (Bupalus piniaris) in the Netherlands and Baltensweiler's (1968) records of the larch tortix (<u>Zeiraphera</u> <u>griseana</u> in the Alps. All these data give clear evidence from the field, of population oscillations within certain limits. Anderson and May (1979) have most recently analysed these further and provide a strong indication that viral infections may play an important role. Moran plots for such oscillating populations (Fig. 2) immediately demonstrate the wide scatter of points around the equilibrium line, the cycling of the population level around some equilibrium point and the suppression of the population below its potential rate of growth by density independent (and probably density dependent) factors.

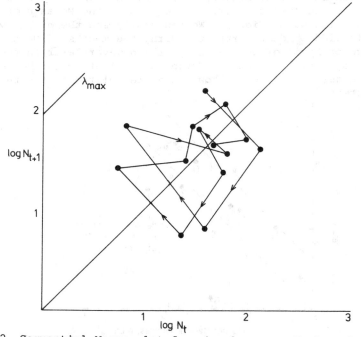

Fig. 2 Sequential Moran plot for pine looper moth (<u>Bupalus</u> <u>piniarius</u>) populations (data from Klomp, 1966).

Time delays are features of the mechanisms underlying such cycling; but the biological interactions are of two main types (and this will affect the patterns of the Moran plots):-

1. The action of an 'overcompensating' direct density dependent factor, one whose mortality effects expressed as $\underline{k}$ - value ($= \log N_{i+1} - \log N_i$) rise exponentially with population density.

2. The action of delayed density dependent factors, such as insect parasitoids whose population tracks that of their hosts, but with a time delay. Thus the $\underline{k}$ - value plotted against prey density is approximately circular or elliptical.

    The first category is characteristic of a single species population close to the carrying capacity of the habitat and is well exemplified by Nicholson's (1954) blowflies (see May et al. 1974; May, 1974). The second is characterised by two species interactions where the prey density is well below the carrying capacity of its resources (May 1976; Hassell 1979).

Generally population behaviour is less regular: Moran plots may help distinguish population growth from instability and real stability, in the region of an equilibrium, from mere numerical consistency. This use of Moran plots can be shown with population data from studies made by Dr. P.M. Reader and myself on Viburnum white fly (Aleurotrachaelus jelenkii). We studied the numbers on three bushes of laurustinus (Vibirnum tinus) at Silwood Park from 1962 for over ten years (Southwood and Reader 1976): the populations were isolated, there was one generation a year and, most important, the larval stages are stationary and inconspicuous on the underside of leaves. Thus once a year, in April/May, every individual on the bush could be censused by examining the underside of each leaf in turn and counting the number of, clearly visible, white dots; - only when the number of larvae exceeded 10, 000 was sampling introduced, but for the years described here at least one fifth of the population was directly enumerated. Errors are thus very much less than is usual in field data and exceptionally are least at the lower population levels (when every leaf was examined).

The first question is how to express the population level: total size or numbers per leaf, a measure of population intensity? As two of the bushes grew, increasing the number of their leaves roughly five fold over the ten years, their carrying capacity must have changed and thus numbers/leaf should be used as more closely relating population to habitat size. When this

is done it is found that the <u>relative</u> number of larvae per leaf
in the spring increased greatly in two bushes, but remained
apparently stable on the third:-

	Bush A	Bush B	Bush C
1964	12	1.5	1
1974	491	9	0.7

However, if a Moran plot is constructed (Fig.3), Bush C may
be seen to be the most unstable. Furthermore, bearing in mind
the remarks made earlier about the accuracy of these counts of
4th stage larvae, I submit that this is a striking demonstration
of what May (1973) termed 'demographic stochasticity', the
impact of random events on small populations. Our studies also
showed that, because of differences in the biochemical composition of the leaves on the bushes, their carrying capacities
may be considered as different; a further correction has been
made, the population sizes have been weighted to bring them
within a common density range (Fig.4). The weighting coefficient was simply the proportional relationship between the total
population densities on the different bushes and is analogous
to Rogers' (1979) method of expressing populations as a percentage of the total.

From other evidence I am confident that this is justified in
relation to bushes AB and B and the Moran plots (Fig.4) are now
very similar and indicate the slow, continuous, growth of the
populations on these bushes after the heavy mortality in the
exceptional winter of 1962/3 (the first point). Mortality was
density independent, thereby confirming the conclusions of
Southwood and Reader (1976) based on conventional key-factor
analysis. The last point for Bush A could represent the
commencement of some density-dependent mortalities. The third
bush (C) conforms to the general area of the plot, but shows
the greater instability (greater variance, as already discussed).

These data from field studies show how the variation in
population size from generation to generation (which is Wolda's
(1978a) 'AV' and is visually represented by the Moran plot) may
be relatively large due to:-

1. Density independent factors, as in the tsetse fly; at very
    low densities the variability due to these may be enhanced
    by random events (as with the low whitefly population
    density).

2. Density dependent factors associated with time lags and other parameter values that lead to oscillations and other behaviour as discussed by May (this volume) and Anderson (this volume).

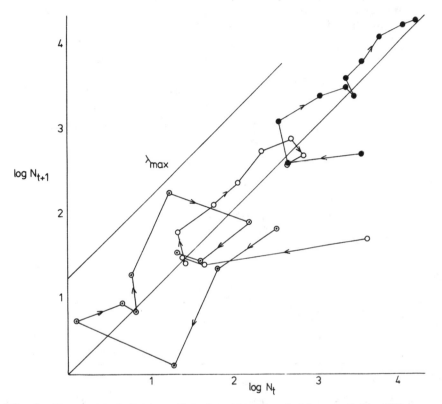

Fig. 3 Sequential Moran plot for the populations of the Viburnum whitefly (<u>Aleurotrachaelus jelenkii</u>) on three bushes (data from Southwood and Reader, 1976).

Thus although populations with high values of AV are by definition unstable, they are not necessarily lacking in resilience to perturbation: the risk of extinction may be low as much of the variation is due to density dependent factors.

The effects of these two components of mortality (density dependent and independent) on population behaviour are related because the fecundity necessary to give a particular value of the intrinsic rate of increase, on which May (1974) has shown dynamic behaviour depends, will be determined by the level of

density independent factors (May 1975; Southwood 1975). Indeed
I would like to make a plea for more consideration of the role
of density independent factors in our theoretical analyses of
population dynamics. They are of course by definition unrelated to density, but as Rogers (1979) shows may exhibit a clear
pattern in relation to time. Their general level for the
populations of any species may well have a range much more
restricted than the 0 - 100% possible.

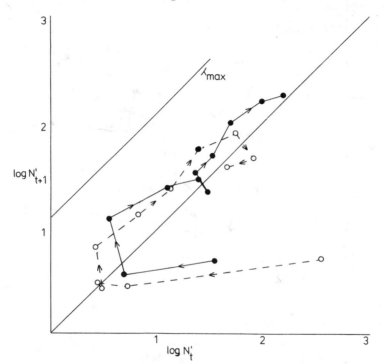

Fig. 4   Sequential Moran plots for two of the populations of the
         Virburnum whitefly (see Fig.3), weighted to correct for
         variations in capacity.

So far I have considered populations whose field data can at
least be interpreted in terms of a single theoretical equilibrium
density. However, as long ago as 1946, on the basis of a lifetime's experience, Voûte (1946) stated that, for most of the
time, phytophagous insect populations are low, but when they
pass an 'escape point', outbreaks occur. The idea was extended
by Milne (1962) and utilized by Clark (1964) as the basis of the
explanation for the changes in population levels observed in his
long study of the eucalyptus psyllid, Cardiaspina albitextura
he referred to endemic and epidemic levels.

Models that provide an explanation based on the existence of
at least two equilibria on the population growth curve have been
developed by Takahashi (1964), Holling (1973), Southwood (1975)
and Southwood and Comins (1976) and have been placed in a general framework by May (1977). The model of Southwood and Comins
(1976) (Fig.5) depends on an irregular form of the mortality
curve, in relation to population density, derived from the total
response of natural enemies, that becomes 'saturated' at the
unstable equilibrium point R (the release or escape point): the
upper equilibrium point (U) depends on intraspecific competition.
With most insects the populations will not remain indefinitely
around this epidemic level, because either density independent
factors or the time delays associated with density dependent
factors (causing them to overcompensate), will take it beyond
the domain of stability (R - C) of the locally stable point (U).
Another model that produces a locally stable point (S) and an
upper unstable equilibrium (R) is that of Hassell and Comins
(1978), based on a sigmoid response by a polyphagous predator
to its prey's density, whilst May and Anderson (1979) show how
life cycle structure and dynamics can generate multiple stable
states in disease-host interactions.

The Moran (or Ricker curve) thus provides a useful framework
for the exploration of mechanisms that underlie the existence
of multiple stable points in field populations, as well as for
their description.

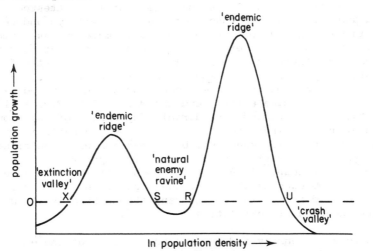

Fig. 5 A section through the 'natural enemy ravine' of the
         synoptic model of Southwood and Comins (1976)

2. STABILITY IN MULTISPECIES POPULATIONS

Population models (e.g. Southwood and Comins, 1976) often
have a lower unstable equilibrium point (X), below which the
population runs to extinction. Generally this is based on the
so-called "Allee effect", a marked lowering of the reproductive
rate when the population is below a certain density.

In the temporal sequence of an ecosystem there are two phases
of extinction. In a young ecosystem the rate of colonisation
is high and greatly exceeds the rate of extinction, but as the
habitat changes some of the early colonisers are no longer able
to survive, they become extinct and will not survive again even
if colonists arrive, so long as the habitat follows its natural
succession. It is easier to be confident that a plant species
is absent in a habitat, than an insect, therefore I illustrate
this with reference to data for plants in a Young Field
(Southwood, Brown and Reader, 1979). Eventually the curves
will flatten out and the distance between them will become more
or less constant: this represents the species equilibrium
density of Macarthur and Wilson, for that habitat.

However there will always be some extinctions (and coloni-
sations, but this process does not now concern us), these
species may or may not be regained later; frequently they will
be species present in low numbers that are geographically at
the edge of their range. The anecdotal but well attested
waxing and waning of the ranges of the hornet (Lloyd and Benson
1945) in Britain may well be related to climate cycles (Lamb,
1965). Unfortunately there is little precise population data
on these, but there is some information on another butterfly,
the large copper, Lycaena dispar. The East Anglian colony is
right on the edge of its range: one population, studied by
Duffey (1968), became extinct and the Moran plot (Fig.6) clearly
shows the continuous and considerable depression of the population by density independent factors below the maximum growth
rate. This point is emphasised by comparison with the cinnabar
moth (Tyria jacobaeae) using the data of Dempster (1971) and
Dempster and Lakhani (1979). This common moth has the same
fecundity (300 eggs/female), but the population shows great
resilience and in several of the generations relatively low,
density independent mortalities.

The role of density independent mortalities at the edge of
the range is more precisely demonstrated in Rogers' (1979)
analysis of tsetse fly populations: he plots density independent mortalities in climograms for the habitats in question and
the high values occur in the driest hottest localities (or
seasons), the limit of the fly's local distribution.

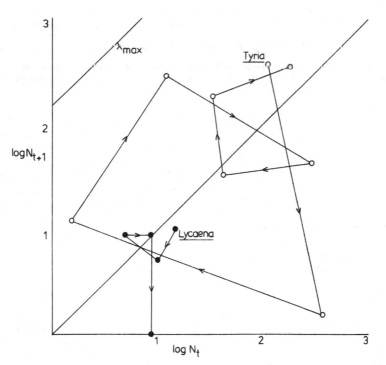

Fig. 6   Sequential Moran plots for the large copper butterfly
         (Lycaena dispar), a colony on the edge of its range,
         and for the cinnabar moth (Tyria jacobaeae) (data from
         Duffey (1968) and Dempster (1971)).

Instability in multi-species populations is therefore due
either to major changes in the habitat, i.e. to succession, or
to fluctuations in density independent factors that then drive
to extinction those species whose Moran plots, in these habitats,
have previously shown considerable depression below the potential logistic growth line.

3. HABITATS AND STABILITY

The relationship between habitats and the stability of the
populations of their denizens may be assessed using a number of
criteria. The variance of log R, Wolda's (1978a and b, 1980) AV
is a useful measure and he gave data for many species and a wide
variety of habitats. Values of AV range from 0.2 to over 0.6
and are especially high in habitats at early stages of colonisation, e.g. polders (see also Meijer 1980): but the synthesis
of these data is at an early stage and fluctuations in rainfall
seem more significant than the temperature regime of the species
habitat. However the development by Wolda of this useful index
of variation has facilitated the quantitative comparison of much

published information. Taylor and Woiwood (1980) have also
considered temporal stability and used the variance of their
log transformed trap catches in different seasons (S^2_{log}) as an
instability measure; they conclude that the amount of variance
is closely related to the density, and that this relationship
is species specific.

The behaviour of the populations of individual species will
be governed by various key parameters in the population growth
equation (May et al.1974; May 1974 and this volume; Hassell et
al 1976 and Southwood et al 1974); that there are evolved
characters of the species, seems to be confirmed by Taylor and
Woiwood's (1980) findings. An attempt to examine the components
was made by Stubbs (1977) who was able to show that, in general,
species with more permanent habitats (in terms of the habitat's
durational stability) had lower reproductive rates than species
that exploit temporary habitats. The value of b, the density
dependent moderator, also showed trend in two groups, being
highest in temporary habitats.

Ecologists sometimes speak as if stability was a virtue: it
is not, it is merely a property of a population. The expression
of this by populations depends on the possession of certain
attributes by the individuals that constitute it: the analyses
of May (1974) and Hassell (1979) have identified these parameters: fecundity level, interference constant, handling time,
etc. We must remember that the characteristic values of these,
for a species, have evolved not because they provide stability,
but because they increased the fitness of the individuals
concerned.

4.   ACKNOWLEDGEMENTS

I am greatly indebted to Professor R.M. May and Dr. D.J.
Rogers for stimulating discussions and valued help.

5.   REFERENCES

Anderson, R and May, R.M. (1979) Population biology of infectious diseases: Part 1, *Nature*, **280**(5721), pp. 361-367.

Baltensweiler, W. (1968) The cyclic population dynamics of the
grey larch tortrix, Zeiraphera griseana Hübner (= Semasia
diniana Guenee) (Lepidoptera: Tortricidae), *In* "Insect Abundance"(T.R.E. Southwood, ed), *Symp. Roy. Ent. Soc.* **4**, pp. 88-97.

Benedek, P. (1970) The Hungarian countrywide light-trap network
in the service of plant protection forecasting. Europe.
Mediterranean Plant Protection Organ. *Pub. A*, pp. **57**, pp. 163-
167.

Clark, L.R. (1964) The population dynamics of Cardiaspina albitextura (Psyllidae), *Aust. J. Zool*, **12** (3), pp. 362-80.

Dempster, J.P. (1971) The population ecology of the cinnabar moth, Tyria jacobaeae L. (Lepidoptera, Arctiidae), *Oecologia (Berl.)*, **7**, pp. 26-67.

Dempster, J.P. and Lakhani, K.H. (1979) A population model for cinnabar moth and its food plant, ragwort, *J. Anim. Ecol*, **48** (1), pp. 143-163.

Duffey, E. (1968) Ecological studies on the large copper butterfly Lycaena dispar Haw. batavus Obth. at Woodwalton fen National Nature Reserve, Huntingdonshire, *J. Appl. Ecol*, **5**(1), pp. 69-96.

Hassell, M.P. (1975) Density-dependence in single-species populations, *J. Anim. Ecol*, **44**, pp. 283-295.

Hassell, M.P. (1979) The dynamics of predator-prey interactions: polyphagous predators, competing predators and hyperparasitoids, Chapter 13, *In* 'Population Dynamics' (R.M. Anderson, B.D. Turner, and L.R. Taylor, eds) *20th Symp. Br. Ecol. Soc.*, pp. 283-306.

Hassell, M.P., Lawton, J.H. and May, R.M. (1976) Patterns of dynamical behaviour in single-species populations, *J. Anim. Ecol*, **45**, pp. 471-486.

Hassell, M.P. and Comins, H.N. (1978) Sigmoid functional responses and population stability, *Theor. Pop. Biol*, **14**(1), pp. 62-67.

Holling, C.S. (1973) Resilience and stability of ecological systems, *Ann. Rev. Ecol. Syst.*, **4**, pp. 1-23.

Klomp, H. (1966) The dynamics of a field population of the pine looper Bupalus piniarius L. (Lep. Glom.), *Adv. Ecol. Res.*, **3**, pp. 207-305.

Lamb, H.H. (1965) Britain's changing climate, *In* "The Biological Significance of Climatic Changes in Britain" (C.G. Johnson and L.P. Smith, eds), *Symp. Inst. Biol.*, **14**, pp. 3-34.

Lewontin, R.C. (1969) The meaning of stability, *In* "Diversity and Stability in Ecological Systems", Report of Symposium held on May 26-28 at Brookhaven National Laboratory, N.Y., pp. 13-24.

Lloyd, B. and Benson, R.B. (1945) Hornets in Hertfordshire, *Trans. Herts. Nat. Hist. Soc.*, **22** (3), pp. 87-88.

May, R.M. (1973) Stability and complexity in model ecosystems, Princeton University Press, Princeton.

May, R.M. (1974) Biological populations with non-overlapping generations: stable points, stable cycles, and chaos, *Science*, **186**, pp. 645-647.

May, R.M. (1975) Patterns of species abundance and diversity, *In* 'Ecology of Communities' (J. Diamond and M. Cody, eds), Harvard University Press, Cambridge, Mass., pp. 81-120.

May, R.M. (1976) Simple mathematical models with very complicated dynamics, *Nature*, **261**, pp. 459-467.

May, R.M. (1977) Thresholds and breakpoints: ecosystems with a multiplicity of stable states, *Nature*, **269**, pp. 471-477.

May, R.M., Conway, G.R., Hassell, M.P. and Southwood, T.R.E. (1974) Time delays, density dependence and single-species oscillations, *J. Anim. Ecol.*, **43**, pp. 747-770.

May, R.M. and Oster, G.F. (1976) Bifurcations and dynamic complexity in simple ecological models, *Am. Nat.*, **110**, pp. 573-559.

May, R.M. and Anderson, R.M. (1979) Population biology of infectious diseases, Part II, *Nature*, **280**, pp. 455-461.

Meijer, J. (1980) The development of some elements of the arthropod fauna, *Oecologia (Berl.)*, **45** (2), pp. 220-235.

Milne, A. (1962) On a theory of natural control of insect population, *J. Theoret. Biol.*, **3**, pp. 19-50.

Nicholson, A.J. (1954) An outline of the dynamics of animal populations, *Aust. rev. Zool.*, **2** (1), pp. 9-65.

Rogers, D. (1979) Tsetse population dynamics and distribution: a new analytical approach, *J. Anim. Ecol.*, **48**, pp. 825-849.

Schwerdtweger, F. (1935) Studien über den Massenwechsel einiger Forstschädlinge, *Z. Forst-u. Jagdw.*, **67**, pp. 15-38, 85-104, 449-482, 513-540.

Schwerdtweger, F. (1941) Über die Ursachen des Massenwechsels der Insekten, *Z. angew. Ent.*, **28**, pp. 254-303.

Southwood, T.R.E. (1975) The dynamics of insect populations, *In* "Insects, Science and Society", (D. Pimentel, ed) Academic Press, N.Y.

Southwood, T.R.E., May, R.M., Hassell, M.P. and Conway, G.R. (1974) Ecological strategies and population parameters, *Am. Nat.* **108** (964), pp. 791-804.

Southwood, T.R.E. and Comins, H.N. (1976) A synoptic population model, *J. Anim. Ecol.*, **45**, pp. 949-965.

Southwood, T.R.E. and Reader, P.M. (1976) Population census data and key factor analysis for the viburnum whitefly, Aleurotrachelus jelinikii (Frauenf.), on three bushes, *J. Anim. Ecol.*, **45**, pp. 313-325.

Southwood, T.R.E., Brown, V.K. and Reader, P.M. (1979) The relationships of plant and insect diversities in succession, *Biol. J. Linn. Soc.*, **12** (4), pp. 327-348.

Stubbs, M. (1977) Density dependence in the life-cycles of animals and its importance in K- and r-strategies, *J. Anim. Ecol.*, **46**, pp. 677-688.

Takahashi, F. (1964) Reproduction curve with two equilibrium points: a consideration on the fluctuation of insect population, *Res. Popul. Ecol.*, **6**, pp. 28-36.

Taylor, L.R. and Woiwod, I.P. (1980) Temporal stability as a density-dependent species characteristic, *J. Anim. Ecol.*, **49**, pp. 209-224.

Voûte, A.D. (1946) Regulation of the density of the insect-population in virgin-forests and cultivated woods, *Arch. Néer. Zool.*, **7**, pp. 435-70.

Watt, K.E.F. (1969) A comparative study on the meaning of stability in five biological systems: insect and furbearer populations, influenza, Thai hemorrhagic fever, and plague, *In* "Diversity in Ecological Systems". Report of Symposium held on May 26-28 at Brookhaven National Laboratory, N.Y., pp. 142-150.

Wolda, H. (1978a) Fluctuations in abundance of tropical insects, *Am. Nat.*, **112** (988), pp. 1017-1045.

Wolda, H. (1978b) Seasonal fluctuations in rainfall, food and abundance of tropical insects, *J. Anim. Ecol.*, **47** (2), 369-381.

Wolda, H. (1980) Seasonality of tropical insects. I. Leafhoppers (Homoptera) in Las Cumbres, Panama., *J. Anim. Ecol.*, **49**, pp. 277-290.

INFECTIOUS DISEASE AGENTS AND
CYCLIC FLUCTUATIONS IN HOST ABUNDANCE

R.M. Anderson

(Imperial College of Science & Technology, London)

1. INTRODUCTION

Many animal species are known to exhibit regular non-seasonal
cyclic changes in abundance within their natural habitats.
Among numerous examples recorded in the ecological literature,
the 3-4 year cycles of lemmings and voles in Europe (Shelford
1943; Elton 1942); the 6-7 year cycles of red grouse in Britain
(Mackenzie 1952); the 8-10 year cycles of certain forest insects
in Central Europe (Varley, Gradwell and Hassell 1973) and the
10 year cycles of hare and lynx in North America (Leopold and
Ball 1931) are particularly remarkable.

To account for these observations ecologists have put forward
many theories, some based on the dynamical properties of two
species population interactions (e.g. predator-prey, host-para-
sitoid, host-pathogen and plant-herbivore associations) others
implicating climatic change or evolutionary factors (Lack 1954;
Krebs 1978; Bulmer 1975; May 1975).

The observation that many directly transmitted viral and bacterial diseases of man exhibit regular fluctuations in prevalence
within urban communities in Europe and North America has also
generated much interest in cyclical population phenomena among
epidemiologists. The two year cycles of measles and the 3-4
year cycles of whooping cough in Britain and the United States
are well documented phenomena (Bartlett 1957; Yorke et al. 1979).
These patterns are often referred to as recurrent epidemic
behaviour. The are, in part, the result of man's ability to
acquire lasting and often life long immunity to such diseases
subsequent to recovery from first exposure. Epidemics severely
deplete the pool of susceptible hosts and further outbreaks are
conditional on the replenishment of the susceptible pool by new
births within the population.

The early deterministic work of Soper (1929) employed mathematical formulations describing the flow of hosts between com-
partments containing susceptible, infected and immune individuals. These compartmental models generated damped epidemic
waves, the system eventually settling to a stable equilibrium
point. The inclusion of factors such as disease incubation
periods and the continual replenishment of the susceptible stock
did not result in undamped epidemic behaviour. The important
work of Bartlett (1956, 1957), however, revealed that stochastic
formulations of these models lead to the.perpetuation of cyclic
epidemic waves indefinitely within large communities where the
probability of disease fade out is small. More recently, Yorke
and co-workers, and Dietz have shown that undamped non-seasonal
oscillations may be produced by deterministic models incorpora-
ting disease incubation periods and annual periodicity in transmission; features which are intrinsic to the biologies of many
human viral and bacterial infections (Yorke and London 1973;
London and Yorke 1973; Dietz 1976; Yorke et al. 1979). These
workers have cogently argued that such a mechanism is responsible
for the regular biennial cycle, alternating between years of
high and low incidence, for measles in New York City between
1948 and 1964.

This paper aims to bring together the two separate litera-
tures - one dealing with cyclic fluctuations in animal abundance
and the other dealing with recurrent epidemic behaviour - in
order to explore the role played by pathogens in inducing periodic fluctuations in host abundance. Theoretical developments
are based on deterministic compartmental models, describing the
flow of hosts between for example, susceptible and infected
categories, but in contrast to the majority of published models,
the pathogen is assumed to play an important role in the regulation of host abundance (Anderson and May 1979; May and Anderson
1979).

Attention is specifically focused on directly transmitted
viral and protozoan infections of forest insects, and rabies
within fox populations. The choice of these two types of infection is in part stimulated by the observation that both forest
insects and fox populations often exhibit periodic fluctuations
in abundance in the presence of these pathogens. The major
objectives of this paper are (a) to ascertain whether simple
deterministic models of each host-pathogen interaction exhibit
periodic dynamical behaviour, (b) to compare model predictions
with observed patterns and (c) to pursue the implications of
theoretical predictions in light of the use of insect pathogens
as biological control agents and the control of rabies within
fox populations.

2. PATHOGENS OF INSECTS

Recent theoretical work has clearly demonstrated the potential of many directly transmitted microparasites (viruses, bacteria and protozoa) to regulate the abundance of their arthropod hosts, even in the absence of other constraints such as predators and resource limitations (Anderson and May 1980; Anderson and May 1981). This work is based on the construction of simple deterministic models which describe the major biological features of disease transmission.

In this section we consider one specific group of disease agents, the members of which are directly transmitted between hosts by means of an infective stage with a not insignificant lifespan in the external environment. Many viral and protozoan infections of insects possess this characteristic (Tinsley 1979). The dynamical properties of simple deterministic models of such infections are extensively discussed by Anderson and May (1981) and the treatment outlined below is based on this work.

Population models of the transmission of these pathogens are somewhat simpler than those for vertebrate infections as a consequence of the observation that invertebrates do not appear to develop an affective degree of acquired immunity to infectious disease agents (Maramorosch and Shope 1975; Lackie 1980). Although arthropods are often able to mount cellular or humoral responses to parasitic invasion those individuals which recover do not seem to possess an enhanced degree of resistance to further infection. Recovered individuals therefore pass directly back into the pool of susceptible hosts.

Our model of disease transmission consists of three coupled differential equations describing the rates of change through time of the densities of susceptible hosts, infected hosts and infective stages in the external habitat; denoted respectively by $X(t)$, $Y(t)$ and $W(t)$ at time t. Since our interest lies in the impact of the pathogen on host population growth, hosts are assumed in the absence of the pathogen to reproduce and die at per capita rates $\underline{a}$ and $\underline{b}$ respectively. The disease free host population, $N(t)$, therefore grows exponentially where

$$N(t) = N_O \exp (rt). \tag{1}$$

N_O is the initial density of hosts at time t=O, and r is the natural intrinsic growth rate of the host ($r = a-b$) which is assumed to be positive.

The pathogen is assumed to influence host survival such that the per capita death rate of infected hosts is $b+\alpha$ where α

denotes the disease induced mortality rate. Infected hosts may
recover from infection at a rate v (passing back into the susceptible pool) such that the average duration of infection is
$1/(v+b+\alpha)$ time units. The total number of infective transmission stages (W) produced by an infected host throughout its expected life span $(1/(v+b+\alpha))$ is denoted by Λ and the per capita
rate of production is represented by λ where

$$\lambda = \Lambda(\alpha+b+v). \tag{2}$$

For simplicity we assume that there is no incubation period;
hosts being able to produce infective stages immediately on
acquisition of infection. The total number of infective stages
Λ is typically of the order of 10^6 or more for many viral and
protozoan pathogens of insects (Anderson and May 1981).

    Initially we assume that transmission between hosts is solely
horizontal in nature. Following conventional lines, the net
rate of transmission is taken to be directly proportional to the
density of susceptible hosts (X) times the density of infective
stages (W); namely βWX where β is a transmission coefficient.
The quantity $\frac{1}{\beta}$ measure the average time interval between contacts
of hosts and infective stages which result in infection. The
free-living infective stages (W) are lost at a per capita rate
$\mu+\beta N$ where μ represents natural mortality and βN represents
losses as a result of being picked up by hosts (either infected
(Y) or susceptible (X)).

    These assumptions lead to the following equations

$$dX/dt = a(X+Y) - bX - \beta XW + vY \tag{3}$$

$$dY/dt = \beta XW - (b+\alpha+v)Y \tag{4}$$

$$dW/dt = \lambda Y - (\mu+\beta N)W \tag{5}$$

The total host population N, where N = X+Y, is given by

$$dN/dt = rN - \alpha Y. \tag{6}$$

    Despite the comparative simplicity of the biological assump-
tions made above the model represented by equations (3) to (6)
possesses a rich spectrum of dynamical behaviour a brief summary
of which is as follows.

Pathogen persistence

    If we define R as the expected number of secondary infections
that an infected host gives rise to during its infectious life

span if introduced into a population of susceptible hosts, it is clear that the quantity R, commonly referred to as the "basic reproductive rate" (Dietz 1974; Anderson 1981), must be greater than unity if the disease is to persist. The basic reproductive rate R is precisely analogous to the demographers "expected number of offspring" R_O (Fisher 1930). The state R = 1 therefor defines a transmission threshold above which the pathogen persists within the host population and below which it becomes extinct. From equation (4), the basic reproductive rate R within a population of N_O susceptible hosts is

$$R = \left[\frac{\lambda}{(b+\alpha+v)}\right]\left[\frac{\beta N_O}{\mu+\beta N_O}\right] \tag{7}$$

R is clearly greater than unity provided

$$\lambda > (\alpha+b+v) \tag{8}$$

or alternatively,

$$\Lambda > 1 \tag{9}$$

These equations simply state that each infected host must produce on average more than one infective stage. As noted earlier many viral and protozoan infections produce in excess of 10^6 infective stages per host and hence persistence is ensured.

Equation (7) also illustrates a further point of epidemiological interest, since by putting R = 1, the threshold density of susceptible hosts for disease maintenance, N_T, may be derived where

$$N_T = \left[\frac{\mu}{\beta\,\lambda}\right]\left[\frac{(\alpha+b+v)}{(1 - (\alpha+b+v)/\lambda)}\right] \tag{10}$$

Since λ is typically very large this essentially reduces to

$$N_T = (\alpha+b+v)/\hat{\beta} \tag{11}$$

where $\hat{\beta} = \beta\lambda/\mu$. $\tag{12}$

Note the similarity of equation (11) with the threshold conditions derived from conventional epidemiological models of human diseases (Kermack and McKendrick 1927).

Regulation of host population growth

Provided R > 1, the pathogen will be able to regulate host

population growth if and only if,

$$\lambda > \alpha(\alpha+b+v)/(\alpha-r) > 0. \tag{13}$$

For λ large, as is the case for most microparasites, this expression is essentially met provided

$$\alpha > r. \tag{14}$$

In other words the parasite is able to regulate population growth provided pathogenicity, α, exceeds the intrinsic growth rate, r, of its host.

If equation (14) is not satisfied, but $R > 1$, the host population grows exponentially at a rate P, until other constraints such as resource limitation restrict growth. Asymptotically the growth rate P (where $P < r$) is

$$P = r-\alpha y, \tag{15}$$

where y is the prevalence of infection, namely Y/N. Interestingly, the prevalence settles to a constant value as N becomes large such that

$$y \rightarrow \frac{(\alpha+b+v)(\Lambda-1) - r}{\Lambda(\alpha+b+v) - \alpha} \tag{16}$$

Clearly in the exponentially growing (unregulated) population, the disease will only persist (y positive) provided

$$\lambda - (\alpha+b+v) > r, \tag{17}$$

since $\Lambda(\alpha+b+v) = \lambda$.

Of more interest, however, is the disease controlled equilibrium. This state is locally stable provided

$$AB > C, \tag{18}$$

where

$$A = \mu\Delta + \alpha(\alpha+b+v)/(\alpha-r) - r \tag{19}$$

$$B = \mu r\Delta(a+v)/(\alpha-r) \tag{20}$$

$$C = r\mu(\alpha+b+v) \tag{21}$$

and the quantity Δ is

$$\Delta = (\alpha-r)/(\alpha-r-\alpha/\Lambda) \tag{22}$$

(Anderson and May 1981).

In cases where Λ is effectively infinite, as for most insect pathogens, equation (18) reduces to

$$(\mu+\alpha D-r)(D-1) - (1/L) > 0, \qquad (23)$$

where L is the expected life span of an infected host ($1/(\alpha+b+v)$) and $D = 1/(L(\alpha-r))$.

Provided equation (18) is satisfied the disease controlled level of host abundance, N*, is

$$N^* = \frac{\mu(\alpha+b+v)}{\lambda\beta[1 - (r/\alpha) - (1/\Lambda)]} \qquad (24)$$

and the equilibrium prevalence, or incidence of infection y* is given by

$$y^* = \frac{Y^*}{N^*} = \frac{r}{\alpha}. \qquad (25)$$

Note that highly pathogenic organisms (α large) although more likely to regulate host population growth (see equation 14) will persist at very low prevalances at equilibrium. This is a consequence of the often observed relationship in biology between "standing crop" and rate of turnover. Highly pathogenic organisms lead to the rapid removal of their host and hence the "standing crop" of infected hosts is low.

A clear biological interpretation of equation (18) is not straightforward but in general a stable disease controlled equilibrium will be achieved if (a) the disease agents pathogenicity α exceeds the host population's intrinsic growth rate r (equation 14); (b) the rate of production of infective stages λ is large (equation 17) and (c) the expected life span of the infective stage, $1/\mu$, is short (equation 18).

Numerical studies reveal that if $R > 1, \alpha > r$, and equation (18) is not satisfied, the population variables (host and infective stage density) oscillate in stable cycles, the period, amplitude and characteristic shape of which are determined by the biological properties of the host-pathogen association (i.e. the rate parameters of the model). In particular it can be seen from equation (18) that periodic behaviour is most likely to occur when (a) the infective stage is long lived (μ small), (b) the intrinsic growth rate of the host is low (r small), (c) the parasite is highly pathogenic (α large) and (d) when very large numbers of infective stages are produced by one infected host (λ very large). Fig. 1, based upon extensive numerical studies, illustrates these points and furthermore shows the period of the cycles in host abundance (and prevalence of infection) as a func-

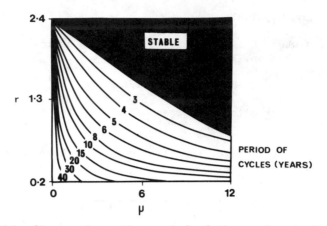

Fig. 1   This figure shows the period of the cycles in host abun-
         dance and prevalence of infection predicted by the
         insect pathogen model, as a function of the intrinsic
         growth rate of the host r, and the death rate of the
         infective stage μ.   In the shaded region, there is a
         stable equilibrium point.   Rate parameters (expressed
         in units of 1/years): $\lambda = 10^6$, $\alpha = 9.0$, b = 3.3, v = 0
         (from Anderson and May 1980).

tion of the expected life span of the infective stages $(\frac{1}{\mu})$ and
the intrinsic growth rate of the host population (r).

   The four patterns of dynamical behaviour exhibited by the
model may be summarised as follows: (1) pathogen becomes extinct;
(2) pathogen persists but is unable to regulate host population
growth; (3) pathogen persists and stably regulates the host population and (4) pathogen persists, regulating abundance but inducing cyclical changes in population size.   The regions of a
section of the λ-α parameter space which give rise to these
various patterns of behaviour are shown in Fig. 2 for fixed
values of the other parameters (i.e. β, r, v).

   The major conclusion to be drawn is that directly transmitted
pathogens are able to induce non-seasonal cyclic changes in the
abundance of their host and in the prevalence of infection.   We
briefly consider this conclusion with respect to forest insects
and their pathogens in the following section.

3.   CYCLIC CHANGES IN THE ABUNDANCE OF FOREST INSECTS

   Cyclic changes in the abundance of forest insects, many of
which are pest species, have been reported in numerous temperate
forest regions in Europe and North America (Varley, Gradwell and
Hassell 1973).   The pest species have been much studied by

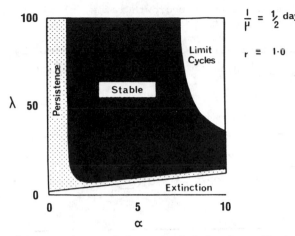

Fig. 2 The four regimes of dynamical behaviour that can be exhibited by the insect pathogen model are here illustrated in the λ-α parameter space (see text). Rate parameters (expressed in 1/weeks): $r = 1.0$, $b = 1.0$, $v = 0$, $\mu = 14$ (the infective stages are short lived).

entomologists and the long term records of insect abundance are among the best that exist in the ecological literature. Many of these studies reveal a striking degree of regularity in the cyclic changes in insect abundance. The larch budmoth, *Zeiraphera diniana,* in the European Alps, for example, has predictable population peaks every 8 to 10 years (Auer 1968).

Certain workers have noted that epidemic outbreaks of viral or protozoan parasites are often observed in years of peak pest abundance and have argued that such pathogens, although unlikely to drive the cyclic changes in host abundance, are important in causing dramatic reductions in host population density (Bird and Whalen 1953; Morris 1963; Stairs 1972).

The most frequently observed pathogens of lepidopteran forest pests, such as the larch budmoth, are protozoan microsporidia and baculoviruses (Tinsley 1979; Stairs 1972). Interestingly, these pathogens often possess long lived infective stages which survive exceptionally well in damp habitats protected from direct sunlight, such as the soil environment of temperate forests. Furthermore these parasites are invariably highly pathogenic and produce infective stages in very large numbers (in excess of 10^6 per infected host). Diseased insects do not in general recover from these infections (v=0). Finally, it is striking that in addition to these properties, many forest insect pests are univoltine (one generation per year) and character-

istically have low intrinsic growth rates (r) often close to
unity in value (in units/year).

These properties are precisely those predicted by the theoretical model of the previous section, to induce cyclic changes in
host abundance and disease prevalence.

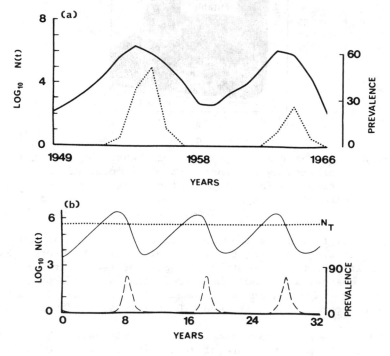

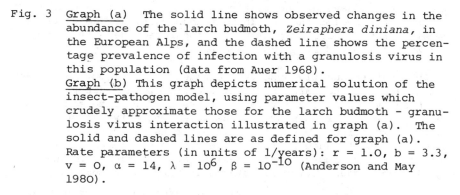

Fig. 3   Graph (a)   The solid line shows observed changes in the
         abundance of the larch budmoth, *Zeiraphera diniana,* in
         the European Alps, and the dashed line shows the percen-
         tage prevalence of infection with a granulosis virus in
         this population (data from Auer 1968).
         Graph (b) This graph depicts numerical solution of the
         insect-pathogen model, using parameter values which
         crudely approximate those for the larch budmoth - granu-
         losis virus interaction illustrated in graph (a).   The
         solid and dashed lines are as defined for graph (a).
         Rate parameters (in units of 1/years): $r = 1.0$, $b = 3.3$,
         $v = 0$, $\alpha = 14$, $\lambda = 10^6$, $\beta = 10^{-10}$ (Anderson and May
         1980).

A remarkable set of data described by Auer (1968) records the
abundance of the larch budmoth in the European Alps, and the
prevalance of infection with a granulosis virus, over a 20 year
period (Fig. 3).   Also shown in Fig. 3 are the same quantities,

namely insect abundance and disease prevalence, as calculated
from equations (3) - (5) with numerical values of the parameters
estimated independently of the population data by Anderson and
May (1980). These authors used the information given by Baltensweiler et al (1977), Baltensweiler (1964), Benz (1962) and Auer
(1968) to assign rough estimates of the parameter values. The
agreement between the data and theoretical results in Fig. 3 is
striking both with respect to the period of the cycles (9-10
years) and the general shape of the oscillations in budmoth
density and viral prevalence. In particular note that the prevalence always peaks just after the peak in host abundance. This
is a commonly observed feature of epidemic outbreaks of disease
within arthropod populations and is to be expected if the pathogen is the cause of the decline in host abundance (see Fig. 3b).

A second general feature of population cycles driven by such
pathogens is that the prevalence of infection declines effectively to zero during the years in which host density falls
below the threshold level N_T. The disease thus appears to have
disappeared from its host population. This observation has led
many ecologists to conclude that such pathogens are not responsible for the cyclic changes in host abundance. This conclusion
is incorrect since during periods in which N is below N_T, the
pathogen survives as a free living infective agent by virtue of
its long expected life span and the enormous numbers of such
stages produced during an epidemic. Stairs (1972), for example,
reports that an epidemic of a nuclear-polyhedrosis virus in
North American tent caterpillars, *Malacosoma* sp., can result in
an increase by a factor of 10^{10} in virus polyhedra in forest
environments within a period of 20 days. If these infective
stages have an average life span of 4 months,out of a population
of 10^{20} roughly 10^{8} will still be alive after 10 years (assuming
a constant death rate).   This population is more than adequate
to initiate the next epidemic once host density again rises
above the threshold level.

4.   THE USE OF PATHOGENS AS BIOLOGICAL CONTROL AGENTS

Theoretical models of the dynamics of insect-pathogen associations are of more than purely academic interest. In recent
years, for example, invertebrate pathologists have become increasingly aware of the potential of viruses and protozoa as biological control agents of pest species (Tinsley 1979; Huffaker
1974; DeBach 1974). Baculoviruses and microsporidia, in particular, appear to have great promise as control agents.

Two of the most important questions in this area of research
are a) what characteristics does a pathogen require if it is to
be an effective control agent? and b) in what quantities should

the pathogen be introduced? Insights into both questions can be
achieved by some minor modifications of the model outlined in
section 2 (equations 3 - 5).

For example, if a biological control program introduces infective stages of a pathogen into the habitat of the pest at a
constant rate A, the model remains essentially as before but
with equation (5) replaced by

$$dW/dt = A + \lambda Y - (\mu+\beta N)W. \tag{26}$$

The new model (equations (3), (4)   and (26)) has the same
general dynamical properties as those outlined earlier in
section 2. The condition that must be satisfied if the disease
is to regulate host population growth is, as before, equation
(13). Clearly, disease agents of high pathogenicity (α large)
and which produced large numbers of infective stages (λ large)
will be effective regulators of host population growth.

Given that the pathogen is able to regulate host population
growth, the disease will eradicate the host provided the introduction rate of infective stages A, exceeds a critical value A_c
where,

$$A > A_c = \frac{\mu r (\alpha+b+v)}{\beta (\alpha-r)}. \tag{27}$$

If $A > A_c$ the system, in the absence of immigration of new
hosts, settles to a stable equilibrium with $N^* = 0$, $Y^* = 0$ and
$W^* = A/\mu$. If the introduction rate is not large enough to satisfy equation (27) the pathogen regulates the host population
either to a stable equilibrium or a stable cycle (Anderson and
May 1981).

From equation (27) it is clear that control is more likely to
be effective if the parasite (a) is highly pathogenic (α large),
(b) has a high transmission efficiency (β large) and (c) produces
long lived infective stages (μ small). In addition it is obvious
that pest species with high intrinsic growth rates will be more
difficult to control than those with small r values. These
notions are displayed in Fig. 4 where the patterns of dynamical
behaviour produced by various combinations of the parameters A
and r are recorded. Note that for the parameter values used in
the construction of this figure, when r is roughly 2 per annum
an introduction rate A of 10^{10} would be necessary to eradicate
the pest. Given a virus which produces over 10^6 infective particles per infected host, this would require the rearing of 10^4
infected insects per year and the collection and application of
the infective particles produced by these. This numerical
example suggests that pests with high r values may be difficult

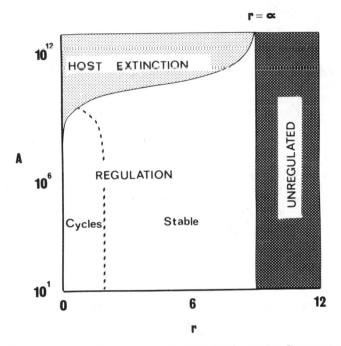

Fig. 4   The use of pathogens as biological control agents.   The
         five regimes of dynamical behaviour that can be exhi-
         bited by the biological control insect pathogen model
         (equations (3), (4) and (26)) are here illustrated in
         the A - r parameter space (see text) A = introduction
         rate of virus, r = intrinsic growth rate of host.   Rate
         parameters (expressed in units of 1/years):
         $\beta = 10^{-10}$, $\mu = 3.0$, $b = 3.3$, $\lambda = 10^{6}$, $\alpha = 9.0$.

to eradicate by the continual introduction of a pathogen on
purely practical grounds.

   Considerable improvements in effectiveness, however, may be
achieved by the choice of pathogens with specific properties.
For example, many viruses and protozoa are able to transmit
themselves between hosts, vertically from parent to offspring.
Vertical transmission always occurs in conjunction with the
ability to transmit horizontally by means of infective stages.
If we assume, that in addition to horizontal transmission, a
proportion p of offspring from infected hosts are themselves
infected, our biological control model takes the form:

$$dX/dt = rX + (1-p)aY - \beta XW + vY \qquad (28)$$

$$dY/dt = paY + \beta XW - (\alpha+b+v)Y \qquad\qquad (29)$$

$$dW/dt = A + \lambda Y - (\mu+\beta N)W \qquad\qquad (30)$$

The general dynamical properties of this model are as outlined earlier for equations (3), (4) and (27) except that the critical introduction rate A_c now becomes

$$A_c = \frac{\mu r(\alpha+b+v-pa)}{\beta(\alpha-r)}. \qquad\qquad (31)$$

For pest eradication, the introduction rate A must exceed A_c and this is clearly more easily achieved by the use of a pathogen which possesses the ability to transmit itself vertically (compare equation (27) with equation (31)).

Certain invertebrate pathogens, such as many species of insect viruses and protozoa, act to reduce the survival and reproductive capabilities of infected hosts. It has been suggested that the ability to reduce fecundity as well as survival is a desirable attribute for biological control agents. Interestingly, however, theory does not support this suggestion. For example, if the pathogen in question is able to transmit vertically and horizontally, but in addition acts to reduce the fecundity rate of infected hosts by a fraction f in comparison to uninfected individuals, equations (28) and (29) become:

$$dW/dt = rX + f(1-p)aY - \beta XW + vY \qquad\qquad (32)$$

$$dY/dt = fpaY + \beta XW - (\alpha+b+v)Y \qquad\qquad (33)$$

For pest eradication ($N^* = 0$, $W^* = A/\mu$), the introduction rate A must again exceed a critical level, A_c, but this level is now

$$A_c = \frac{\mu r(\alpha+b+v - fpa)}{\beta[\alpha-(af-b)]}. \qquad\qquad (34)$$

Given that all the parameter values of the pathogen are the same, except that $1 \geqslant f > 0$, the critical level A_c of equation (34) is greater than that given by equation (31). In other words, for host eradication, pathogens which reduce fecundity and survival must be introduced at a higher rate than those which solely act on host survival.

In summary, the ideal pathogen for biological control is one with the following properties: (1) high pathogenicity relative

to the intrinsic growth rate of the host where the parasite acts
principally to reduce host survival rather than fecundity;
(2) efficient horizontal and vertical transmission capabilities
and (3) long lived infective stages for horizontal transmission.

5. RABIES AND THE DYNAMICS OF FOX POPULATIONS

The simple compartmental framework of the models outlined in
the preceding sections can be employed, with certain modifications, to examine the dynamics of rabies, an important viral
disease of mammals. Rabies is a directly transmitted infection
of the central nervous system to which man and all mammals are
thought to be susceptible. It is one of the most pathogenic
viruses known to man and once clinical signs of infection appear,
the disease is almost invariably fatal (Kaplan 1977).

Two rabies epidemics have affected much of Europe since 1900.
During the first (1915-1924), dogs accounted for 74% of all
registered cases and wildlife species were thought to have
played a minor role in disease propagation. The present epidemic, which appears to have originated in Poland in 1939, is
characterised by a high incidence in the red fox, *Vulpes vulpes*
(70-80% of all reported cases) and in Central Europe this host
species is thought to be principally responsible for disease
maintenance and transmission (Winkler 1975). In parts of USSR
and North America, however, other species are known to be important hosts (i.e. the wolf (*Lupus lupus*), skunk (*Mephitis mephitis*), racoon (*Procyon lotor*) and the racoon dog (*Nyctereutes
procyonoides*)) (Baer 1975).

The current epidemic in Europe has spread outwards from
Poland at an annual rate of 30-60 km, the present epidemic front
in France being only 40 km from the Channel coast line. The
introduction of this disease into Britain therefore appears a
very real possibility.

A remarkable feature of rabies epidemiology in foxes is the
regular 3 to 5 year cycle in incidence of the disease which
appears to coincide in time with fluctuations in fox density
(Lloyd 1976; Plummer 1954; Kantorovich 1964). Such patterns
have been reported in Europe and North America, and are most
apparent in areas where fox densities were high prior to the
introduction of the disease (Johnston and Beauregard 1969; Toma
and Andral 1977).

In this section we focus on the dynamics of rabies within red
fox (*V.vulpes*) populations in Europe. A number of features of
the biologies of the host and pathogen are relevant to the development of a model framework. (1) Once infected, few hosts, if
any, recover and an immune category of animals is therefore

effectively absent from the fox population. (2) The disease has
a long and often variable incubation period during which the
host is infected but not infectious. The average length of the
incubation period in foxes appears to be roughly 28-30 days.
(3) Once clinical symptoms of the disease appear (the fox becomes
rabid) the expected life span of the host is short, being
roughly 3-6 days. On average infected foxes are thought to be
infectious for roughly 5 days. (4) The density of foxes per
unit area varies widely according to habitat type. For example
figures of between 0.7 to 1.4 mature foxes per km^2 appear to be
common in many areas of Europe but densities of 20-24 per km^2
have been reported by Macdonald (1980) in some urban and suburban districts of England. The density of animals per unit area
appears to be tightly constrained by habitat type, resource
limitations (food and social territory) being an important feature of fox population dynamics.

Our model framework will assume that in the absence of infection, the fox population grows logistically to a disease-
free carrying capacity of K animals/sq. km, where the value of K
is determined by habitat type. For simplicity density-dependence is placed on fox survival where the per capita mortality
rate in a population of density N is taken to be b+γN. The per
capita birth rate is denoted by a and in the absence of rabies
the equilibrium fox density K is defined as

$$K = (a-b)/\gamma = r/\gamma. \qquad (35)$$

The rate at which infected foxes become infectious is denoted
by σ where $\frac{1}{\sigma}$ is the average incubation period (28 days).

Infectious foxes are assumed to die at a disease induced
mortality rate α where $\frac{1}{\alpha}$ is taken to be roughly 5 days.

These assumptions lead to the following three differential
equations for the temporal dynamics of the number of susceptible
X(t), infected but not yet infectious I(t), and infectious Y(t),
animals;

$$dX/dt = rX - \gamma NX - \beta XY \qquad (36)$$

$$dI/dt = \beta XY - (b+\gamma N)I - \sigma I \qquad (37)$$

$$dY/dt = \sigma I - (b+\alpha+\gamma N)Y. \qquad (38)$$

Here transmission between foxes is horizontal in nature where
the net rate is proportional to the densities of susceptible and
infectious foxes, namely, βXY where β is a transmission coefficient. Since the duration of infection is short, infected foxes
are assumed to be unable to reproduce. The total density of
foxes N, where N = X + I + Y, is given by

$$dN/dt = rX - (b+\gamma N)N - \alpha Y. \tag{39}$$

This model (equations (36) to (38)) is somewhat more complex than that detailed for the insect pathogens, but its equilibrium and local stability properties are easily determined.

Pathogen persistence

The 'basic reproductive' rate of rabies, R(where R is as defined earlier in section 2), after the introduction of a few infecteds into a population of N_O susceptibles, is directly obtainable from equations (37) and (38) by noting that for disease persistence dI/dt and dY/dt must initially be positive:

$$R = \frac{\beta \sigma N_O}{(\sigma+b+\gamma N_O)(\alpha+b+\gamma N_O)}. \tag{40}$$

Alternatively, if the fox population is at its carrying capacity, K, (consisting solely of susceptibles) prior to the introduction of the disease, equation (40) may be expressed as

$$R = \frac{\beta \sigma K}{(\sigma+a)(\alpha+a)}. \tag{41}$$

For disease persistence R > 1, and hence from equation (41) it is clear that an epidemic will only occur provided fox density, K, is above a critical threshold level K_T where

$$K > K_T = \frac{(\sigma+a)(\alpha+a)}{\beta\sigma}. \tag{42}$$

This expression is analogous to the threshold density condition derived from the classical epidemic model of Kermack and McKendrick (1927).

If R < 1, (or alternatively K < K_T) the fox population will settle to its disease-free equilibrium level K.

Provided R > 1, the disease will suppress fox density to a disease controlled equilibrium level, N*, such that N* < K, where

$$N* = \frac{[(\sigma+a)(\alpha+a) - ar]}{[\sigma\beta - a\gamma]}. \tag{43}$$

At this equilibrium the prevalence of rabies y*, where
$y* = (I* + Y*)/N*$, is

$$y* = \left(\frac{\alpha+\sigma+a-v}{\sigma+a}\right)\left(\frac{r}{\alpha+a}\right)\left[\frac{1 - \dfrac{1}{R}}{1 - \dfrac{ar}{(a+\alpha)(a+\sigma)}}\right], \qquad (44)$$

where v is defined for convenience as

$$v = r(1 - N*/K) \qquad (45)$$

and N* and R are defined in equations (41) and (43) respectively.

The degree of depression of the fox population, d, below its
rabies free level where $d = 1 - N*/K$ (Anderson 1979) is simply

$$d = \frac{(\sigma+a)(\alpha+a) - ar}{K(\sigma\beta - a\gamma)} . \qquad (46)$$

It is interesting to note that depression is more severe in
habitats where fox density is high (K large). Furthermore,
within the disease regulated fox population the prevalence of
infection, y*, also rises as K becomes large (Fig. 5).

Neighbourhood stability analysis of the rabies model (using
standard methods as detailed in May (1975)) reveals that the
disease controlled equilibrium defined by equations (43) and (44)
for R > 1 is stable to small perturbations if, and only if,

$$(2b+\alpha+\sigma+3\gamma N*)[(b+\sigma+\gamma N*)N*+\alpha(N*-Y*)+aN*] - C > 0. \qquad (47)$$

Here the equilibrium densities of susceptible (X*) and infectious (Y*) foxes are given by

$$Y* = (r-\gamma N*)/\beta \qquad (48)$$

$$X* = (b+\sigma+\gamma N*)(b+\alpha+\gamma N*)/(\sigma\beta) \qquad (49)$$

and C is defined for notational convenience as

$$C = X*(K-N*)(\sigma\beta-\gamma a) \qquad (50)$$

Noting that C is always positive provided R > 1, this condition
(equation (48)) is more easily satisfied for low values of K
just in excess of K_T and when the pathogenicity of the disease,
α, is low.

Numerical studies reveal that if R > 1, and equation (47) is not satisfied, fox density (N*) and the prevalence of rabies (y*) oscillate in stable cycles, the period and amplitude of which are determined by the biological properties of the host-pathogen association. The various patterns of dynamical behaviour exhibited by the model and the period of the cycles in the oscillatory region are portrayed in Fig. 6 for various values of K, the carrying capacity of the fox habitat, and $\frac{1}{\sigma}$ the incubation period of the disease.

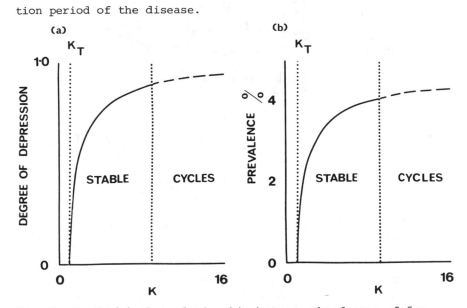

Fig. 5 <u>Graph (a)</u> The relationship between the degree of fox population depression, d, where d = 1 - N*/K and the carrying capacity of the habitat, K, in the absence of rabies. Parameter values (expressed as units of 1/years): a = 1.05, b = 0.5, α = 73, σ = 13, β = 80. <u>Graph (b)</u> The relationship between the prevalence of infection y* and K (see equation (44) in text). Parameter values as for graph (a).

<u>Oscillatory behaviour</u>

Rough estimates of the values of most of the parameters of the model can be obtained from published information in the literature. For example, the characteristics of the infection within foxes is fairly well known where the incubation period $\frac{1}{\sigma}$, is of the order of 28-30 days on average and the life expectancy of infectious forces, $\frac{1}{\alpha}$, is roughly 5 days. The parameters

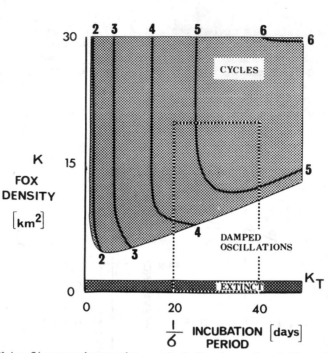

Fig. 6   This figure shows the period (in years) of the cycles in
         fox abundance and rabies prevalence predicted by
         equations (36) to (38) as a function of the carrying
         capacity, K (in km^2) and the incubation period, $\frac{1}{\sigma}$(in
         days). The 3 regimes of dynamical behaviour exhibited
         by the model are also illustrated in this figure (see
         text). The level K_T defines the threshold fox density
         necessary for rabies maintenance, while the rectangular
         area surrounded by a dashed line depicts the region of
         parameter space most relevant to the known biology of
         rabies within fox populations. Parameter values as for
         Fig. 5.

of the fox population clearly vary according to habitat type
where K lies in the region of 0-25 animals per km^2. Lloyd
(1976) provides information concerning the reproductive and survival characteristics of foxes in various European localities.
Female foxes produce litters which on average contain 5 cubs.
The sex ratio of females to males appears to be roughly 1:1 and
on average 80% of the vixens successfully produce cubs. The
instantaneous per capita birth rate a, per annum, is therefore
approximately a = 1.05. Life expectancy, $\frac{1}{b}$, varies in different
habitats, an average value being in the region of 2 years.

Given a, b and K, the parameter γ, measuring the severity of density dependence can be estimated from equation (35).

The estimation of β, the transmission parameter, is more problematic. Fortunately, however, epidemiologists have recorded observations on the density of foxes per unit area necessary to maintain endemic rabies (W.H.O. 1978); the majority of these estimates lie between O.4-1.0 foxes per km^2. If we assume that these values reflect the threshold carrying capacity, K_T, equation (42) may be used to obtain crude estimates of β, knowing σ, α and a. In what follows, the larger estimate of K_T has been employed (i.e. 1.O/km^2) which yields a β value of approximately 8O.

It can be seen from Fig. 6, that the parameter values detailed above give rise to oscillatory behaviour in habitats with a fox carrying capacity, K, greater than 8 per km^2. The period of these cycles lies in the region of 4 to 5 years; a pattern which is in broad agreement with the observed 3-5 year cycles which are most apparent in areas where fox densities were initially high prior to the introduction of rabies (Toma and Andral 1977; Johnston and Beauregard 1969) (Table I). Furthermore, if the value of K_T used to calculate β is taken as O.4 foxes/km^2, the boundary between stable limit cycles and a stable point changes such that oscillatory behaviour is predicted in habitats where K is greater than 4 animals/km^2 (Fig. 7) and these cycles will have a period of between 3-5 years depending on the precise value of K.

TABLE I

Cyclic Patterns in Rabies Epidemics within Fox Populations

Period between major outbreaks (years)	Geographical location	Author(s)
3-5	Canada	Johnston and Beauregard (1969)
3	Germany	Kauker and Zettl (1960)
4-5	USA	Friend (1968)

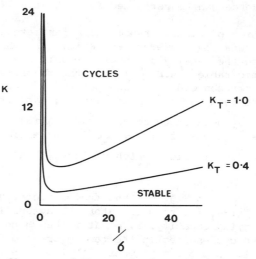

Fig. 7   The influence of K_T on the location of the boundary
         between damped oscillatory behaviour to a stable point
         and undamped limit cycle behaviour in the $K - \dfrac{1}{\sigma}$
         parameter space.   The values of K_T are expressed as
         foxes/km^2.   Parameter values as for Fig. 5.

   In either case, however, even in the region in which a stable
point occurs, the model exhibits damped oscillatory behaviour
and numerical studies reveal that (a) the period of these oscillations lies in the region of 3-4 years and (b) the damping time
is long.   For example, two such numerical simulations are displayed in Figs. 8 and 9 where the trajectories of fox populations density, N, and the prevalence of infection, y, are
plotted over a period of 40 years for two different K values.
These simulations make clear that oscillatory behaviour will be
observed even in poor fox habitats (K small) over a period such
as 40 years which is roughly the time span of the current epidemic in Europe.

   The oscillatory behaviour of the system can be accentuated by
seasonal changes in the value of any one of the population parameters.   Reproduction within the fox population, for example, is
a discrete process; the birth of cubs usually occurring around
March to April.   Furthermore, the behaviour of foxes during the
mating (December to February) and cub production (March-April)
periods appears to enhance the rate of transmission of rabies;
a peak in disease prevalence occurring during the winter and
spring months (Kauker and Zettl 1960).

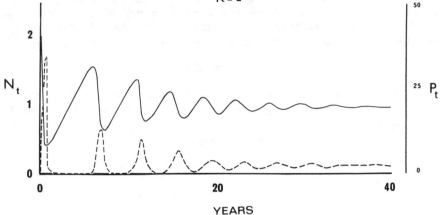

Fig. 8 Numerical solution of equations (36) to (38) over a
period of 40 years for parameter values K = 2, α = 73,
σ = 13, a = 1.05, b = 0.5, β = 80. The model exhibits
damped oscillatory behaviour in this region of parameter
space. The solid line represents fox density, N/km^2,
while the dashed line represents the prevalence of
rabies infection within this population. The period of
the oscillations is between 3-4 years.

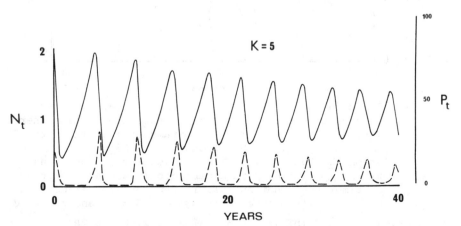

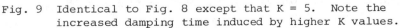

Fig. 9 Identical to Fig. 8 except that K = 5. Note the
increased damping time induced by higher K values.

The impact of seasonal time dependence, in either the birth
rate a or the transmission coefficient β, can be crudely
examined by representing the parameters as periodic functions of
time. For example, seasonal changes in β may be mimicked by the
function

$$\beta(t) = A + B \sin[2\pi(t-\tau)] \tag{51}$$

where t is in units of one year, τ is a phase angle, A is the
average value of β(t) and B is a constant determining the amplitude of the oscillations.

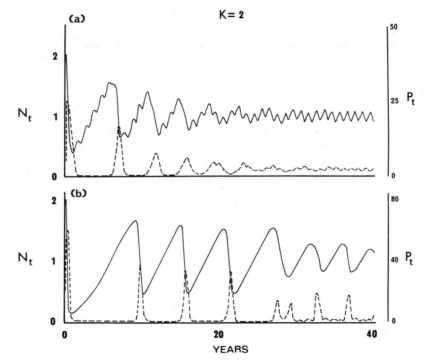

Fig. 10   Graph (a) Identical to Fig. 8 except that the birth
          rate a is a periodic (seasonal) function of time where
          a(t) = A+B sin 2π(t-τ). The parameter t is in units of
          one year, A = 1.05, B = 1.0 and τ = - 3.0.
          Graph (b) Identical to Fig. 8 except that the trans-
          mission parameter β is a periodic (seasonal) function
          of time (see equation (51) in text). The parameter
          t is in units of one year, A = 80, B = 50 and τ = -3.0.

Both graphs (a) and (b) are to be compared with Fig. 8.

Two numerical simulations of the rabies model are shown in
Fig. 10.   The parameter β fluctuates seasonally in Fig. 10b with
an average value of 80 and a range of 30 to 130, while in Fig.
10a a is a periodic function (of the form defined in equation
(51) with an average of 1.05 and a range of 0.05 to 2.05.   The
main conclusions to be drawn from this superficial analysis are
as follows.   (1) Seasonality in transmission may increase the
damping time of the system in its approach to a stable equilibrium (compare Fig. 8 with Fig. 10b) and may in certain circumstances generate undamped waves in a region of parameter space
which, in the absence of time dependence in β, generates damped
behaviour to a stable point.   As noted earlier, such patterns of
behaviour are generated by certain models of human viral infections (Yorke and London 1973; Dietz 1976).   (2) Seasonality in
reproduction does not appear to enhance the oscillatory behaviour of the system beyond imposing seasonal fluctuation on fox
density and disease prevalence (compare Fig. 8 with Fig. 10a).

On a year to year basis, an examination of the range over
which the prevalence of infection, y, fluctuates provides further
qualitative agreement between model predictions and observed
trends. In endemic areas of rabies the prevalence of infection
appears to fluctuate between 0.1-7%; a range which is broadly
similar to that generated by the model (see Figs. 5, 8 and 9).
The high pathogenicity of rabies results in the disease persist-
ing at very low levels within fox populations.   This is, as
noted earlier for insect pathogens, a consequence of the often
observed biological relationship between "standing crop" and
rate of turnover (see section 2 and equation (25)).

One obvious and important consequence of this relationship is
that during the troughs of the disease induced fluctuations in
fox density, when N is less than the threshold density necessary
for pathogen persistence, i.e. R < 1, the prevalence of infection declines to very low levels (< 1%).   This is particularly
apparent when the carrying capacity of the foxes' habitat is
high since the amplitude of the cyclic fluctuations in host density and disease incidence are large in these circumstances.
The danger of disease extinction due to stochastic effects is
clearly high during these troughs in prevalence, particularly
within small areas of good fox habitat.   Over large areas,
however, rabies probably persists endemically as a consequence
of the high degree of spatial mobility exhibited by the host
species.   Young foxes, for example, invariably move from their
place of birth, often travelling distances in the region of 5-10
km in poor fox habitats (Lloyd 1976).   Males tend to move further than females in search of unoccupied territories.   An additional factor in the maintenance of infection during the troughs
may be the involvement of other host species.   In Europe, for
example, badgers, mustelids, rodents and deer are all known to be
susceptible to rabies.

In summary, the simple deterministic model of rabies dynamics
predicts patterns of dynamical behaviour which are in broad
agreement with observation in large areas of fox habitat. This
agreement provides encouragement for the extension of the model
framework to consider the efficiencies of various methods of
rabies control.

6. THE CONTROL OF RABIES WITHIN FOX POPULATIONS

The control of wildlife rabies in Europe during the current
epidemic has been principally based on attempts to reduce fox
density below the threshold level (K_T) necessary for disease
persistence. This approach, however, has in general met with
little success. More recently the possibility of oral vaccination of foxes using baits inoculated with attenuated virus has
been explored.

Suppression of fox density

From a theoretical standpoint, the most obvious way to control the spread of rabies is to maintain fox population density
below the threshold density K_T (equation (42)) by means of culling. In practical terms, this may be achieved by hunting, gas-
sing, poisoning or trapping. The simplest way in which to man-
age such a programme is to set an annual quota of foxes, say Λ,
which must be removed from the population in order to reduce the
density below K_T. The precise level of the quota Λ, will
clearly depend on the carrying capacity K of the fox habitat in
which control is to be initiated.

We can examine the feasibility of such an approach by modification of the rabies model defined in equations (36 to 39) to
include an extra mortality term Λ in equation (39). The problem
is in part similar to that of setting an annual quota of fish
which may be removed from a fishery in order to maximise
sustainable yield. The logistic equation of population growth,
used in the rabies model, also forms the template for many fisheries models (see Beddington 1979). We can therefore make use
of certain theoretical results in the fisheries literature to
examine the problem of fox culling.

In the absence of rabies, our new equation for the dynamics
of the fox population, taking account of the culling programme,
is

$$dN/dt = (r-\gamma N)N - \Lambda \qquad (52)$$

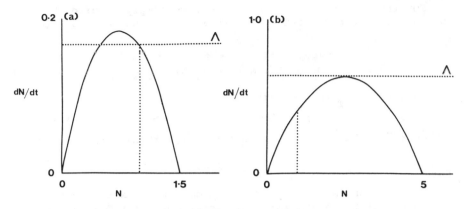

Fig. 11   The relationship between the logistic population
          growth curve, dN/dt (solid line) and the rate of fox
          culling Λ (horizontal dashed line) for various popula-
          tion densities, N.   The dashed vertical line denotes
          the value of $K_T = 1.0$.

          Graph (a) The case where $K_T > K/2$, and a culling rate
          Λ which produces two stable equilibrium points, $N^* = 0$
          and $N^* = N^*_2$ separated by an unstable equilibrium N^*_1.
          To eradicate rabies $\Lambda > rK_T(1-K_T/K)$.   Parameter values,
          $K_T=1.0$, K=1.5.

          Graph (b) The case where $K_T < K/2$ ($K_T = 1.0$, K = 5).

          The culling rate Λ must be in excess of the maximum
          value of the growth curve dN/dt, namely $\Lambda > rK/4$.   In
          such circumstances the system is attracted to the
          stable point $N^* = 0$.

This model has three equilibrium solutions; namely O, N^*_1
and N^*_2 where $N^*_2 > N^*_1$.   These three possible equilibria are
portrayed diagrammatically in Fig. 11 where the relationship
between the logistic population growth curve and the death rate
Λ imposed by culling is plotted.   It is well known that the
equilibria at points O and N^*_2 are locally stable while N^*_1 is
unstable (May 1977; Beddington 1979; Peterman, Clark and Holling
1979).   As the culling rate Λ increases towards the maximum
growth rate, which occurs at a density K/2, the equilibrium
points N^*_1 and N^*_2 draw closer together.   Once Λ exceeds the
growth rate at K/2, the system is attracted to the stable state
$N^* = 0$ and the fox population becomes extinct.

For the purpose of disease control we simply require that $N^*_2 < K_T$. Two cases arise. (1) If $K_T > K/2$ the culling rate Λ must satisfy

$$\Lambda > r\,K_T(1 - K_T/K) \tag{53}$$

For values of K_T in the region of 1 per km^2, this condition applies to areas of poor fox habitat where K is less than 2 foxes/km^2 (Fig. 11a). (2) Alternatively, if $K_T < K/2$,

$$\Lambda > r\,K/4. \tag{54}$$

This condition implies that we must cull the foxes to extinction since the stable state under this regime is $N^* = 0$ (Fig. 11b). In areas of good fox habitat, therefore, our culling programme must ensure the complete eradication of the fox population. This would appear difficult to achieve, particularly in light of the spatial mobility of the hosts and may explain why culling programmes have met with little success in Europe. In poor habitats where $K < 2$, fox culling would appear a feasible objective but its success is conditional on the continual maintenance of N^*_2 below K_T.

Vaccination

To examine the impact of vaccination on the dynamics of rabies, it is necessary to consider an additional population variable, Z, representing the number (or density) of vaccinated foxes within the population which are immune to infection. If we assume that susceptible foxes are vaccinated at a per capita rate ϕ and that immune hosts lose their protection at a per capita rate δ the dynamics of the various categories of the fox population may be represented by the following equations:

$$dX/dt = a(X+Z) - (b+\gamma N)X - \beta XY - \phi X + \delta Z \tag{55}$$

$$dI/dt = \beta XY - (\sigma+b+\gamma N)I \tag{56}$$

$$dY/dt = \sigma I - (\alpha+b+\gamma N)Y \tag{57}$$

$$dZ/dt = \phi X - (\delta+b+\gamma N)Z. \tag{58}$$

Where $N = X + I + Y + Z$, the dynamics of the total fox population is accordingly represented by

$$dN/dt = r(X+Z) - (b+\gamma N)N - \alpha Y. \tag{59}$$

In the context of disease eradication, the equilibrium of interest is the disease - free state defined by;

$$Y^\wedge = I^\wedge = O$$

and

$$N^* = K.$$

Without going into detail concerning the derivation (see Anderson, Jackson, May and Smith, 1981) this state is locally stable provided

$$\phi > (a+\delta)(R-1), \tag{60}$$

where R is as defined in equation (41). At this disease - free equilibrium the proportion of vaccinated foxes, p, is given by

$$p = \frac{Z^*}{(Z^*+X^*)} = \frac{\phi}{(\phi+a+\delta)}. \tag{61}$$

Equation (60) can therefore be expressed as

$$p > [1 - \frac{1}{R}], \tag{62}$$

a condition which defines the proportion p of the population that must be protected by vaccination in order to eradicate rabies.

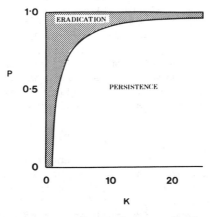

Fig. 12   The proportion p of the fox population that must be protected by vaccination in order to eradicate rabies for various values of K. In the shaded region $p > [1 - \frac{1}{R}]$ (see text). Parameter values as for Fig. 8 except K variable.

This proportion is simply related to R and hence to the
carrying capacity of the fox habitat K (see equation (41)).
The relationship between p and K is portrayed in Fig. 12, from
which it is clear that extremely high levels of protection are
necessary to eradicate rabies in good fox habitats (i.e. many
surburban areas (Macdonald 1979)). For example, if K is in the
region of 5 foxes/km^2, we must protect more than 80% of the population to ensure eradication. In poorer habitats, however,
more practical levels are indicated such as 50+% where K = 2
(Fig. 12).

In summary, the rabies model provides clear guidelines on the
level of either culling or vaccination required to control
rabies. Theory suggests that disease eradication will be difficult to achieve by means of either control method in habitats
where the fox carrying capacity is high. In Britain such areas
are predominantly surburban in nature (Harris 1977). It is precisely in these areas that dog-fox and cat-fox contacts are most
frequent (Macdonald 1980) and hence the risk of human exposure
to rabies is likely to be high. In such circumstances it would
clearly be necessary to reduce fox density as much as possible
but, in addition, the compulsory vaccination of all dogs and
cats would appear essential in order to minimise the risk of
human exposure.

7. CONCLUSIONS

The dynamical properties of the two models discussed in this
paper highlight the ability of infectious disease agents to both
regulate host population growth and induce cyclic fluctuations
in host abundance. The major factors which generate oscillatory
behaviour are high disease pathogenicity in conjunction with low
host reproductive potential, long lived free-living infective
agents and long incubation periods during which hosts are
infected but not infectious. Seasonality in disease transmission accentuates the non-seasonal cyclic behaviour induced by
these mechanisms.

The degree of qualitative agreement between observation and
theory in the forest insect-pathogen and fox-rabies interactions
is encouraging. It argues for a reappraisal of some long term
records of animal abundance in light of the regulatory potential
of pathogens. The relevance of this suggestion is highlighted
by the theoretical prediction that highly pathogenic organisms
are more likely to regulate host population growth yet, paradoxi-
cally, the lower will be their equilibrium incidence. It is
therefore incorrect to conclude, as ecologists have often done,
that a disease of low prevalence is unlikely to be a major factor contributing to the regulation of its host's abundance

(Anderson and May 1979; May and Anderson 1979; Anderson and May 1981).

The deterministic models discussed in this paper are clearly gross oversimplifications of the complex biological processes they profess to mirror. No detailed statistical agreement between theory and observation is to be expected from such models. What is looked for is a comparable pattern with the main features of the host-pathogen association. As we have seen, the models predict important features which conform to reality and they therefore appear worthy of further study and elaboration (Bartlett 1960).

8. REFERENCES

Anderson, R.M. (1979) Parasite pathogenicity and the depression of host population equilibria, *Nature* **279**, pp. 150-152.

Anderson, R.M. (1981) The control of infectious disease agents: strategic models, *In* "Pest and Pathogen Control: Strategy, Tactics and Policy Models" (G.R. Conway ed.), John Wiley (in press).

Anderson, R.M., Jackson, H.C., May, R.M. and Smith, A.M. (1981) The population dynamics of fox rabies in Europe, *Nature* **289**, pp. 765-77.

Anderson, R.M. and May, R.M. (1979) Population biology of infectious diseases, Part I, *Nature* **280**, pp. 361-367.

Anderson, R.M. and May, R.M. (1980) Infectious diseases and population cycles of forest insects, *Science* **210**, pp. 658-661.

Anderson, R.M. and May, R.M. (1981) Population dynamics of directly transmitted microparasites of invertebrates, *Phil. Trans. R. Soc. Series B* (in press).

Auer, C. (1968) Erste Ergenbnisse einfacher stochastischer Modelluntersuchungen uber die Ursachen der Populationsbewegung des grauen Lärchenwicklers *Zeiraphera diniana*, Gn. (= *Z. griseana* Hb.) im Oberengadin, 1949/66, *Zeitschrift für angewandte Entomologie* **62**, pp. 202-235.

Baer, G.M. (ed.) (1975) The Natural History of Rabies, Vols. I and II, Academic Press, New York.

Baltensweiler, W. (1964) *Zeiraphera griseana* Hubner (Lepidoptera: Tortricidae) in the European Alps. A contribution to the problem of cycles, *Canadian Entomologist* **96**, pp. 792-800.

Baltensweiler, W., Benz, G., Borey, P. and Delucchi, V. (1977) Dynamics of larch bud moth populations, *Annual Review of Entomology* **22**, pp. 79-100.

Bartlett, M.S. (1956) Deterministic and stochastic models for
recurrent epidemics, *Proc. Third Berkeley Symp. Math. Statist.
and Prob.* **4**, pp. 81-109, California Press, Los Angeles.

Bartlett, M.S. (1957) Measles periodicity and community size,
J.R. Statist. Soc. Ser. A **120**, pp. 48-70.

Beddington, J.R. (1979) Harvesting and population dynamics,
In "Population Dynamics"(R.M. Anderson, B.D. Turner and L.R.
Taylor eds) Blackwell Scientific Publications, Oxford, pp. 307-
320.

Benz, G. (1962) Untersuchungen über die Pathogenität eines
Granulosis-Virus des grauen Lärchenwicklers *Zeiraphera diniana*
(Guenée), *Agron. Glas.* **1962**, pp. 566-574.

Bird, F.T. and Whalen, M.M. (1953) A virus disease of the European pine sawfly, Neodiprion sertifer (Geoffr.), *Canadian
Entomologist* **85**, pp. 433-437.

Bulmer, M.G. (1975) Phase relations in the ten-year cycle, *J.
Anim. Ecol.* **44**, pp. 609-621.

Debach, P. (1974) Biological Control by Natural Enemies, Cambridge University Press, London.

Dietz, K. (1974) Transmission and control of arbovirus diseases,
In "Epidemiology", SIAMS, Philadelphia, pp. 104-121.

Dietz, K. (1976) The incidence of infectious diseases under the
influence of seasonal fluctuations, *In* "Mathematical Models in
Medicine"(J. Berger, W. Bühler, R. Repges and P. Tautu (eds))
pp. 1-15, Lecture Notes in Biomathematics Vol. 11, Springer
Verlag, Berlin.

Elton, C. (1942) Voles, Mice and Lemmings: Problems in Population Dynamics, Oxford University Press, Oxford.

Fisher, R.A. (1930) The Genetical Theory of Natural Selection,
Clarendon Press, Oxford.

Friend, M. (1968) History and epidemiology of rabies in wildlife in New York, *N.Y. Fish. Game. J.* **15**(1), pp. 71-97.

Harris, S. (1977) Distribution, habitat utilisation and age
structure of a suburban fox (Vulpes vulpes) population, *Mammal.
Rev.* **7**, pp. 25-39.

Huffaker, C.B. (ed.) (1974) Biological Control, Plenum, New York.

Johnston, D.H. and Beauregard, M. (1969) Rabies epidemiology in Ontario, *Bull. Wildlife Disease Assoc.* **5**, pp. 357-370.

Kantorovioh, R.A. (1964) Natural foci of rabies like infection in the far north, *J. Hyg. Epid. Microbiol. and Immunol.* **8**(1), pp. 100-110.

Kaplan, C. (ed.) (1977) Rabies, the Facts, Oxford University Press, Oxford.

Kauker, E. and Zettl, K. (1960) Die Okologie des Rotfuchses und ihre Beziehung zur Tollwut, *Dtsch. Tierarztl.Wschr.* **67**,pp.463-467.

Kermack, W.O. and McKendrick, A.G. (1927) Contributions to the mathematical theory of epidemics, *Proc. Roy. Soc. A.* **115**, pp. 700-721.

Krebs, C.J. (1978) Ecology, the Experimental Analysis of Distribution and Abundance, (2nd. Ed.) Harper and Row, New York.

Lack, D. (1954) The Natural Regulation of Animal Numbers, Oxford University Press, London.

Lackie, A.M. (1980) Invertebrate immunity, *Parasitology* **80**, pp. 393-412.

Leopold, A. and Ball, J.N. (1931) British and American grouse cycles, *Canad. Field Nat.* **45**, pp. 162-167.

Lloyd, H.G. (1976) Wildlife rabies in Europe and the British situation, *Trans. R. S. Trop. Med. Hyg.* **70**, pp. 179-187.

London, W.P. and Yorke, J.A. (1973) Recurrent outbreaks of measles, chickenpox and mumps, I: Seasonal variation in contact rates, *Amer. J. Epidemiol* **98**, pp. 453-468.

Macdonald, D.W. (1980) Rabies and Wildlife: A Biologist's Perspective, Oxford University Press, Oxford.

Mackenzie, J.M.D. (1952) Fluctuations in the numbers of British Tetraonids, *J. Anim. Ecol.* **21**, pp. 128-153.

Maramorosch, K. and Shope, R.E. (1975) Invertebrate Immunity, Academic Press, New York.

May, R.M. (1975) Stability and Complexity in Model Ecosystems, 2nd. Ed. Princeton University Press, Princeton.

May, R.M. (1977) Thresholds and breakpoints in ecosystems with a multiplicity of stable states, *Nature* **269**, pp. 471-477.

May, R.M. and Anderson, R.M. (1979) Population biology of infectious diseases: Part II, *Nature* **280**, pp. 455-461.

Morris, R.F. (1963) The dynamics of epidemic spruce budworm populations, *Memoirs of the Entomological Society of Canada* **31**, pp. 1-332.

Peterman, R.M., Clark, W.C. and Holling, C.S. (1979) The dynamics of resilence: shifting stability domains in fish and insect systems, *In* "Population Dynamics" (R.M. Anderson, B.D. Turner and L.R. Taylor (eds)) pp. 321-341, Blackwell Scientific Publications, Oxford.

Plummer, P.J.G. (1954) Rabies in Canada with special reference to wildlife resevoirs, *Bull. Wld. Hlth, Org.* **10**(5), pp. 767-774.

Shelford, V.E. (1943) The abundance of the Collared Lemming (*Dicrostonyx groenlandicus* (Tr.) var. *richardsoni* (Mer.)) in the Churchill area 1929 to 1940, *Ecology* **24**, pp. 472-484.

Soper, H.E. (1929) Interpretation of periodicity in disease-prevalence, *J.R. Statist. Soc.* **92**, pp. 34-73.

Stairs, G. (1972) Pathogenic micro-organisms in the regulation of forest insect populations, *Annual Review of Entomology* **17**, pp. 355-372.

Tinsley, T.W. (1979) The potential of insect pathogenic viruses as pesticidal agents, *Annual Review of Entomology* **24**, pp. 63-87.

Toma, B. and Andral, L. (1977) Epidemiology of fox rabies, *Adv. Virus Res.* **21**, pp. 1-36.

Varley, G.C., Gradwell, G.R. and Hassell, M.P. (1973) Insect Population Ecology: an Analytical Approach, Blackwell Scientific Publications, Oxford.

W.H.O. (1978) Rabies Bulletin Europe, 1-4 WHO Collaborating Centre for Rabies Surveillance and Research, Tubingen.

Winkler, W.G. (1975) Fox Rabies, *In* "The Natural History of Rabies"Vol. II (G.M. Bauer (ed.)), Academic Press, New York.

Yorke, J.A. and London, W.P. (1973) Recurrent outbreaks of measles, chickenpox and mumps, II, Systematic differences in contact rates and stochastic effects, *American Journal of Epidemiology* **98**, pp. 469-482.

Yorke, J.A., Nathanson, N., Pianigiani, G. and Martin, J. (1979) Seasonality and the requirements for perpetuation and eradication of viruses in populations, *Am. J. Epidemiol.* **109**, pp. 103-123.

THE EVALUATION OF RUBELLA VACCINATION STRATEGIES

K. Dietz

*(Institute of Medical Biometry, University of Tübingen,
Tübingen, Federal Republic of Germany)*

1. INTRODUCTION

The present paper is stimulated by Knox (1980) who compares
alternative rubella vaccination programs by an equilibrium analysis and by simulations based on a dynamic model. It is implicit
in his comparisons that the costs of the vaccination programs
are determined by the <u>proportion</u> effectively vaccinated in a
given age-group of boys and girls. It will be shown that other
rankings of the vaccination strategies result if the costs
depend on the <u>number</u> of vaccinations carried out. Explicit equations are derived which allow the determination of the equilibrium incidence for different vaccination strategies under alternative assumptions about the boosting effect of the wild virus.
For background of the problem and references to the literature
see Knox (1980).

2. THE GENERAL ENDEMIC

Since the occurrence of Congenital Rubella Syndrome (CRS)
depends on the age at infection we have to consider explicitly
the age-specific prevalence of the infection. Dietz (1975) gave
the corresponding equations which are repeated here for ease of
reference.

Let $x(a,t)$, $y(a,t)$, $z(a,t)$ denote the number of susceptibles,
infectives and immunes of age a at time t. Then the general
endemic is described by the following system of integro-
differential equations:

$$\frac{\partial x}{\partial a} + \frac{\partial x}{\partial t} = - (\lambda+\mu) x(a,t)$$

$$\frac{\partial y}{\partial a} + \frac{\partial y}{\partial t} = \lambda x(a,t) - (\gamma+\mu) y(a,t)$$

$$\frac{\partial z}{\partial a} + \frac{\partial z}{\partial t} = \gamma y(a,t) - \mu z(a,t),$$

with

$$\lambda = \beta \int_{0}^{\infty} y(s,t)ds$$

and with the initial and boundary conditions

$$x(a,0) = x_0(a), \ y(a,0) = y_0(a), \ z(a,0) = z_0(a)$$

$$x(0,t) = n\mu, \qquad y(0,t) = 0, \qquad z(0,t) = 0.$$

Here μ denotes the natural death rate of individuals. The recovery rate is γ and the contact rate is β. The incidence λ of the infection is proportional to the total number of all infectives in the population. The total population is assumed to be of constant size n so that the birth rate μ is set equal to the death rate. No differential mortality of infectives is taken into account.

In order to determine the stationary solutions we set the derivatives with respect to time equal to zero. We introduce the new variables u=x/K, v=y/K, w=z/K, where K=x+y+z:

$$\frac{du}{da} = -\lambda u$$

$$\frac{dv}{da} = \lambda u - \gamma v \qquad\qquad (2.1)$$

$$\frac{dw}{da} = \gamma v$$

with the initial conditions u(0) = 1, v(0) = w(0) = 0,

and

$$\lambda = \beta n \int_{0}^{\infty} v(s)\mu e^{-\mu s}ds. \qquad\qquad (2.2)$$

Since u+v+w = 1, the last equation (2.1) is superfluous. For non-trivial equilibria, the incidence λ is a positive constant. Then (2.1) is reduced to a linear system of ordinary differential equations with the solutions

$$u(a) = e^{-\lambda a} \tag{2.3.1}$$

$$v(a) = \begin{cases} \varkappa(e^{-\lambda a} - e^{-\gamma a})/(\gamma - \lambda) & \text{for } \gamma \neq \lambda \\ \lambda a e^{-\lambda a} & \gamma = \lambda \end{cases} \tag{2.3.2}$$

$$w(a) = \begin{cases} 1-(\gamma e^{-\lambda a} - \lambda e^{-\gamma a})/(\gamma-\lambda) & \gamma \neq \lambda \\ 1-e^{-\lambda a}(1+\lambda a) & \gamma = \lambda \end{cases} \tag{2.3.3}$$

If we insert (2.3.2) into (2.2) and cancel the trivial solution $\lambda = 0$, we obtain

$$\lambda = \mu(\beta n/(\gamma+\mu)-1). \tag{2.4}$$

Let $L = 1/\mu$ denote the life expectancy of an individual and $A = 1/\lambda$ the average age at infection. Further, let

$$R = \beta n/(\gamma+\mu)$$

denote the reproduction rate of the infection, i.e. the number of secondary cases that one case could generate if the total population were susceptible. From (2.4) we get

$$\lambda = \mu(R-1) \tag{2.5}$$

and

$$R = 1+L/A \tag{2.6}$$

Equation (2.5) implies the natural condition $R > 1$ for a positive endemic state. If the incidence λ is known, equation (2.6) allows to estimate R. Assuming a life-expectancy $L = 77$ years and taking $\lambda = 0.086$ for rubella according to Knox (1980) we get $R = 7.62$.

If $\bar{u}$, $\bar{v}$, $\bar{w}$ denote the average proportions of susceptibles, infectives and immunes, we have

$$\bar{u} = 1/R, \tag{2.7.1}$$

$$\bar{v} = (1-1/R)/M, \tag{2.7.2}$$

$$\bar{w} = (1-1/R)(1-1/M), \tag{2.7.3}$$

where $M = (\mu+\lambda)/\mu$.

The equation $R\bar{u} = 1$ will be used in the following section to derive the equilibrium incidence for a given vaccination strategy and for given R.

We conclude the present section by specifying the critical proportion to be vaccinated in order to eradicate an infection:

$$p > 1 - 1/R.$$

This lower bound seems to have been given first by Smith (1970). If we apply this to rubella we get

$$p > 0.87,$$

i.e. maintaining 87% of the total population immunised would eventually lead to the elimination of the infection.

3. DERIVATION OF STEADY STATE EQUATIONS FOR SPECIFIC VACCINATION STRATEGIES

3.1 *Specification of the models*

In the following the index i refers to the sex of an individual: i = 1 and 2 denotes male and female, respectively. Let $p_i(a)$ be the proportion vaccinated of sex i at age a. The proportion $u_i(a)$ of susceptibles of sex i at age a satisfies the equations

$$\frac{du_i}{da} = -\lambda u_i - \pi_i(a)u_i + \delta p_i$$

$$\frac{dp_i}{da} = \pi_i(a) - (\delta + \varepsilon)p_i$$

(3.1.1)

where $\pi_i(a)$ determines the age- and sex-specific vaccination schedule and δ is the rate of loss of vaccine immunity. If it is assumed that the wild virus can boost vaccine immunity such that an individual becomes permanently immune, the parameter ε is set equal to λ. Otherwise it is set equal to zero. We assume a sex ratio of 1:1 in the population. Then the equilibrium incidence can be determined from the equation

$$R \frac{1}{2} \sum_{i=1}^{2} \int_{0}^{\infty} u_i(a)\mu e^{-\mu a} da = 1,$$

(3.1.2)

where $u_i(a)$ are solutions of (3.1.1).

For the evaluation of alternative vaccination strategies against rubella we consider the following special case: vaccination of the proportions σ_i at age T_1 and τ_i at age $T_2 > T_1$, $i = 1,2$. It is assumed that the two vaccinations are applied independently of each other and without prior testing for antibodies. These assumptions imply the following relationships at the points of discontinuity of u_i and p_i:

$$u_i(T_1+) = (1-\sigma_i)u_i(T_1-),$$

$$p_i(T_1+) = \sigma_i u_i(T_1-),$$

$$u_i(T_2+) = (1-\tau_i)u_i(T_2-),$$

$$p_i(T_2+) = p_i(T_2-)+\tau_i u_i(T_2-).$$

(3.1.3)

3.2 Vaccine immunity is boosted by wild virus

In this section we assume $\varepsilon = \lambda$ in (3.1.1). According to our assumptions we have to solve (3.1.1) consecutively for the intervals $[0,T_1)$, $[T_1,T_2)$ and $[T_2,\infty)$. After straightforward calculations we get:

$$\left. \begin{aligned} p_i(a) &\equiv 0 \\ u_i(a) &= e^{-\lambda a} \end{aligned} \right\} \quad \text{for } 0 \leq a < T_1,$$

$$\left. \begin{aligned} p_i(a) &= \sigma_i e^{-\lambda a - \delta(a-T_1)} \\ u_i(a) &= (1-\sigma_i e^{-\delta(a-T_1)})e^{-\lambda a} \end{aligned} \right\} \quad \text{for } T_1 \leq a < T_2,$$

(3.2.1)

$$\left. \begin{aligned} p_i(a) &= \left[\sigma_i(1-\tau_i)e^{\delta T_1}+\tau_i e^{\delta T_2}\right]e^{-(\delta+\lambda)a} \\ u_i(a) &= \left[1-\sigma_i(1-\tau_i)e^{-\delta(a-T_1)}-\tau_i e^{-\delta(a-T_2)}\right]e^{-\lambda a} \end{aligned} \right\} \quad \text{for } T_2 \leq a.$$

Inserting the expressions for $u_i(a)$ into (3.1.2) we get the
following equation for the determination of λ:

$$\mu R \frac{1}{2} \sum_{i=1}^{2} \left[\frac{1}{\lambda+\mu} - \frac{\sigma_i}{\lambda+\mu+\delta} e^{-(\lambda+\mu)T_1} - \frac{\tau_i}{\lambda+\mu+\delta} e^{-(\lambda+\mu)T_2} \right.$$

$$\left. + \frac{\sigma_i \tau_i}{\lambda+\mu+\delta} e^{-(\lambda+\mu)T_2-\delta(T_2-1)} \right] = 1.$$

This can be rewritten in analogy to (2.5) as follows:

$$\lambda = \mu \left\{ R \left[1 - \frac{\lambda+u}{2(\lambda+\mu+\delta)} \left((\sigma_1+\sigma_2) e^{-(\lambda+\mu)T_1} + (\tau_1+\tau_2) e^{-(\lambda+\mu)T_2} \right. \right. \right.$$

$$\tag{3.2.2}$$

$$\left. \left. \left. - (\sigma_1\tau_1\sigma_2\tau_2) e^{-(\lambda+\mu)T_2-\delta(T_2-T_1')} \right) \right] - 1 \right\}.$$

If individuals are vaccinated only at one age, T_1 say, then
(3.2.2) reduces to

$$\lambda = \mu \left\{ R \left[1 - \frac{\lambda+\mu}{2(\lambda+\mu+\delta)} (\sigma_1+\sigma_2) e^{-(\lambda+\mu)T_1} \right] - 1 \right\}.$$

Solutions can easily be found iteratively. For a certain λ one
can then determine the risk of CRS as a function of the vaccination strategy. This will be done in section 4.

3.3 *Vaccine immunity is not boosted by wild virus*

Now we set $\varepsilon = 0$ in (3.1.1). This results in the following solutions:

$$p_i(a) = 0$$

$$\text{for } 0 \leq a < T_1$$

$$u_i(a) = e^{-\lambda a}$$

$$p_i(a) = \sigma_i e^{-\lambda T_1 - \delta(a - T_1)}$$

$$u_i(a) = \begin{cases} \left(1 + \dfrac{\sigma_i \lambda}{\delta - \lambda}\right) e^{-\lambda a} - \dfrac{\delta \sigma_i}{\delta - \lambda} e^{-\delta(a - T_1) - \lambda T_1} & \text{if } \delta \neq \lambda \\[3em] e^{-\lambda a}\left(1 - \sigma_i + \sigma_i \lambda(a - T_1)\right) & \text{if } \delta = \lambda \end{cases}$$

$$\text{for } T_1 \leq a < T_2$$

$$p_i(a) = [p_i(T_2 -) + \tau_2 u_i(T_2 -)]e^{-\delta a} \tag{3.3.1}$$

$$u_i(a) = \Bigg\{ [(\delta - \lambda + \sigma_i \lambda)(\delta - \lambda + \tau_i \lambda) - \sigma_i \tau_i \delta \lambda e^{-(\delta - \lambda)(T_2 - T_1)}]e^{-\lambda a}$$

$$-\delta[\tau_i(\delta - \lambda + \sigma_i \lambda)e^{-(\lambda - \delta)T_2} - \sigma_i(\lambda - \delta + \tau_i \delta)e^{-(\lambda - \delta)T_1}]e^{-\delta a}\Bigg\}/(\delta - \lambda)^2$$

$$\text{if } \delta \neq \lambda$$

$$u_i(a) = e^{-\lambda a}\{(1 - \tau_i)[1 - \sigma_i + \sigma_i \lambda(T_2 - T_1)]$$

$$+\lambda(a - T_2)[\sigma_i + \tau_i[1 - \sigma_i + \sigma_i \lambda(T_2 - T_1)]]\} \qquad \text{if } \delta = \lambda$$

$$\text{for } T_2 \leq a$$

Similarly as in the previous section we find the following equation for the determination of λ:

$$\lambda = \mu \left\{ R \left[1 - \frac{\mu}{2(\delta+\mu)} \left\{ (\sigma_1+\sigma_2)e^{-(\lambda+\mu)T_1} + (\tau_1+\tau_2)e^{-(\lambda+\mu)T_2} \right. \right. \right.$$

$$\left. \left. \left. -(\sigma_1\tau_1+\sigma_2\tau_2)e^{-(\lambda+\mu)T_2}[\delta e^{-(\delta-\lambda)(T_2-T_1)}-\lambda]/(\delta-\lambda) \right\} \right] -1 \right\} \quad \text{if } \delta \neq \lambda$$

and   (3.3.2)

$$\lambda = \mu \left\{ R \left[1 - \frac{\mu}{2(\lambda+\mu)} \left\{ (\sigma_1+\sigma_2)e^{-(\lambda+\mu)T_1} + (\tau_1+\tau_2)e^{-(\lambda+\mu)T_2} \right. \right. \right.$$

$$\left. \left. \left. -(\sigma_1\tau_1+\sigma_2\tau_2)e^{-(\lambda+\mu)T_2}(1-\lambda(T_2-T_1)) \right\} \right] -1 \right\} \quad \text{if } \delta = \lambda$$

3.4 No loss of vaccine immunity

If the loss of vaccine immunity is negligible, i.e. $\delta = 0$, the equations for the proportion of susceptibles and for the determination of λ are considerably simplified. One can easily verify that both models lead to the same expressions:

$$u_i(a) = e^{-\lambda a} \qquad \text{for } 0 \leq a < T_1$$

$$u_i(a) = (1-\sigma_i)e^{-\lambda a} \qquad \text{for } T_1 \leq a < T_2$$

$$u_i(a) = (1-\sigma_i)(1-\tau_i)e^{-\lambda a} \qquad T_2 \leq a$$

and

$$\lambda = \mu \left\{ R \left[1 - \frac{1}{2} \left(\sigma_1 + \sigma_2 \right) e^{-(\lambda+\mu)T_1} - \frac{1}{2} \left(1-\sigma_1 \right) \tau_1 \right. \right.$$

$$\left. \left. + \left(1-\sigma_2 \right) \tau_2 \right) e^{-(\lambda+\mu)T_2} \right] - 1 \right\}. \tag{3.4.1}$$

4. COMPARISON OF VACCINATION STRATEGIES

4.1 *Definition of cost functions*

Knox (1980) compares the different strategies on the basis of the relationship between the incidence of CRS and the efficacy f of the vaccination, where f is the product of the coverage among susceptibles and the probability that a vaccination is effective. This method implicitly assumes that the successful vaccination of 80% of 2-year-old boys and girls is as costly as the vaccination of 80% of 14-year-old girls alone, in other words, the costs per vaccination of a two-year-old child are about half the costs per vaccination of a 14-year-old girl. This assumption may perhaps be justified by the possibility that the rubella vaccine could be administered simultaneously with other vaccines which would help to reduce costs. But when it comes to the comparison of his strategies B (vaccination of boys and girls at 2 years old) and C (vaccination of girls at 2 years old) it is not plausible that they should be compared on the basis of different costs per vaccination. We therefore propose to take into account the number of vaccinations applied for a given strategy. The following five strategies are considered:

TABLE I

Vaccination of	Parameters	Costs
S_A : boys at 2 years old	$\sigma_2 = \tau_1 = \tau_2 = 0$	$\frac{1}{2} \frac{\sigma_1}{k} e^{-2\mu}$
S_B : boys and girls at 2 years old	$\sigma = \sigma_1 = \sigma_2 ; \tau_1 = \tau_2 = 0$	$\frac{\sigma}{k} e^{-2\mu}$
S_C : girls at 2 years old	$\sigma_1 = \tau_1 = \tau_2 = 0$	$\frac{1}{2} \frac{\sigma_2}{k} e^{-2\mu}$

TABLE I (cont.)

Vaccination of	Parameters	Costs
S_D : girls at 14 years old	$\sigma_1 = \sigma_2 = \tau_1 = 0$	$\frac{1}{2}\tau_2 e^{-14\mu}$
S_E : girls at 2 years old and girls at 14 years old	$\sigma = \sigma_2 = \tau_2$, $\sigma_1 = \tau_1 = 0$	$\frac{1}{2}\sigma\left[\frac{1}{k}e^{-2\mu} + e^{-14\mu}\right]$

Here k is the ratio of the costs of a vaccination at age 14 to a vaccination at age 2. For our comparisons we shall only assign the values k = 1 or k = 2. The costs also depend on the relative size of the age group to be vaccinated. Since we have so far assumed an exponential age-distribution, the relative costs are multiplied by $e^{-\mu T}$ if vaccination takes place at age T. Fig. 1 a and b show the coverage that can be achieved in the various age- and sex groups of a vaccination program as a function of the costs. Following Knox (1980) we take as criterion I for comparing the strategies the number of susceptibles transferring to the immune state between the age b and b+g, where b is the average age at conception and g the average duration of the period during which a fetus is at risk to CRS. Hence

$$I = \lambda \int_b^{b+g} u_2(a)\,da.$$

If $\delta = 0$ this yields $u_2(b) - u_2(b+g)$. For $\delta > 0$ we get

$$I_1 = \left[1 - \frac{\lambda}{\lambda+\delta}\left\{\sigma_2(1-\tau_2)e^{-\delta(b-T_1)} + \tau_2 e^{-\delta(b-T_2)}\right\}\right]e^{-\lambda b}$$

$$- \left[1 - \frac{\lambda}{\lambda+\delta}\left\{\sigma_2(1-\tau_2)e^{-\delta(b+g-T_1)} + \tau_2 e^{-\delta(b+g-T_2)}\right\}\right]e^{-\lambda(b+g)}$$

$$(4.1.1)$$

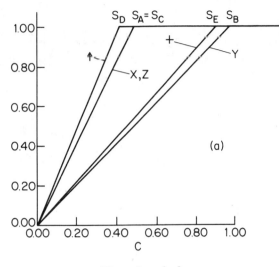

Fig. 1a   k=1

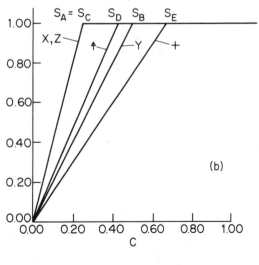

Fig. 1b   k=2

and

$$I_2 = \left\{ \left[(\delta-\lambda+\sigma_2\lambda)(\delta-\lambda+\tau_2\lambda)-\sigma_2\tau_2\delta\lambda e^{-(\delta-\lambda)(T_2-T_1)} \right] e^{-\lambda b}(1-e^{-\lambda g}) \right.$$

$$\left. -\lambda\left[\tau_2(\delta-\lambda+\sigma_2\lambda)e^{-(\lambda-\delta)T_2} -\sigma_2(\lambda-\delta+\tau_2\delta)e^{-(\lambda-\delta)T_1} \right] e^{-\delta b}(1-e^{-\delta g}) \right\}/(\delta-\lambda)^2,$$

$$\text{if } \delta\neq\lambda$$

$$(4.1.2)$$

$$I_2 = e^{-\lambda b}(1-e^{-\lambda g})(1-\tau_2)[1-\sigma_2+\sigma_2\lambda(T_2-T_1)]+$$

$$[(1+\lambda(b-T_2))e^{-\lambda b}(1-e^{-\lambda g})-\lambda g e^{-\lambda g}][\sigma_2+\tau_2(1-\sigma_2+\sigma_2\lambda(T_2-T_1))],$$

$$\text{if } \delta=\lambda$$

Here the indices 1 and 2 of I refer to the situations where the wild virus boosts (j = 1) or does not boost (j = 2) vaccine immunity. The numerical values for b and g are taken as 25 years and 0.1 year as in Knox (1980). The following values for R will be compared.

TABLE II

R - reproduction rate, λ - incidence of the infection, A - average age at infection, I - incidence of CRS, p* - minimum proportion of total population to be immunised for reduction of λ to zero.

R	$\lambda=\mu(R-1)$	$A=\lambda^{-1}$	$I=e^{-\lambda b}(1-e^{-\lambda g})$	$p^*=1-1/R$
7.615	0.086	11.63	$1.0\cdot10^{-3}$	0.87
4.000	0.039	25.64	$1.5\cdot10^{-3}$	0.75
2.000	0.013	76.92	$0.9\cdot10^{-3}$	0.50

For R = 4, the incidence I is approximately at its maximum value if one takes b = 25. The curves in the next section were calculated according to the following steps:

1. For a given value of the cost function c the proportion σ_i, τ_i for each strategy was calculated using the specifications in Table I, e.g. S_D: $\sigma_1 = \sigma_2 = \tau_1 = 0; \tau_2 = \min (1; 2ce^{14\mu})$.

2. Depending on the assumptions about loss of vaccine immunity, the equilibrium incidence λ was calculated iteratively according to (3.2.2), (3.3.2) or (3.4.1), respectively.

3. Finally the incidence I_1 and I_2, respectively, is calculated according to (4.1.1) and (4.2.2), respectively.

If the following inequality holds for a given vaccination strategy, then the equilibrium incidence λ of the infection is reduced to zero:

$$\frac{1}{2} \frac{\mu}{(\mu+\delta)} \left[(\sigma_1+\sigma_2) e^{-\mu T_1} + (\tau_1+\tau_2) e^{-\mu T_2} \right.$$

$$\left. -(\sigma_1\tau_1+\sigma_2\tau_2) e^{-\mu T_2 - \delta(T_2-T_1)} \right] > 1-1/R.$$

This inequality is independent of the assumption about the boosting effect of the wild virus.

For δ = 0.01 it turns out that it is impossible to eradicate the infection for R > 2.53 even if 100% girls <u>and</u> boys were vaccinated twice at ages 2 and 14.

The loss rate would have to be less than approximately 0.00185, if this vaccination strategy should be sufficient for reducing λ to zero from its initial value of 0.086 for R = 7.615. The best available estimate for δ is 0.00183 which is based on 28 individuals who became seronegative out of 3832 seropositive vaccinated individuals after 4 year follow-up (Herrmann et al. 1976).

4.2 Summary of results

Because of lack of space it is impossible to give a complete survey of all the results that have been obtained. Only typical cases are reproduced here for illustration. The following symbols are utilised for the five strategies:

S_A	S_B	S_C	S_D	S_E
X	Y	Z	↑	+

In Fig. 2 the R value is 7.615. Fig. 2a, b assume $\delta = 0$.
They only differ in the value k. If k = 1, i.e. costs for vaccination are independent of age, then (Fig. 2a) S_D is the best one
for all levels of cost. The second best strategy is S_C, i.e.
vaccination of two-year-old girls. Strategy S_B ranks third. If
k = 2 (Fig. 2b), then S_C is now optimal and S_D is the second
best one. If k were increased even further, then S_C would stay
the best, but the line for S_B will cross the one for S_D as it
happens in Fig. 3 of Knox (1980). Zero incidence of infection
and CRS is obtained for less than 100% efficacy which is in contrast to the Fig. 3 of Knox (1980). (It is however not clear
whether the broken line for strategy B is not supposed to hit
the abscissa at 0.87 instead of 1.0.) If there is no loss of
vaccine immunity the choice of the optimal strategy for R = 7.615
depends uniquely on the relative costs per vaccination of 2-year-
old and 14 year-old girls. There is no point in vaccinating any
boys.

If we consider the effect of loss of vaccine immunity by
assuming $\delta = 0.01$, we notice that it is no longer possible to
reduce the incidence of CRS to zero, no matter which strategy is
applied, even at maximum coverage. In Fig. 2c it is assumed
that the wild virus boosts vaccine-immunity, whereas in Fig. 2d
the contrary is assumed. For Fig. 2c and d, the cost ratio is
equal to 2. If there is no boosting of vaccine immunity (2d)
then strategy D is optimal. But even 100% efficacy of vaccination leads only to a reduction of the CRS incidence to 18.2% of
its original level. In Fig. 2c the choice between strategy C
and D depends on the coverage that can be achieved for both
methods. Strategy D is only to be preferred if the achievable
coverage is more than about 82% corresponding to a c value of
0.34 at which the D strategy reaches lower incidence values than
the C strategy.

Fig. 3a and b assume R = 4. Fig. 3a is comparable to Fig. 2b
since both have $\delta = 0$ and k = 2. In both cases the optimal
strategy is C. But the second best is now B instead of D. Even
strategy A (vaccination of two-year-old boys) leads to a moderate
reduction in the incidence of CRS. If $\delta = 0.01$ and vaccine-
immunity is boosted (Fig. 3b) the optimal strategy depends again
at the achievable coverage. Strategy B is only optimal if 95%
coverage can be exceeded. If also D does not achieve more than
91% coverage, the best strategy turns out to be C.

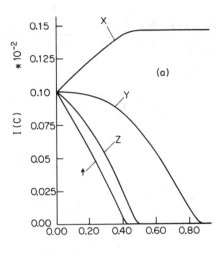

Fig. 2a   R=7.615, k=1

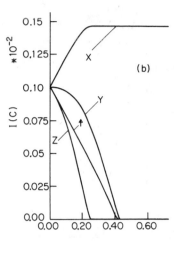

Fig. 2b   R=7.615, k=2

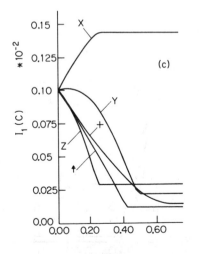

Fig. 2c   R=7.615, k = 2

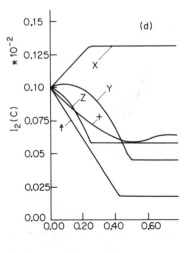

Fig. 2d   R=7.615, k=2

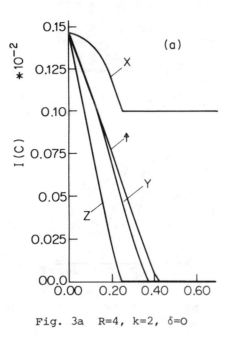

Fig. 3a   R=4, k=2, δ=0

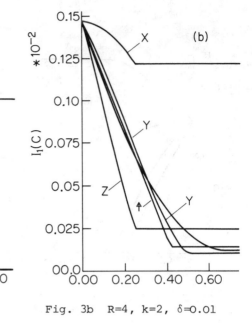

Fig. 3b   R=4, k=2, δ=0.01

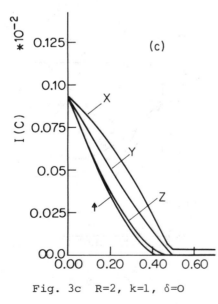

Fig. 3c   R=2, k=1, δ=0

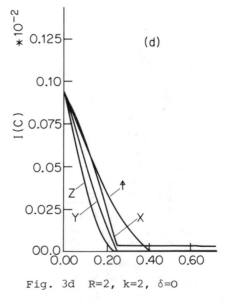

Fig. 3d   R=2, k=2, δ=0

Finally we look at the situation R = 2, δ = 0 (Fig. 3c and d). Here vaccination of 2-year-old boys has greater effects and is even preferable to vaccination of 14-year-old girls if k = 2. But also here the optimal choice is between strategy D and C, depending on k.

5. CONCLUSIONS

The present equilibrium analysis of rubella vaccination strategies has shown that the strategy adopted in the United States of America (strategy B) is less effective than the strategy adopted in the United Kingdom and other European countries (strategy D) for the actual reproduction rate. But it turns out that vaccination of two year old girls may be preferable depending on relative costs and on achievable coverage.

It is admitted that the present equilibrium analysis has to be complemented by further investigations of the dynamic equations but it offers the possibility to take into account different assumptions about vaccine-immunity in order to rank complicated vaccination strategies on the basis of their long term performance. The stability of these equilibrium solutions needs further analysis.

6. ACKNOWLEDGEMENTS

A pertinent question of Roy Anderson led to a considerable revision of the present paper. I would like to thank Mr. H. Renner for his help with the calculations and the production of the plots.

7. REFERENCES

Dietz, K. (1975) Transmission and control of arbovirus diseases, *In* "Epidemiology - Proceedings of a SIMS Conference, Alta, Utah, 1974", (D. Ludwig and K.L. Cooke, eds), SIAM, Philadelphia, pp. 104-121.

Herrmann, K.L., Halstead, S.B., Brandling-Bennett, A.D., Witte, J.J., Wiebenga, N.H. and Eddins, D.L. (1976) Rubella immunization. Persistence of antibody four years after a large-scale field trial, *JAMA,* **235**, pp. 2201-2204.

Knox, E.G. (1980) Strategy for rubella vaccination, *Int. J. Epidemiology,* **9**, pp. 13-23.

Smith, C.E.G. (1970) Prospects for the control of disease, *Proc. Roy. Soc. Med.,* **63**, pp. 1181-1190.

THE IMPORTANCE OF DEMOGRAPHIC STOCHASTICITY
IN POPULATION DYNAMICS

D. Mollison

(Heriot-Watt University)

1. INTRODUCTION AND SUMMARY

Demographic stochasticity is inherent in population processes.
In detail all such processes consist of discrete individuals
subject to chance: for instance, chances of moving or giving
birth, or chances of catching a disease from another particular
individual. However, demographic stochasticity has often been
regarded as unimportant in the description of the gross behaviour
of population processes.

After discussing the circumstances in which this view is
justified (§2), I shall give examples to show that demographic
stochasticity plays a crucial role in the qualitative behaviour
of some spatial population processes, especially in determining
whether and how fast they spread.

2. NEGLECTING DEMOGRAPHIC STOCHASTICITY

What might be called the classical view is that a population
process can be analysed deterministically, and that its detailed
behaviour will be a minor stochastic deviation from that of the
deterministic model. Such an analysis is likely to be accurate
over a bounded time period when the population sizes and numbers
with whom an individual interacts are large, as for instance in
describing the course of a simple epidemic in a large homogeneous population (Bailey 1975).

A hybrid analysis can be used if there are one or more periods
when numbers are small, for instance in the initial stages of an
epidemic with removal in a large homogeneous population (Kendall
1965), or in a cyclic population model where extinction is possible at one or more points of each cycle (Bartlett 1960; Stirzaker 1975). In such cases differential equations adequately
describe the main course of the process, but a stochastic analysis is needed for the critical periods when numbers are small.

General results on the convergence of a class of population
processes to solutions of differential equations are given by
Kurtz (1980) and Barbour (1980). Though very interesting theoretically, these results appear a little remote from applications, at least in the case of spatial processes. For instance,
Kurtz (1980)'s theorem on spatial competition processes whose
mean numbers are asymptotically described by the KPP/Fisher
equation

$$u_t = u_{xx} + u(1-u) \qquad\qquad (1)$$

(Kolmogoroff, Petrovsky and Piscounoff 1937; Fisher 1937)
requires the following: the population density and number of
possible contacts of each individual tend to infinity, while the
area over which such contacts are made, the inter-generation
time and the competitive advantage of the superior species all
tend to zero. Also, if we seek to justify the neglect of demographic stochasticity, it might be more relevant to consider the
converse of this approach; that is, for a fixed stochastic process, to find a sequence of deterministic models converging on
it.

A less formal justification for the classical view was the
belief that deterministic models were easier to analyse than
stochastic ones, which seemed likely to be true if apparently
simple non-linear differential equations such as the KPP/Fisher
equation could be used to approximate non-linear stochastic processes. (A linear population process is one whose mean numbers
satisfy a linear equation, and therefore grow exponentially;
more realistic models for which the population remains bounded
are thus inevitably non-linear.) While Kurtz's theorem provides
some justification for the latter view, McKean (1975) found a
closer connection between the KPP/Fisher equation and a linear
stochastic model, the diffusion birth process (a simple birth
process in which the individuals execute independent Brownian
motion): if, for the diffusion birth process, $u(s,t)$ denotes
Prob (there is an individual to the right of s at time t), then
$u(s,t)$ satisfies the KPP/Fisher equation. Bramson (1978) has
subsequently used the 'McKean connection' to prove the sharpest
result presently known on the speed of propagation of solutions
to the KPP/Fisher equation, thus reversing the traditional role
of the deterministic model as helping us analyse a more difficult stochastic model.

Incidentally, the McKean connection illustrates that a stochastic model, in this case the diffusion birth process, can be
closely related to two quite distinct deterministic models, since
the density for the expected numbers in this process satisfies

$$u_t = u_{xx} + u \qquad\qquad (2)$$

a linear equation which is much more easily analysed than the
KPP/Fisher equation. (On the other hand a deterministic model
can relate to several quite distinct stochastic models: for
instance, this linear equation also describes the density for
the expected numbers in a process with birth rate 1 + d and
death rate d in which, unlike the diffusion birth process,
extinction is possible.)

Another argument for neglecting demographic stochasticity is
that its effects in a population of size N will be of order
$N^{1/2}$, whereas variations in environmental parameters ('environmental stochasticity') will have effects of order N.   This
argument is persuasive in large homogeneously mixing populations,
but requires caution when, as in many spatial processes, the
number with whom each individual interacts is small.

3.   THRESHOLDS AND EXTINCTION PROBABILITIES

An epidemic is said to be 'above threshold' if its parameters
are such that a pandemic, infecting a significant proportion of
the population, can occur; similarly, we may say that a species
in an ecological model is 'above threshold' if it has a non-zero
probability of becoming established.

For the 'general epidemic' (actually a relatively simple
Markovian model, but allowing for removal of infected cases) we
can, as was mentioned above, carry out a successful hybrid analysis (Kendall 1965; Whittle 1955). Deterministic analysis
suggests that if the average number of potentially infectious
contacts per infected individual (the 'reproduction rate' of the
epidemic), R say, is less than or equal to one, then a pandemic
cannot occur; while if R > 1, a proportion z(R) of the population will become infected during the epidemic outbreak.

A stochastic analysis of the early stages, comparing the
epidemic with a simple birth and death process, shows that for
the case where $R \leqslant 1$ the deterministic analysis is substantially
correct: with near certainty only a few individuals will be
infected. When R > 1, the epidemic may still only infect a few
individuals, the probability of this being approximately the
same as for the birth and death process, i.e. R^{-M}, where M is
the initial number of infected; but if it survives its initial
stages, a pandemic will occur in which the proportion who become
infected is close to the value z(R) predicted by the deterministic analysis.

However for spatial epidemics the correspondence between
stochastic and deterministic models is less close. In one or
two dimensions the deterministic result remains essentially the

same as in the non-spatial case: if the reproduction rate R is
less than or equal to unity no epidemic occurs, if R > 1 an
epidemic wave spreads out infecting a proportion z(R) of the
population (Kendall 1957, 1965; Atkinson and Reuter 1976). For
stochastic epidemics we find that in one dimension extinction is
certain for all values of R (Kelly 1977), while in two dimensions a pandemic is possible but the threshold value of R may be
considerably greater than unity. (For instance, for the classical bond percolation process, which can be regarded as a discrete
time nearest neighbour epidemic model, the threshold value of R
is 2 (Kesten 1980), and for the corresponding continuous time
process it is at least 2 (Kuulasmaa 1981).)

4. VELOCITIES OF SPREAD

   For the KPP/Fisher equation (1) the possible velocities turn
out to be the same as for the linear equation (2), which is not
surprising considering the close connections they both have with
the same stochastic model, the diffusion birth process (see §2
above). In each case the minimal velocity, $c^* = \sqrt{2}$, is of most
practical relevance: higher velocity waves require an initial
forward tail to 'pull them along', and it can, for instance, be
shown that a solution of the KPP/Fisher equation which is initially non-zero only on a bounded interval develops into a pair of
minimal velocity waves, one in each direction (Weinberger 1980,
§2). It is of interest to note that in numerical calculations
even very small rounding errors significantly reduce the velocity
(Mountford, in Skellam 1973); in this sense even the minimal
velocity wave is 'pulled' by its forward tail.

   Similar results hold for the linear and non-linear equations
with equivalent relations to the contact birth process (Mollison
1977; Aronson 1977). (The contact birth process, with contact
distribution V, is another simple birth process, but with individuals having fixed locations; the position of each individual
relative to its parent is independently chosen according to the
probability distribution V.)

   For both diffusion and contact birth processes, results on the
convergence of solutions of the associated non-linear differential equation to a waveform can be interpreted as showing that
the variability of the front of the process is only O(1). This
indicates that it is the exponentially growing population around
the origin of the process that determines its outward spread.
Fluctuations in the boundary area where the population density
is low and the model thus rather more realistic have no lasting
effect.

   More realistic non-linear stochastic models appear to have
rather lower velocities than their associated birth processes

and deterministic models, and can indeed have finite velocity
when the latter do not. I shall illustrate this in terms of
simple epidemic models. The simple epidemic with contact distribution V consists of a population of bounded density in which
infected individuals remain permanently infectious, and the probability of infection of a susceptible by a particular infective
depends on the (vector) distance between them according to the
probability distribution V. A simple epidemic can be thought of
as a contact birth process with a probability of perinatal mortality proportional to population density, so that the population
density remains bounded (Mollison 1977,§1). Perhaps the best
known examples of the simple epidemic are percolation processes
(Hammersley and Welsh 1965; Smythe 1980), in which there is one
individual at each point of a regular lattice, and the contact
distribution is concentrated on an individual's nearest neighbours.

For one-dimensional simple epidemics with exponentially
bounded contact distribution V, simulations reveal lower velocities than the minimal velocity c_V of the contact birth process
and its associated non-linear differential equation, the 'deterministic simple epidemic' (Mollison 1972; 1977). It is possible
that the velocity tends to c_V as the population density tends to
infinity, but any such convergence must be fairly slow. (For
instance, in the case where V is a two-sided geometric distribution with standard deviation 2, the velocity is still more than
20% below c_V when the population density is 30.) Fluctuations
in the velocity of the simple epidemic are also greater than for
the contact birth process; the statistical variability of the
position of the front (infected) individual at time t appears to
be $O(\sqrt{t})$ instead of $O(1)$ (Mollison 1977).

In cases where the contact distribution does not have exponentially bounded tails but still has finite variance, the one-
dimensional simple epidemic still has finite velocity although
c_V is infinite. For such contact distributions the simple epidemic displays interestingly irregular behaviour (Mollison 1972)
which is qualitatively different from that of the 'deterministic
simple epidemic'.

In two dimensions less is known about simple epidemics with
widely spread contact distributions: theoretical analysis is
more difficult, and simulations can hardly follow such a process for an adequate period. Results on nearest-neighbour
models, i.e. percolation processes, are reviewed by Smythe
(1980). For instance, for the continuous-time Markov process
case, where infection times between neighbours are exponentially
distributed with unit parameter, the velocity along an axis lies

between 1.68 and 3.35, as compared with 4.46 for the contact birth process; simulations by Downham and Green suggest that the true value is about 2.4. (Green 1977, reports values of 2.8 to 2.9 for a biologically more realistic model on an irregular lattice.)

While the differences of velocity between the stochastic process and associated deterministic models is less in this case in two dimensions than in one, the manner of spread appears to depend crucially on the 'crinkliness' of the edge of the set of infected (Mollison 1974; 1977), and thus on the assumption that only nearest neighbours can be infected.

5. CONCLUSIONS

Populations consist of discrete individuals subject to chance; the use of a deterministic model to approximate a population process therefore requires some justification, preferably supported by an estimate of the order of magnitude of the errors involved. Nevertheless there are circumstances in which demographic stochasticity is negligible, some of which can be precisely specified (§2).

It is less easy to be precise when denying the existence of a close deterministic approximation to a process, but there are sufficient examples (§3, §4) to show that demographic stochasticity cannot easily be neglected for spatial processes. The main reason for this would seem to be that small numbers are important: in most spatial population processes each individual interacts mainly with a fairly small set of neighbours or near neighbours, and what goes on at the frontof the process, where numbers are by definition small, is of particular importance. A secondary reason is that we are often concerned with long periods of time: as in considering the asymptotic velocity of a process, or whether fluctuations from equilibrium can eventually cause extinction: so that apparently negligible differences have scope to compound into essential ones.

Historically, a principal reason for the neglect of demographic stochasticity in spatial processes has been the assumed difficulty of analysing non-linear stochastic models, as compared with differential equations for which there was an established theoretical background. I hope that the examples given here show that it is possible to obtain worthwhile results for non-linear stochastic spatial processes, and that these reveal enough differences from those for deterministic models to justify continuing such work.

Two important areas for further work are on the velocity and manner of spread of two-dimensional epidemics where contacts are not restricted to nearest neighbours, and on endemicity and other equilibrium problems, where again existing results are only for simple nearest-neighbour models (Liggett 1980).

6. REFERENCES

Aronson, D.G. (1977) "The asymptotic speed of propagation of a simple epidemic" In"Non-linear diffusion"(W.E. Fitzgibbon and H.E. Walker eds), *Research Notes in Maths*. 14, Pitman, London, pp. 1-23.

Atkinson, C. and Reuter, G.E.H. (1976) Deterministic epidemic waves, *Math. Proc. Camb. Phil. Soc*. 80, pp. 315-330.

Bailey, N.T.J. (1975) The mathematical theory of infectious diseases and its applications, Griffin, London.

Barbour, A.D. (1980) "Density dependent Markov population processes" *In* Jäger, Rost and Tautu, pp. 36-49.

Bartlett, M.S. (1960) Stochastic population models in ecology and epidemiology, Methuen, London.

Bramson, M. (1978) Maximal displacement of branching Brownian motion, *Comm. in Pure and Appl. Math*. 31, pp. 531-581.

Downham, D.Y. and Green, D.H. (1976) Inference for a two-dimensional stochastic growth model, *Biometrika* 63, pp. 551-554.

Fisher, R.A. (1937) The wave of advance of advantageous genes, *Ann. Eugen*. 7, pp. 355-369.

Green, P.J. (1977) *In* Discussion of Mollison (1977), pp. 317-318.

Jäger, W., Rost, H. and Tautu, P. (1980) (eds) Biological growth and spread: mathematical theories and applications, *Springer-Verlag Lecture Notes in Biomathematics* 38, Berlin and Heidelberg.

Hammersley, J.M. and Welsh, D.J.A. (1965) "First-passage percolation, subadditive processes, stochastic networks and generalized renewal theory" *In* Bernouilli, Bayes, Laplace Anniversary Volume (J. Neyman and L.M. LeCam eds), Springer-Verlag, Berlin, pp. 61-110.

Kelly, F. (1977) *In* Discussion of Mollison (1977), pp. 318-319.

Kendall, D.G. (1957) *In* Discussion of Bartlett, M.S., Measles periodicity and community size, *J. Roy. Statist. Soc. A*, 120, pp. 64-67.

Kendall, D.G. (1965) "Mathematical models of the spread of infection" *In* Mathematics and Computer Science in Biology and Medicine, MRC, HMSO, pp. 213-225.

Kesten, H. (1980) On the time constant and path length of first-passage percolation, *Adv. in Appl.Prob.* **12**, pp. 848-863.

Kolmogoroff, A.N., Petrovsky, I.G. and Piscounoff, N.S. (1937) Etude de l'équation de la diffusion avec croissance de la quantité de matière et son application a un problème biologique, *Bull. de l'Univ. d'État a Moscou (sér. intern.)* **A 1** (6), pp. 1-25.

Kurtz, T.G. (1980) "Relationships between stochastic and deterministic population models" *In* Jäger, Rost and Tautu, pp. 449-467.

Kuulasmaa, K. (1981) Locally dependent random graphs and the spatial general epidemic, private communcation.

Liggett, T.M. (1980) "Interacting Markov processes" *In* Jäger, Rost and Tautu, pp. 145-156.

McKean, H.P. (1975) Application of Brownian motion to the equation of Kolmogorov-Petrovskii-Piscunov, *Comm. in Pure and Appl. Math.* **28**, pp. 323-331.

Mollison, D. (1972) The rate of spatial propagation of simple epidemics, *Proc. 6th Berkeley Symp. on Math. Statist. and Prob.* **3**, pp. 579-614.

Mollison, D. (1974) Percolation processes and tumour growth, *Adv. in Appl. Prob.* **6**, pp. 233-235.

Mollison, D. (1977) Spatial contact models for ecological and epidemic spread (with discussion), *J. Roy. Stat. Soc.* **B 39**, pp. 283-326.

Skellam, J.G. (1973) "Models for spatial diffusion" *In* The mathematical theory of the dynamics of biological populations (M.S. Bartlett and R.W. Hiorns eds), Academic Press.

Smythe, R.T. (1980) "Percolation models in two and three dimensions" *In* Jäger, Rost and Tautu, pp. 504-511.

Stirzaker, D.R. (1975) A perturbation method for the stochastic recurrent epidemic, *J. Inst. Maths. Appls.* **15**, pp. 135-160.

Weinberger, H.F. (1980) "Some deterministic models for the spread of genetic and other alterations" *In* Jäger, Rost and Tautu, pp. 320-349.

Whittle, P. (1955) The outcome of a stochastic epidemic - a note on Bailey's paper, *Biometrika* **42**, pp. 116-122.

FAMILIAL DISEASES IN MAN

R.N. Curnow

*(Department of Applied Statistics, University of Reading,
Reading, England)*

1. INTRODUCTION

Questions concerning stability and control arise naturally in
the study of familial diseases and in the discussion of the
policy decisions that sometimes have to be made about them.
Familial diseases are most easily defined as those diseases,
physical and mental, that tend to "run in families". The assumption is made, not always correctly, that these diseases have
some genetic component in their causation. Futhermore, geneticists often assume that genes related to human diseases have,
until recently, been held in some form of approximate stable
equilibrium. Improved and more effective genetic counselling
has, for some diseases, disturbed this equilibrium and should
lead to a reduction in the frequency of such diseases. In this
paper, I shall discuss the other major change of recent years,
the relaxation of selection acting against individuals with certain diseases. This change will inevitably lead to increases
in the frequencies of the diseases concerned. We need to know
the likely magnitude of these increases before deciding our
attitude towards the relaxation of selection and so as to be prepared for its consequences.

There are many reasons for the increased interest over recent
years in familial diseases. First, the reduction in the frequency of diseases caused by poor environment or poor nutrition
and the effectiveness of preventive measures and improved treatment of infectious diseases has increased the proportion of
still-births and early morbidity and mortality that are caused
by diseases with a genetic component in their aetiology. Second,
the fatalistic attitude toward "genetic" disease as incurable
has given way to the realisation that improved treatment or care
can, at the very least, alleviate the effects of these diseases.
The treatment of children suffering from phenylketonuria is an
obvious example. Third, the possibility of elective abortion
has led to a search for factors that will identify mothers at
risk who can then be offered antenatal diagnosis. This, and

other forms of genetic counselling, require some knowledge of the
mode of inheritance of specific diseases. The fourth reason for
the increased interest in familial diseases is the recent explo-
sion of knowledge about molecular biology and the development of
improved techniques for chromosomal analysis, both of which have
already increased our knowledge of the mode of action of genes
and chromosomes and promise much more. The fifth and final
reason is that recent statistical work, sometimes requiring considerable computing powers, has highlighted and investigated
alternative models for the inheritance of disease. Unfortunately,
it has also demonstrated that discrimination between these alternative models is likely to be very difficult. A major problem,
that there is not time to discuss in this paper, is the difficulty in unravelling the effects of genes from the effects of
the common environments generally experienced by close relatives.

Holloway and Smith (1975) list the new practices that are
affecting the human gene pool, dividing them into those that are
largely dysgenic and those that are principally eugenic. I
shall take just one of the practices listed by Holloway and Smith
to illustrate the importance of the ideas of stability and control in the study of the inheritance of human disease. The
"practice" is the increased proportion of individuals affected
by a disease who, through improved treatment, may now survive to
adulthood and become parents. This will clearly increase the
frequency of the disease in future generations. The improved
treatment may be such that affected individuals can lead normal
lives. If this is so, then there may be no problem. Generally,
however, affected individuals do still suffer and their relatives
do still carry a burden, as does the State in its provision of
services for the individual and the family. Argument about the
division of advantage for the present generation and disadvantage
for future generations is obviously difficult. A key element in
the argument must be the size of the increase in frequency to be
expected from the reduced selection against those suffering from
the disease.

In this paper the expected increase will be calculated for
three models of inheritance, involving one locus, two loci and
many loci, respectively.

For a review of clinical genetics, including estimates of the
frequencies of the various genetic diseases, see the MRC Review
(1978).

2. MODELS OF INHERITANCE

2.1 *One locus-autosomal recessive*

Many diseases are known to be caused by the presence of two deleterious alleles at a particular locus. Examples are cystic fibrosis and phenylketonuria. We shall denote the deleterious allele by a and all other alleles by A; the frequency of the a allele by q and the frequency of the A allele by p, where p+q=1; and the relative selective disadvantage of the aa individuals by 1-s. At conception, following random mating of those surviving to adulthood, we have:-

	AA	Aa	aa	
Frequencies	p^2	$2pq$	q^2	1
Relative selective values	1 :	1 :	1-s	

The frequency of the disease is q^2, the frequency of the aa genotype.

The frequency of the allele a in the next generation will be

$$q' = \frac{2pq \times \frac{1}{2} + q^2(1-s)}{1 - sq^2} = q - \frac{psq^2}{1-sq^2}$$

$$\simeq q - sq^2, \quad \text{if q is small.}$$

Thus $\Delta q = q' - q = -sq^2$.

If the relative selective disadvantage of the aa individuals, s, is reduced by Δs, then the decrease in the frequency of the a allele in a generation will be reduced by $q^2\Delta s$ and the decrease in the frequency of the disease by about $2q.q^2\Delta s$.

As an example, consider s = 1, q = .05 and Δs = .3. The disease frequency will be q^2 = .0025 and before the change in selective disadvantage will be declining by about $2q^3$ = .000250 per generation. After the reduction in selective disadvantage, Δs = .3, the rate of decline of disease frequency will be reduced from .000250 by about $2q^3\Delta s$ = .000075 to .000175. If no other forces are acting then the new rate of decline, .000175, will, despite its dependence on the gene frequency q, continue at approximately the same level as long as the selective disadvantage maintains its new value of s = .7.

This approach is too simple because there is generally no evidence that diseases are on the decline as would be expected if the only force acting was selection against the aa individuals. The balancing force which is often assumed to be holding the gene frequency in a stable equilibrium is recurrent mutation from allele A to allele a. To balance the effect of the selection against the a allele, the mutation rate, u, from A to a would need to be such that the total change in gene frequency,

$$-\frac{psq^2}{1-sq^2} + u\left[1-q + \frac{psq^2}{1-sq^2}\right]$$

is zero. This means that the disease incidence, q^2, will be

$$q^2 = u/s \qquad\qquad (2.1.1)$$

If we now consider the extreme case where selection ceases entirely, s = 0, then the change in gene frequency from generation t to generation t + 1 will be

$$q_{t+1} - q_t = u(1-q_t).$$

Therefore,

$$q_t = 1 - (1-q_0)(1-u)^t \qquad\qquad (2.1.2)$$

If s was originally s = 1, i.e. the disease was genetically lethal, then (2.1.2) shows that, with mutation rates assumed to be about u = 10^{-5}, the disease frequency, initially $q_0^2 = 10^{-5}$, will take 130 generations, 3,000 years say, to double to a frequency of $q^2 = 2 \times 10^{-5}$.

With rare diseases and low mutation rates we have seen that the relaxation of the selection acting against individuals with the disease will not lead to a rapid increase in the incidence of of the disease. Even with a complete relaxation of selection, an unlikely event, the only increases after the small increase in the single generation the population requires to reach Hardy-Weinberg equilibrium will be due to new mutations, which occur at a very low rate.

2.2 Two loci models

Davie, Smith, Curnow and Holloway (1978) have discussed the effects of the removal of selection against individuals with a disease when there are two loci involved in the causation of the disease. They show that if the only individuals affected are the double recessives, aabb, and the two loci are unlinked, then, with no other balancing forces, the disease incidence P(=0.006 say) will increase in the first generation by about $2P^{3/2}$(=0.00093). The increase will then halve every generation to give a total change after many generations of $4P^{3/2}$(=0.00186). If some balancing force was maintaining an equilibrium prior to the removal of selection, then an increase each generation of $4P^{7/4}$ = .00052, needs to be added. With linkage between the two loci the fall-off of increases can be much less than one-half per generation and the eventual incidence therefore considerably increased.

Again the largest increase in disease will be in the first generation but the increases per generation are always likely to be not more than a few per cent of the initial frequency of the disease.

Merry, Roger and Curnow (1979) discuss the results of relaxed selection for some rather more speculative two loci models. They find, for some values of the parameters, substantial increases in the frequency of the diseases over a relatively small number of generations.

2.3 Multifactorial models

Multifactorial models are models in which many loci and environmental factors are assumed to be involved in the causation of the disease. They have been introduced in an attempt to explain the continued existence at quite high frequency, certainly higher than the frequency equal to the mutation rate implied by the single locus equation (2.1.1), of highly disadvantageous diseases, such as spina bifida. These diseases are often characterised by relatively low recurrence risks in close relatives and by these recurrence risks increasing with the number of affected relatives and with the severity of the disease in these affected relatives. The multifactorial model is equivalent to hypothesizing an underlying continuous trait with the disease occurring only if the trait exceeds some threshold value. The continuous trait is assumed to be inherited in the same way as many continuous characteristics such as height in man, milk yield in cattle and seed weight in maize.

Davie, Smith, Curnow and Holloway (1978) show how the effects
of reduced selection can be calculated for a disease with a
multifactorial aetiology. As an example, consider a disease with
a frequency of 0.00591 and a heritability for the underlying
continuous trait of h^2 = 0.5. Heritability is most easily interpreted as twice the regression coefficient of the value of the
trait for an offspring on the value of the trait for one of the
parents. The disease frequencies for two further generations of
complete selection followed by the removal of the selection
against the disease would be as follows:

	Generation	Disease frequency
Selection	0	0.00591
operating	1	0.00577
	2	0.00564
No selection	3	0.00579
	4	0.00585
	5	0.00588
	6	0.00589

The disease would eventually reach a new equilibrium at a frequency of 0.00590.

Again we note that the largest increase is in the first
generation after the removal of selection. The increases in
later generations reflect the breakdown of linkage disequilibrium. The disease frequency quickly reaches a new equilibrium
very little above the value when selection ceased.

The conclusions are different if, prior to the relaxation of
selection, the disease frequency is assumed to be at some equilibrium with a compensating force balancing the effects of
selection. If the compensating force is selection against
individuals with low values of the underlying trait, and if the
heritability is again h^2 = 0.5, then a typical sequence of
disease frequencies in successive generations following the
removal of selection would be:

Generation	Disease frequency
0	0.00610
1	0.00641
2	0.00663
3	0.00683
4	0.00700
5	0.00717
6	0.00734
7	0.00751
8	0.00768

Again the largest change occurs in the first generation after
the removal of selection. The increase in each generation then
stabilises quickly to that determined by the selection against
those with low values of the underlying trait.

3. CONCLUSIONS

   The results presented above are reassuring in that the
increases in disease frequency following the relaxation of selection are small even in the first generation following complete
relaxation. This has been the general conclusion in studies of
this kind. There is one exception to the general reassurance.
There may well be genes, or blocks of closely linked loci, that
are involved in the causation of more than one disease. In this
case relaxation of selection against one disease may lead to
increases in the frequencies of other diseases. Clearly this
could have serious consequences.

   The prediction of the effects of relaxed selection depend on
the nature and magnitude of the other forces acting on the frequency of the disease, and in some cases holding it in a stable
equilibrium. This underlines the importance of discovering more
about these other forces.

   In our present state of knowledge this is probably as far as
we can go. The hope must be that we can discover more about the
mode of ineritance of the important diseases. With the multifactorial model, this would have to include an identification of
the nature of the underlying trait involved and of its genetic
and environmental components. The overlap in the causation of
alternative diseases also needs elucidation. Purely descriptive
techniques will eventually give way as we gain an understanding,
partly from these advances, of the biochemical and physiological
determinants of disease and the way in which environmental and
genetical factors influence these determinants.

4. REFERENCES

Curnow, R.N. and Smith, C. (1975) Multifactorial models for familial diseases in man - with discussion, *J. R. Statist. Soc. A,* **138**, pp. 131-169.

Davie, A.M., Smith, C., Curnow, R.N. and Holloway, Susan M. (1978) On effects of relaxed selection in familial disorders, *Ann. Hum. Genet.,* **41**, pp. 481-489.

Holloway, Susan M. and Smith, C. (1975) Effects of various medical and social practices on the frequency of genetic disorders, *Amer. J. Hum. Genet.,* **27**, pp. 614-627.

Merry, Alyce, Roger, J.H. and Curnow, R.N. (1979) A two-locus model for the inheritance of a familial disease, *Ann. Hum. Genet.,* **43**, pp. 71-80.

M.R.C. Review of Clinical Genetics (1978) A report by the MRC Subcommittee to review Clinical Genetics, London: Medical Research Council.

PART II

BEHAVIOUR AND STRUCTURE OF

BIOLOGICAL POPULATIONS

POPULATION AND COMMUNITY STRUCTURE AND INTERACTION

M.S. Bartlett

(formerly University of Oxford)

ABSTRACT

A cursory survey is made of the various factors to be considered in any realistic population model, such as age structure,
sex, spatial structure, genetic structure, with all the possible
interactions even for a single species, before the more intricate
problems of community structure are broached.

It is convenient to refer to the various population models
first in deterministic terms, treating stochastic variability as
one extra factor to be considered in its effect on population
structure. However, in view of growing interest in what May
terms <u>environmental</u> stochasticity, a short Appendix on <u>doubly
stochastic</u> models (which include both environmental and demographic stochasticity) has been added.

This survey includes brief notes on recent theoretical work
on ecological-genetical populations, and on genetic models invok-
ing (a) frequency - dependent selection or (b) environmental
variability, as explanations of polymorphisms. It emphasises
also, however, the difficult task of matching models with Nature,
this requiring ideally an assessment of the relevance and importance <u>both</u> of the models and of observed biological data.

1. INTRODUCTORY REMARKS

The vast literature on population models now in existence is
indicative of the growing awareness of the complexities of models
purporting to mirror Nature in any realistic way. Thus while
the population equations I noted at a previous Oxford conference
(Bartlett, 1973) could represent in principle most population
models (moreover in a stochastic form), it may help to highlight
the dilemma of simplicity versus complexity if I recall some of
the more obvious attributes in a real population or community
that may have to be incorporated in our models viz. age, sex,
spatial structure, genetic structure, social structure, with all
the possible interactions among these various factors. This is
so just for a single species, before we even begin to turn our
attention to the structure and interactions among populations in
a whole community.

Stochastic effects may at times be important, but in this concentration on structure it is convenient to refer to the various situations firstly in deterministic terms, treating stochastic variability as one extra factor to be considered in its effect on the structure to be expected with any specific population model. However, the increasing relevance of what I call doubly stochastic models (cf. Bartlett, 1980) in which the parameters of the model themselves become random, usually to mimic environmental variability in space and/or time, calls for one or two remarks of a technical nature, which are made in an Appendix. Such stochasticity is referred to by May (1973) as environmental stochasticity, as against intrinsic stochasticity in the population model, which he terms demographic.

For definiteness, I shall as a rule discuss factors in a continuous time formulation, even though some real populations may be better envisaged in terms of generations, especially when their genetic evolution is involved. Even then, diffusion models (see, for example, Kimura 1964) are often used as an approximation, such models representing the next stage of approximation (in which variance is not neglected) to the deterministic model. My very cursory survey must obviously be supplemented by reference to the relevant literature (see in particular Part II of the volumes edited by Levin, S.A., 1978).

2.   AGE STRUCTURE FOR A SINGLE POPULATION

This problem (for one sex only) is a standard one for birth and death rates $\lambda(u)$ and $\mu(u)$ dependent on age u, but not otherwise dependent on the epoch or the population size. The deterministic age-density $n_t(u)$ (or the expected age-density $E\{dN_t(u)\}/du$ in a full stochastic formulation) satisfies the continuity equation (cf. Bartlett 1970 or 1973)

$$\frac{\partial n_t}{\partial t} + \frac{\partial n_t}{\partial u} = -\mu(u)n_t, \quad (0<u<t),$$ (1)

together with the "renewal" equation at $u = 0$,

$$n_t(0) = \int_0^\infty \lambda(u)n_t(u)du.$$ (2)

These equations determine $n_t(u)$ from given initial conditions; and in particular, under fairly general conditions for the functions involved, we have the asymptotic solution as t increases,

$$n_t(u) \to Ce^{K(t-u)} \exp\left[-\int_0^u \mu(v)\,dv\right], \tag{3}$$

where $\underline{K}$ is the dominant root of the equation

$$\int_0^\infty \lambda(u)e^{-Ku} \exp\left[-\int_0^u \mu(v)\,dv\right] du = 1 \tag{4}$$

Continuity equations like (1) were rather curiously in the context of growing cell populations referred to by S.I. Rubinow (1978) as Scherbaum-Rasch-von Foerster equations, though in an Addendum he notes that they had already appeared in the work of McKendrick (1926).

The effect of immigration or emigration is of course readily added to the equations. If we put $\lambda(u) = 0$, and add an immigration rate $\nu(u)$ dependent on age, we have the case of a Society recruited by election. If the total intake rate is constant, so that $\nu(u) = \alpha g(u)$, say, where $g(u)$ is the age-distribution of new Fellows, it is clear that we obtain an ultimate steady population

$$n_t(u) \to \alpha \int_0^u g(w)P(u|w)\,dw, \tag{5}$$

where

$$P(u|w) = \exp\left[-\int_w^u \mu(v)\,dv\right]$$

denotes the probability that a Fellow alive at age $\underline{w}$ is still alive at age $\underline{u}$. The total ultimate size of the Society, attained by integrating over all $\underline{u}$, may be written

$$n_t \to \alpha E, \tag{6}$$

where $\underline{E}$ is the average life expectation of new Fellows. From the present standpoint, the interesting formula is the ultimate age structure (5), depending on the distribution on entry. An example using Royal Society statistics was given in Bartlett (1970). A further point on age structure which I noted is that the entry age distribution varies by subject, so that the ultimate age distribution also varies by subject. I quote in Table I the relevant total percentage composition by subject, making use of the statistics of ages at entry for individual subjects.

3. AGE AND SEX

The extra complication of sex is less straightforward. For animal populations under random encounter conditions it might be appropriate to assume matings and hence offspring at rates proportional to the product of numbers of males and females (compare

TABLE I
(Bartlett 1970)

SUBJECT	AT ENTRY (1954-61)	ULTIMATE (estimated)
Mathematics	12.0	14.6
Physics	13.5	14.4
Chemistry	13.5	14.0
Engineering	7.5	6.5
Geology	6.5	4.9
Botany	8.0	7.2
Zoology	12.5	11.9
Physiology	17.5	17.2
"Borderline"	9.0	9.3

the assumption in epidemiology of new infections proportional to
the product of numbers of infective and susceptible individuals).
However, in human populations at least it is usually considered
more reasonable to assume that births are linearly proportional
to population size (as in the uni-sex case), so that one possible
assumption would be to assume births proportional to the square-
root of the product of male and female numbers. This leads to
some difficulty of formulation when ages are taken into account,
which may be resolved by introducing a weight function (cf. Das
Gupta, 1972; Bartlett, 1973). Thus to summarize the model gen-
eralising equations (1) and (2), we denote male and female den-
sities by ages $\underline{u}$, $\underline{v}$ respectively, as $m_t(u)$, $f_t(v)$. The continuity equations now read

$$\left.\begin{array}{l} \dfrac{\partial m_t(u)}{\partial t} + \dfrac{\partial m_t(u)}{\partial u} = -\mu_m(u)m_t(u) \\[3em] \dfrac{\partial f_t(v)}{\partial t} + \dfrac{\partial f_t(v)}{\partial v} = -\mu_f(v)f_t(v) \end{array}\right\} \tag{7}$$

and equation (2) is replaced by

$$\left.\begin{array}{l} m_t(0) = \displaystyle\int_0^\infty \int_0^\infty \Lambda_m\{m_t(u), f_t(v)\}\,dudv \\[3em] f_t(0) = \displaystyle\int_0^\infty \int_0^\infty \Lambda_f\{m_t(u), f_t(v)\}\,dudv \end{array}\right\}, \tag{8}$$

say, where we are assuming in particular that the __functionals__ Λ_m, Λ_f are of the form, say

$$
\left.
\begin{aligned}
\lambda_m(u,v) \left[\int w_m(u,u')m_t(u')du' \int w_t(v,v')f_t(v')dv' \right]^{\frac{1}{2}}, \\
\lambda_f(u,v) \left[\int w_m(u,u')m_t(u')dv' \int w_f(v,v')f_t(v')dv' \right]^{\frac{1}{2}}
\end{aligned}
\right\}
\tag{9}
$$

An alternative approach (Federickson, 1971) for human populations assigns births to marriages (neglecting illegitimate births), so that the population is divided into __unmarried__ males $m_t(u)$, __unmarried__ females $f_t(v)$, and married couples $n_t(u,v)$. Equations may be similarly written down, with three continuity equations for $m_t(u)$, $f_t(v)$, and $n_t(u,v)$, and birth equations of the form

$$
\left.
\begin{aligned}
m_t(0) &= \int \int \lambda_m(u,v)n_t(u,v)dudv, \\
f_t(0) &= \int \int \lambda_f(u,v)n_t(u,v)dudv
\end{aligned}
\right\}
\tag{10}
$$

There is still a formulation difficulty analogous to that for births in the previous model, this time for the rate of marriages. More importantly, the solutions of the equations are not so readily developed; and as they still neglect such aspects as divorces, unmarried mothers, family planning, etc., it seems doubtful whether the model possesses any advantages over reasonably formulated two-sex models not explicitly introducing marriages, even for human populations.

For some populations, especially in the plant or insect realms, the sex structure may of course be markedly different from that appropriate for models of human populations.

The problem in population genetics of defining "fitness", especially for sexual populations, is apparent from the above discussion. Even for uni-sex populations, the fitness should ideally be defined in terms of the root K in equation (4). If we denote the integral on the left of the equation by $L(K)$, then if $L(0)$, which may be termed the net reproduction rate, is not much different from unity, say $1 + \varepsilon$, then

$$
K \sim \varepsilon / \left[\frac{\partial}{\partial K}L(K) \right]_{K=0} = \varepsilon/T
\tag{11}
$$

where T is the mean generation time. For a short reproductive period at age $u = T_0$, the equation for K reduces to

$$me^{-KT_O} \sim 1;$$

and again, very approximately, $K \sim \varepsilon / T_O$, or $K \sim \varepsilon$ if the generation time T_O is scaled to unity.

4. GENETIC STRUCTURE

It is perhaps a matter of definition whether we define two or more markedly different genotypes as part of a single population, but in the case of interbreeding groups it seems logical to do so. This implies that most populations, as they are unlikely to be homozygous for more than a fraction of their genes, have a formidably complex genetic structure, for which, at least until recently, very simplified models concentrating on one, or maybe two, loci have been considered.

The genetic diversity observed in Nature implies a considerably degree of heterozygosity, part of which is explicable in terms of transient selection situations, part in terms of stochastic effects for finite populations (Sewall Wright's random drift), and part in terms of stable polymorphisms. A classical example of the last is that arising when a heterozygote is more fit than either homozygote, but other explanations of polymorphism have been stressed in recent years, including variable environments (see § 6) and selection which is frequency dependent, the latter associated with Maynard Smith's concept of evolutionarily stable strategies (ESS).

A special kind of stable polymorphism is of course sex, and the usual (approximately) 1 : 1 sex ratio may be regarded as a particular case of an ESS (the usual ratio being a value to which there are exceptions in exceptional circumstances*).

The importance of genetic structure as such cannot be mirrored by any systematic details here, but, as mentioned in the introductory remarks, reference should be made to the relevant literature (in the present context see, for example, genetical papers at this conference, or in Levin, S.A., (ed.) 1978, Fisher's classical 1930 work, Ewens' 1979 book on mathematical population genetics, and, for a non-technical account, including discussion of ESS, Dawkins, 1976). Various comments are, however, made in relation to the other topics listed in the present survey.

---

*see, for example, Bulmer and Taylor (1980)

5. SPATIAL AND/OR SOCIAL STRUCTURE

Spatial structure is becoming of increasing interest in population theory, but largely because of interaction with other factors, and is better mentioned in such a context. Ordinary diffusion of populations in space presents no great difficulty; for small-scale movements it is reasonable to assume the standard diffusion equation

$$\frac{\partial f_t(\underset{\sim}{r})}{\partial t} + \text{divm}(\underset{\sim}{r}) f_t(\underset{\sim}{r}) = \frac{\sigma^2 \nabla^2}{2} f_t(\underset{\sim}{r}) \qquad (12)$$

if for simplicity isotropic and homogeneous dispersion is assumed. The space vector coordinate is $\underset{\sim}{r}$, and the second term on the left of equation (12) represents a systematic mean drift.

In some circumstances, when the dispersion term σ^2 is balanced by an attractive drift to a centre focus, the model will result in an equilibrium distribution (analogous to the Sewall Wright distribution in one dimension representing a gene frequency), and has been used in this way by D.G. Kendall (1974) in a discussion on the migration of birds. In a further discussion by myself (Bartlett, 1978), the velocity of movement is explicitly retained (it is infinite in (12)), and in particular is assumed constant in magnitude. The possibilities are now more complicated, but under appropriate conditions an equilibrium distribution can still result. A particular one-dimensional case of this model also appears in a paper by L. Segel (1978) as a model of bacterial diffusion.

The spatial structure of a herd has been considered by Hamilton (1971) in relation to immunity to attack. The empirically observed structure of herds of sheep in relation to the quality of forage have been discussed by Dudziński et al. (1978). It is evident that a considerable ecological literature bears on this topic.

Social structure is also a concomitant of other variables, e.g. genetic, and may be relevant in animal populations if interpreted broadly enough, - for example, "pecking order", or spacing regularity in the nesting habits of gulls.

6. STOCHASTIC EFFECTS AND INTERACTIONS

Stochastic effects, as remarked in §1, may be classified into those arising (a) from population sampling variability, especially when numbers are small, and (b) from random variation in parameters of the model due to variable environment. The best known example of (a) is perhaps the survival history of a mutant gene at a locus. If the population is effectively infinite, then the mutant will not survive unless it has a fitness in terms of expected progeny greater than one. Notice that it is the _absolute_ fitness that is relevant, not that relative to the normal gene. It is usual, however, to assume that the normal fitness is one. Then if the mutant fitness is $1 + \varepsilon$, where ε is small, its chance P of extinction is approximately

$$P \sim e^{-2\varepsilon/\sigma^2} \tag{13}$$

where σ^2 is the variance in the number of progeny. For a Poisson distribution of progeny, $\sigma^2 = 1 + \varepsilon \sim 1$, and so $P \sim e^{-2n\varepsilon}$. While for small ε this is near one, it becomes $e^{-2n\varepsilon}$ after $\underline{n}$ mutations, and becomes small as $\underline{n}$ increases.

These formulae are modified for finite total population size $\underline{N}$, and in particular even an unfavourable mutant may survive in a constant total population. The change of survival of a neutral mutant (in a diploid population) is $1/(2N)$.

To turn to interaction between genetic and spatial factors, a discussion by Hamilton and May (1977) showed that it may pay a parent organism to disperse its progeny even when mortality of such dispersing progeny is high. This conclusion did not depend on any assumption of heterogeneous or random habitat.

Interaction between genetic structure and temporal randomness in environment is illustrated by the following example of a polymorphism arising without any superiority of the heterozygote (Gillespie, 1974). Let the fitness for the diploid genotypes A_1A_1, A_1A_2, A_2A_2, be additive and denoted by $1 + s$, $1 + \frac{1}{2}(s+t)$, $1 + t$. However, $\underline{s}$ and $\underline{t}$ vary from generation to generation with $E(s) = \mu_s$, $E(t) = \mu_t$, $\mathrm{corr}(\bar{s},t) = \rho$. Gillespie shows that a polymorphic stationary distribution exists if $|\alpha| < 1$, where

$$\alpha = 4 \frac{\left[\mu_s - \mu_t + \frac{1}{2}(\sigma_t^2 - \sigma_s^2)\right]}{\sigma_s^2 + \sigma_t^2 - 2\rho\sigma_s\sigma_t} \tag{14}$$

In particular, if $\sigma_s^2 = \sigma_t^2$ and $\rho = 0$, this expression for α becomes

$$\alpha = 4 \frac{\left[\mu_s - \mu_t\right]}{\sigma_s^2 + \sigma_t^2}. \tag{15}$$

The frequency distribution of A_1 is given by

$$f(x) = Cx^{\alpha}(1-x)^{-\alpha} \tag{16}$$

Gillespie has also considered combined temporal and spatial variability in the environment (see also Ewens, 1979 for further references), showing that polymorphism is facilitated by such additional heterogeneity (and also by higher polyploidy).

Density dependence

A common necessity with animal populations is a density-dependent factor, so that, in the simplest case of one type of individual (no age structure) the growth equation for the population size n_t would read

$$\frac{dn_t}{dt} = \lambda n_t (1-n_t/m) \tag{17}$$

the well-known logistic model with n_t increasing to its maximum m. May (1978) notes that the effect of age-structure might approximately be incorporated into equation (17) by replacing it by

$$\frac{dn_t}{dt} = \lambda n_t (1-n_{t-\tau}/m) \tag{18}$$

In this case a limit cycle ensues when $\lambda\tau > \frac{1}{2}\pi$, and in a discussion of data showing oscillations of sheep blow-fly numbers (Nicholson, 1954) May suggests the value $\lambda\tau = 2.1$. Such limit cycle oscillations in a model are not likely to be affected much by stochastic variability, except in conditions for which the oscillations become violent. Thus for $\lambda\tau = 2.4$, the ratio N(max) to N(min) has risen to 1,040, so that if N(max) were 10,000, N(min) would be only 10, and stochastic effects would no longer be negligible.

The limiting factor in equation (17) is of course itself a shorthand version of some extraneous limiting factor, such as space or food, which in some contexts would require more explicit formulation.

Theory of epidemics

It is convenient to classify any epidemiological situation where a single population is divided into two or more groups, such as infective and susceptible individuals in relation to, say, a virus, as a multi-group problem, as the various groups are

conveniently listed in a model as if distinct species. Thus in
a simple model of a closed population of i_t infected individuals
and $s_t = n - i_t$ susceptible, infection being by effective "contact",
the deterministic version of the model is

$$\frac{di_t}{dt} = \lambda i_t s_t = \lambda i_t (n - i_t) , \qquad (19)$$

which is merely the logistic model (17). If the infected individuals are removed, however, either by death, or recovery (and
subsequent immunity), then (19) is replaced by

$$\left. \begin{array}{l} \dfrac{di_t}{dt} = \lambda i_t s_t - \mu i_t , \\[2em] \dfrac{ds_t}{dt} = \lambda i_t s_t . \end{array} \right\} \qquad (20)$$

If new susceptibles are entering the population at rate ν, then
the second equation in (20) is replaced by

$$\frac{ds_t}{dt} = \nu - \lambda i_t s_t , \qquad (21)$$

the equations now permitting a steady endemic state when $s_t = \mu/\lambda$,
$i_t = \nu/\mu$. This simple model roughly represents some epidemic situations such as measles, but must be amplified by further terms
in other cases, to allow, for example, for temporary immunity,
deaths, population growth or decline (cf. e.g. Bartlett 1973,
Anderson and May 1979). In the case of the last equation (21),
there are two distinct aspects of stochastic variability.
Formally, with the deterministic equations, small oscillations
about the endemic equilibrium point are damped down, and this
may be shown (e.g. Bartlett, 1960) to be true for any size
oscillations (and also if a more realistic incubation period is
introduced into the model). However, for moderate size populations stochastic variability maintains these natural oscillations which may also be driven by seasonal factors. There is
also a further complication arising from the alternative possibility (if there are no new _infected_ individuals coming from
outside) of i_t becoming zero. In that case s_t steadily increases with $\underline{\nu}$. The stochastic switch from i_t to $i_t = 0$ can arise
when i_t is small, especially in the course of the epidemic
cycle when s_t has dropped below its critical value μ/λ (see

below). This gives rise to a very different pattern of behaviour for measles epidemics in small and large communities (Bartlett, 1960).

In the case (20) of the closed populations, the stochastic effect is simpler and more apparent, for at the start of infection when the number i_t of infectives is small, and the number s_t of susceptibles is large, s_t may be treated as approximately constant; the stochastic version of (20) is then a population of infective individuals with birth rate λs_0 and death rate μ. It then follows that the chance of "extinction" of the infectives is 1 below the threshold $\lambda s_0/\mu$, and $\left[\mu/(\lambda s_0)\right]^{i_0}$ if $s_0 > \mu/\lambda$.

7. POPULATIONS IN ECOLOGY

The deterministic theory of ecological systems stemming from the classical Lotka-Volterra equations and more recent generalisations of them is the starting point for Levin's 1978 compilation on populations and communities, both in his own introductory remarks and in May's following contribution. As in the case of population genetics, the purpose of the present survey is not to look at these developments in ecological models in detail, but in relation to each other, and to their relevance to real population and community structure.

A fundamental difficulty with this general problem at the present time, as in genetics, is that the growing complexity of models is more than matched by the variation in the living world. It is thus not so much a question as whether any model is relevant, in the sense of finding somewhere a counterpart in Nature, as how important and central it is in the biological scheme of things; this is a much more difficult question to answer. Any attempt at an answer requires ideally a comprehensive knowledge of, on the one hand, real animal populations, present and past, and their environments, and on the other, a knowledge and understanding of the various models available to represent them. This is a formidable and almost impossible requirement, and in its absence we must expect much more laboured progress.

On the theoretical side, May (1977) has suggested that complex communities may often be approximately split up into a number of "low order systems" with loose linkage between them. The other systems may then be treated as an environment (possibly heterogeneous) for the particular low order system under discussion.

Three topics are mentioned below. The first is variable environment and other stochastic effects, the second is the

interaction between ecology and genetics, and the third the impact of the concept of an evolutionarily stable strategy on ecology and animal behaviour.

With regard to the first, a valuable survey of models involving spatial and temporal heterogenity will be found in
Levin (ed.)(1978); for example, May includes a discussion on the
limit set on the number of viable species in the traditional
niche formulation by a fluctuating environment, and Levin himself
discusses the effect of heterogeneous spatial environments. An
extreme example of diversity associated with spatial dispersal
is that of habitats completely or partially isolated from each
other, such as a group of islands, considered by MacArthur and
Wilson (1967). Their model involved the chances of extinction
depending on the sizes of the islands, and was essentially a
stochastic model in the demographic sense; it was also an example
of interaction between ecology and evolutionary genetics.

A more formal marriage of ecology and evolutionary genetics
has been begun in, for example, the work of Roughgarden (1976;
cf. also Ewens, 1979).

The deterministic discrete-time formulation of the Lotka-
Volterra equations may be denoted by

$$\Delta n_i(t) = n_i(t)\{\alpha_i - \Sigma\beta_i \, n_j(v)\}, \; (i=1...K),$$
(22)

for $\underline{K}$ interacting species of population sizes $n_i(t)$. For each
species we may write

$$x_i(t+1) = x_i(t) \, \overline{w}_i,$$
(23)

where $\overline{w}_i$ is the absolute mean fitness of this species in relation to alleles A_1 and A_2, say, at a gene locus. If the frequency of A_1 is x_i and A_2 $1-x_i$; the formula for $\overline{w}_i$ under random
mating is

$$\overline{w}_i = (w_{11})_i x_i^2 + 2(w_{12})_i x_i(1-x_i) + (w_{22})_i(1-x_i)^2,$$
(24)

where the $(w)_i$'s are allowed to depend on all the $n_j(j=1....K)$.
The change in x_i is (e.g. Ewens 1979)

$$\Delta x_i = x_i(1-x)\{(w_{11})_i x_i + (w_{12})_i(1-2x_i) - (w_{22})_i(1-x_i)\}/\overline{w}_i.$$
(25)

Let $G = \{g_{ij}\} = \{\partial\Delta n_i/\partial n_j\}$ at equilibrium,

$\qquad = \{n_i\partial\overline{w}_i/\partial n_j\}$ at equilibrium.

If the $(w)_i$'s are not directly affected by other x_j, only through the n_j, Roughgarden shows that the combined ecological-genetical evolution is determined by (23) and (25). Moreover, if for fixed $x_1 \ldots x_K$, there is a unique locally stable equilibrium for the purely ecological model, then

(i) an equilibrium point in the co-evolutionary model is
     locally stable if and only if $\overline{w}_i$ is maximised locally
     at that point with respect to x_i; and

(ii) the equilibrium size of the $\underline{i}$th species is either maxi-
     mised or minimised, at a stable equilibrium, at the
     equilibrium value of x_i (maximisation occurs if $F_i < 0$
     and minimisation at $F_i > 0$ where $F_i = (-1)^K|G_i|$, $|G_i|$
     denoting the determinant obtained from G by striking
     out the $\underline{i}$th row and column).

   Roughgarden has also considered the situation when the $(w)_i$'s may be affected directly by the other gene frequencies x_i.

   The question whether genetic considerations are relevant in population ecology is of course partly a question of time-scales. Even for purely ecological (or epidemiological) pro-blems, the problem may be simplifiable if some time-scales are long compared with others, as, for example, in the approximation of a constant number of susceptibles at the beginning of an epi-demic (§6) (cf. also May 1977b).

   To illustrate the impact of the concept of evolutionarily stable strategies (ESS) in ecology, we may note the arguments advanced by Hastings and Conrad (1979) for short food chains in natural ecosystems. The impact on theories of animal behaviour has become well-known since the publication of Dawkins' book (1976), and is founded particularly on the work of Hamilton (1964).

8. CONCLUDING REMARKS

   It is encouraging to see these beginnings of a theory of community structure developing in recent years, both ecologically and genetically, and we are likely to see considerable further development in the future. Further empirical study of species abundances and diversity by ecologists and geneticists, and statistical analyses of such data by biometricians (cf. Engen. 1978), will be needed to complement this theoretical development.

On genetic diversity, the existence of various population models, including in particular (a) frequency-dependent selection and (b) environmental heterogeneity, raises the question noted in §7 of what are the more relevant models; e.g. for the class of genetic models in (b), does the amount of environmental hete-rogeneity required to explain the genetic diversity tally with what actually exists?

9. REFERENCES (see also references in starred items)

*Anderson, R.M., Turner, B.D. and Taylor, L.R. (eds) (1979) Populations Dynamics, Blackwell Scientific Publications, Oxford.

Anderson, R.M. and May, R.M. (1979) Population biology of infec-tious diseases, *Nature,* **280**, pp. 361-367 and pp. 455-461.

Bartlett, M.S. (1960) Stochastic Population Models in Ecology and Epidemiology, Chapman and Hall, London.

Bartlett, M.S. (1970) Age distribution, *Biometrics,* **26**, pp. 377-385.

Bartlett, M.S. (1973) Equations and models of population change (see Bartlett, M.S. and Hiorns, R.W. (1973) pp. 5-21).

Bartlett, M.S. (1978a) Introduction to Stochastic Processes, Cambridge, 3rd edition.

Bartlett, M.S. (1978b) A note on random walks at constant speed, *Adv. App. Prob.,* **10**, pp. 704-707.

Bartlett, M.S. (1980) The development of population models, *In* Statistics and Probability: Essays in honour of C.R. Rao, North-Holland Publ, Co.

Bartlett, M.S. and Hiorns, R.W. (eds) (1973) The Mathematical Theory of the Dynamics of Biological Populations, Academic Press.

Bulmer, M.G. and Taylor, P.D. (1980) Dispersal and the sex ratio, *Nature,* **284**, pp. 448-9.

Charlesworth, B. (1976) Natural selection in age-structured popu-lations, *Lectures on Mathematics in the Life Sciences,* **8**, pp. 69-87.

*Christiansen, F.B. and Fenchel, T.M. (1977) Theories of Populations in Biological Communities, *Ecological Studies*, **20**, Springer-Verlag, New York.

*Dawkins, R. (1976) The Selfish Gene, Oxford Univ. Press.

Dudzinski, M.L., Schuh, H.J., Wilcox, D.G., Gardiner, H.G. and Morrissey, J.G. (1978) Statistical and probabilistic estimates of forage conditions for grazing behaviour of Merino sheep in semi-arid environment, *App. Anim. Ethol.*, **4**, pp. 357-368.

*Engen, S. (1978) Stochastic Abundance Models, Chapman and Hall, London.

*Ewens, W. (1979) Mathematical Population Genetics, Springer-Verlag, New York.

Fisher, R.A. (1930) Genetical Theory of Natural Selection, Oxford Univ. Press.

Frederickson, A.G. (1971) A mathematical theory of age structure in sexual populations; random mating and monogamous marriage models, *Math. Biosciences*, **10**, pp. 117-143.

Gillespie, J. (1974) Polymorphism in patchy environments, *The Amer. Nat.*, **108**, pp. 145-151.

Hamilton, W.D. (1964) The genetical theory of social behaviour (I & II), *J. Theor. Biol.*, **7**, pp. 1-16; 17-32.

Hamilton, W.D. (1971) Geometry for the selfish herd, *J. Theor. Biolog.*, **31**, pp. 295-311.

Hamilton, W.D. and May, R.M. (1977) Dispersal in stable habitats, *Nature*, **269**, pp. 578-581.

Hastings, H.M. and Conrad, M. (1979) Length and evolutionary stability of food chains, *Nature*, **282**, pp. 838-839.

Kendall, D.G. (1974) Pole-seeking Brownian motions and bird navigation, *J.R. Statist. Soc.*, B**36**, pp. 365-417.

Kimura, M. (1974) Diffusion models in population genetics, *J. App. Prob.*, **1**, pp.177-232.

Levin, S.A. (1978) Population models and community structure in heterogeneous environments, (see Levin, S.A. (ed.), 1978, pp. 439-476).

*Levin, S.A. (ed.) (1978) Studies in Mathematical Biology: Part I Cellular Behaviour and the Development of Patterns; Part II Populations and Communities, Maths. Association of America.

MacArthur, R.H. (1970) Species packing and competitive equilibrium for many species, *Theor. Pop. Biol.*, **1**, pp. 1-11.

MacArthur, R.H. and Wilson, E.O. (1967) The Theory of Island Biogeography, Princeton Univ. Press.

McKendrick, A.G. (1926) Applications of mathematics to medical problems, *Proc. Edin. Math. Soc.*, **44**, p. 98.

May, R.M. (1973) Stability and Complexity in Model Ecosystems, Princeton Univ. Press.

May, R.M. (1977a) Population genetics and cultural inheritance, *Nature*, **268**, pp. 11-13.

May, R.M. (1977b) Thresholds and breakpoints in ecosystems with a multiplicity of stable states, *Nature*, **269**, pp. 471-477.

May, R.M. (1978) Mathematical aspects of the dynamics of animal populations, (see Levin, S.A. (ed.) 1978, pp. 317-366).

Maynard Smith, J. (1976) Evolution and the theory of games, *Amer. Sci.*, **61**, pp. 41-45.

Milne, R.K. and Westcott, M. (1972) Further results for Gauss-Poisson processes, *Adv. App. Prob.*, **4**, pp. 151-176.

Nicholson, A.J. (1954) An outline of the dynamics of animal populations, *Austral. J. Zool.*, **2**, p. 9.

Oaten, A. (1977) Optimal foraging in patches: a case for stochasticity, *Theor. Pop. Biol.*, **12**, pp. 263-285.

Roughgarden, J. (1976) Resource partitioning among competing species - a coevolutionary approach, *Theor. Pop. Biol.*, **3**, pp. 338-424.

Rubinow, S.I. (1978) Age-structured equations in the theory of cell populations, (see Levin, S.A. (ed.), 1978, pp. 389-410).

Segel, L. (1978) Mathematical models for cellular behaviour, (see Levin, S.A. (ed.), 1978, pp. 156-190).

APPENDIX

Doubly stochastic models

The basic equations for population models summarised by Bartlett (1973) did not explicitly include random variability in the parameters of the model, though such additional randomness, if fully and unambiguously specified, does not introduce any new principle. Such additional variability, to represent temporal (or spatial) heterogeneity in the environment, is sometimes, however, introduced in a rather *ad hoc* way into models which have been approximately formulated in deterministic or diffusion equation terms and care is then needed to avoid ambiguities or errors (cf. May 1973, Appendices IV and II). In the case of genetic problems where selection parameters become random, but vary from generation to generation (i.e. in discrete time) there is less risk of ambiguity, though Ewens (1979, §5.8) notes that errors have arisen in passing to the diffusion (i.e. continuous time) approximation.

To demonstrate the further generalization of my basic equation

$$\frac{\partial M_t(\underset{\sim}{\theta})}{\partial t} = H M_t(\underset{\sim}{\theta}), \tag{A1}$$

where $\underset{\sim}{H}$ is an operator, $M_t(\underset{\sim}{\theta})$ is the moment-generating function (or probability-generation function $\Pi_t(\underset{\sim}{z})$ if $\underset{\sim}{\theta} = \log \underset{\sim}{z}$) let $\underset{\sim}{H}$ be linear in parameters α_i, and of the form

$$H = H_0 + \Sigma_i \alpha_i H_i. \tag{A2}$$

Then if the parameters α_i are replaced by stochastic processes $\{A_i(t)\}$, the formal solution of (A1) now becomes

$$M_t(\underset{\sim}{\theta}) = E \left\{ e^{\left\{ H_0 t + \Sigma_i \int_0^t A_i(t) H_i dt \right\}} \right\} M_0(\underset{\sim}{\theta}) \tag{A3}$$

where E denotes averaging over the $A_i(t)$. Let the characteristic functional (see Bartlett 1978a) of the $A_i(t)$ be

$$\Lambda\{\phi_i(t)\} = E\{\exp[\Sigma_i \int_0^t A_i(t) \phi_i(t) dt]\}. \tag{A4}$$

Then equations (A3) and (A4) determine in principle the solution of the doubly stochastic model. For example, if the $A_i(t)$ are Gaussian stationary processes, then the $\Lambda\{\phi_i(t)\}$ are known. In particular, if $H = \alpha(z-1)$, corresponding to the Poisson (or immigration) process, with solution (for α constant)

$$\Pi_t(z) = e^{\alpha t(z-1)}, \tag{A5}$$

and $\phi(t)$ has mean α, variance σ^2 and covariance structure $w(t)$, so that

$$\Lambda\{\phi(t)\} = \exp\{\alpha\int_0^t\phi(t)\,dt + \tfrac{1}{2}\int_0^t\int_0^t\phi(u)\,\phi(v)\,w(u-v)\,du\,dv\} \tag{A6}$$

then in place of (A5) we obtain

$$\Pi_t(z) = \exp\{\alpha(z-1)t + \tfrac{1}{2}\int_{-t}^t (t-|x|)\,w(x)\,dx(z-1)^2\} \tag{A7}$$

an example of what is called in the literature a Gauss-Poisson process (see e.g. Milne and Westcott, 1972, equation 7.5). In the particular case of "white noise", where $w(x)$ is zero for $x\neq0$, but the variance still increases as $\sigma^2 t$, the second term in (A7) formally reduces to $\tfrac{1}{2}t\sigma^2(z-1)^2$. This would be a rather dubious model generalizing (A5), as it would imply that two individuals can arise with comparable probability to one however small t may be, and should not be taken too literally for small t. (A spatial version of it would replace t in equations (A6) and (A7) by an appropriate vector spatial variable r, say). The difficulty with the limiting case of "white noise" does not apply to the more realistic model (A7) (which is consistent with (A5) for small t), and merely reminds us to be especially cautious in making use of "white noise" in our models, even if it is sometimes convenient.

As a second example, let the immigrating individuals die at rate μ per individual (μ taken constant for simplicity). Then

$$H = \nu(t)(z-1) - \mu(1-z)\frac{\partial}{\partial z} \tag{A8}$$

and (for $\Pi_0(z) = 1$)

$$\Pi_t(z) = E\{\exp\{\int_0^t\nu(u)\,e^{-\mu(t-u)}(z-1)\,du\} \tag{A9}$$

As $\nu(t-u)$ has the same properties as $\psi(u)$, this gives from (A6)

$$\Pi_t(z) = \exp\{\frac{\nu}{\mu}(z-1)(1-e^{-\mu t}) + \tfrac{1}{2}(z-1)^2\int_0^t\int_0^t w(u-v)\,e^{-\mu(u+v)}\,du\,dv \tag{A10}$$

or, in the limiting case of "white noise",

$$\Pi_t(z) = \exp\{\frac{\nu}{\mu}(z-1)(1-e^{-\mu t}) + \frac{1}{4}\frac{\sigma^2}{\mu}(1-e^{-2\mu t})(z-1)^2\} \quad \text{(A11)}$$

As $t \to \infty$, this gives the equilibrium distribution

$$\Pi(z) = \exp\{\frac{\nu}{\mu}(z-1) + \frac{1}{4}\frac{\sigma^2}{\mu}(z-1)^2\}. \quad \text{(A12)}$$

Note that for equilibrium distributions, <u>in the case of "white noise"</u>,

$$\Pi_t(z) = E\{e^{Ht}\}\Pi_0(z)$$

$$= E\{e^{H\tau}\}\Pi_{t-\tau}(z)$$

whence, as $t - \tau \to \infty$, and $\Pi_{t-\tau}(3) \to \Pi(z)$, say,

$$\Pi(z) = E\{e^{H\tau}\}\Pi(z)$$

for any $\underline{\tau}$, whence

$$(H_0 + \Sigma\alpha_i H_i + \frac{1}{2}\Sigma w_{ij}H_i H_j)\Pi(z) = 0. \quad \text{(A13)}$$

Thus we obtain the last solution more readily from the equation

$$\left[\nu(z-1) + \frac{1}{2}\sigma^2(z-1)^2 + \mu(1-z)\frac{\partial}{\partial z}\right]\Pi(z) = 0. \quad \text{(A14)}$$

More generally, in the case of a birth-rate λ as well, but $\mu-\lambda$ positive and only ν subject to fluctuation, the equation becomes

$$\{\nu(z-1) + \frac{1}{2}\sigma^2(z-1) + \left[\mu(1-z)-\lambda(z^2-z)\right]\frac{\partial}{\partial z}\}\Pi(z) = 0, \quad \text{(A15)}$$

leading to the equilibrium distribution

$$\Pi(z) = \left[1 - \frac{\lambda(z-1)}{\mu-\lambda}\right]^{-\left(\frac{\nu}{\lambda} + \frac{(\mu-\lambda)\sigma^2}{2\lambda^2}\right)} e^{-\left(\frac{\sigma^2}{2}\frac{z-1}{\lambda}\right)} \quad \text{(16)}$$

Similarly the effect of fluctuations on extinction probabilities may be studied though more conveniently from the equivalent "backward equation" (cf. Bartlett 1973). Further details, for example, for the birth-and-death process, will be reported elsewhere.

SEX VERSUS NON-SEX VERSUS PARASITE*

W.D. Hamilton

*(Museum of Zoology, University of Michigan,
Ann Arbor, Michigan, USA)*

1. INTRODUCTION

Given acellular simple organisms in the early history of
life it is not difficult to imagine selection that would favour
multicellularity. Provided cell aggregates were clonal, so that
they would cooperate well, differentiation of somatic cells
could give several advantages. There are parallels with the
trends to eusociality currently occurring in some insects. Here
defence against predators and parasites - including conspecific
parasites - and increasing ability of a colony to buffer local
changes of the physical environment seem to be very important.
Similar factors most probably applied to simple multicellular
organisms. Achievements with regard to the second factor permit
occupation of new habitats.

Specialized somatic cells can increase the sophistication of
defence but also introduce new vulnerability. One new weakness
is in the inevitable slowing of the intrinsic growth rate due to
physico-chemical logistics. Thus all parasites that remain much
smaller than a host (these parasites might be called, in a broad
sense, pathogens) have an advantage in rate of evolution which
will help them to keep abreast.

A second weakness, brought in by multicellularity and crucial
to the theme of this essay, is that body-building in itself
requires that cells adhere to cells: the difficulty then may be
to recognize as non-self, and to deny attachment, all other cells
that present themselves at a cell surface. Non-self cells are
potential parasites. Attached without having alerted any
defence system in the host, an alien parasite cell is strongly
placed with regard to further exploitation. Somewhat similar
considerations can apply rather more weakly to unicellular
organisms as hosts under attack by smaller and still shorter-
lived parasites, notably viruses: here the argument would be
cast in terms of chemical systems and organelles.

*This paper appeared in Oikos, Volume 35 (1980).

Thus an ongoing antagonistic co-evolution is to be expected over the matter of recognition. The parasite evolves towards a presentation which is either so bland that to the victim it seems like being touched by an inert body or by nothing at all or else involves some positive mimicry of attributes of host cells. The host on its side would evolve ever keener methods for discriminating what are truly the cells of its own clone. Provided each individual host is able to know its own idiosyncracy, mimicry by the pathogen is an incentive to variation by the host, for a host which has a new mutation in a recognition substance is able to react to the existing mimetic race of pathogen. But the pathogens by virtue of short generation time can be expected to evolve an appropriate mimetic presentation soon after the new type's advantage has made it common. Obviously a frequency dependent polymorphic equilibrium is likely. Thus in somewhat vague outline we can imagine this coevolution becoming more complex and diversified, with arbitrary password-like identification substances (histo-compatibility antigens?) and facultative responses (current pathogen strains matched by clone proliferation of specific defence cells, as in immune system?) being brought in by the host, and special difficulties for the host (such as mimicking common small particles like pollen grains or self-enwrapping in the membranes of the previous host) being invented by the parasite.

To elaborate on this coevolution in terms of immunology and microbiology is beyond my present competence and beyond the scope of this paper. Instead I intend to consider very simple model systems involving the general kind of frequency dependence just outlined and consider what "steps" the host might take (to adopt for the moment a loose teleology) to make a password system as effective as possible - effective, I will assume, not through facultative adjustment, as with an immune system, but through continual random recreation of "passwords" by sex and recombination.

Historically my theme makes up a thread concerning the role of parasitism in evolution recently followed by Clarke (1976) in pursuit of reason for the abundance of protein polymorphism. Before Clarke the thread started perhaps (as so often) with Haldane (1949); after Clarke it was traced in my present direction - decisively towards sex although not very far - by Jaenike (1978). Besides the stimulus of Jaenike's paper, a similar suggestion from William Irons (pers. comm.), emphasizing pathogen mimicry of host self-recognition antigens, contributes direction to the present paper.

Randomness *per se* in recreation of passwords will not be a particular focus in this account. However, it seems worth noting here in passing that randomness of that kind first identified in the rules of Mendel and subsequently proven so universal in sexual processes, already suggests a theme of escape from enemies. Such randomness, in other words, might be a parallel to that entering the solution of the game of "matching pennies" and others of similar conflictual coevolutionary slant (Fisher 1934). Thus randomness in cellular events, which it is as easy to imagine following fixed courses as random ones, seems a further hint that in this area of antagonistic coevolution may lie the answer to why sex arose and how it is maintained (Hamilton 1975).

Specifically, in the models that follow, a cell is supposed to be able to make antibodies to a certain class of substances and actually to make them to those variants within the class that it itself possesses. Detection, by use of these antibodies, of self-antigens in another cell results in a pacification of the defence system and facilitation of attachment. Any exterior living object in which the self-antigens are not detected is not allowed attachment and is treated as potentially dangerous.

2. ONE-LOCUS MODEL

In the case of a diploid there are imagined to be two quasi-independent genomes checking for their own passwords: hostility results if either genome fails to find its password. A pattern of genetical partial resistance that is interpretable roughly on these lines is that shown by mice to three strains of a leukemogenic virus (Lilly 1972). This particular virus, however, seems unlikely to be a major selection factor in the wild.

In general the heterozygote might be expected to have an advantage over homozygotes since it imposes a harder test on a mimetic parasite cell and will be harder to fool. However, where the parasites are abundant and short-lived, heterozygote-mimetic strains can be expected to appear all the same. This is especially true because in the balanced polymorphism earlier outlined heterozygotes tend to be the commonest genotype. Once the heterozygote mimic is present and itself common the tendency of the heterozygote to be common is to its disadvantage, so that it is likely, over a series of generations, to become the least fit class. But because of the frequency dependence neither homozygote will fix; we see the possibility of an interesting interaction of stabilizing and destabilizing influences.

Before proceeding to examine this interaction in a specific case it may be noted, by way of introduction to the later model of this paper, that for a host to make its password depend on two syllables coded at independently segregating loci increases the range of passwords. So also, of course, does adding new alleles at a single locus. But eventually adding alleles

distributed between two loci makes the number of types rise as
a fourth power instead of as a square. For this among other
reasons multi-locus password systems certainly merit attention.

Here it also seems appropriate to note that while the story
has been told so far in terms that imply microbial parasites,
it is by no means only these that practise highly specific wiles
against their hosts, or that are short-lived enough to show the
very reactive frequency dependence that the models will be found
to require. Special resistance in particular genotypes of host,
special virulence in particular genotypes of parasite, and
matched polymorphic systems for attributes of these kinds, are
being found ever more widely. In the case of wheat and hessian
fly (Hatchett and Gallun 1970), for example, it is seen that the
parasite in such a system does not have to be a microbe. The
models that follow are much too simple to fit any such known
cases but hopefully their very simplicity may serve to bring out
basic principles that might apply in a wide set of more complex
realistic interactions.

Consider a population with three mutant genotypes of an
asexual host species (A,B,C). To each genotype a parasite species has produced a virulent pathotype. The presence of these
pathotypes affects the fitness of each host genotype in the same
frequency-dependent fashion: let $w_i(f_i)$ be the fitness where i
is the genotype symbol, f_i is the frequency of type i in the population and w is a fitness function that monotonically declines
with increasing f and is such that always $w(1/3) = 1$. Thus the
system has a fixed point at (1/3, 1/3, 1/3) in the frequency
space, and the decline of w with frequency means that at least
for some functions this point represents a stable equilibrium.
If, however, the decline of w is steep in the neighbourhood of
the fixed point it can happen that the equilibrium becomes unstable. Then any disturbance gives rise to an oscillating
departure.

For example, suppose the fitness function is

$$w_i = r^{1-3f_i}$$

If $r = e^g$ and $f_i = \frac{1}{3} + d_i$ then this may also be written

$$w_i = \exp(-3gd_i)$$

In the neighbourhood of the fixed point (gd = 0), this is
approximately

$$w_i = 1 - 3gd_i$$

Multiplying by the frequency, $1/3 + d_i$, summing for all three
types, normalizing (actually unnecessary here because mean fitness approximates to 1 near the fixed point), and neglecting
terms in d^2, the approximate frequency in the next generation is
$\frac{1}{3} + d_i(1-g)$. Hence the recurrence relations near the fixed
point are of the simple form

$$d'_i = d_i(1-g).$$

This shows that for $0<g<1$ there is monotonic approach to the
fixed point; for $1<g<2$ there is oscillatory approach; and for
$g>2$ there is an oscillatory departure from which a permanent
oscillatory state can be predicted to result.

A more general analysis using a Taylor Theorem expansion of
w gives the recurrence equation

$$d' = d \{1 + \frac{1}{3}\dot{w}(\frac{1}{3})\}$$

where $\dot{w}$ is the first derived function of w with respect to f.

Now consider a sexual host population with two alleles at a
single locus such that antigenically, relative to the asexuals
just considered, we have equivalences $AA \equiv A$, $AB \equiv C$ and $BB \equiv B$.
Suppose the fitness function is the same. This sexual system
in the presence of the parasite species does not have a fixed
point for the three phenotypes at (1/3, 1/3, 1/3); for if A and
B are equally frequent genotype AB occurs with frequency 1/2
and hence has lower fitness than the homozygotes.

It is clear, however, that equal frequencies of alleles
corresponds to a fixed point. Stability at this point can be
examined. It is now convenient to cast the argument in terms of
gene frequencies. Thus d will now be used differently, as the
measure of the departure of a gene frequency from 1/2.

Using the Hardy Weinberg ratio and working with objective
as before we obtain

$$d' = 2 \frac{w(\frac{1}{4}) + \frac{1}{4}\dot{w}(\frac{1}{4})}{w(\frac{1}{4}) + w(\frac{1}{2})} d$$

which can be abbreviated to $d' = \lambda_s d$.

With the fitness function as before, $w(f) = r^{1-3f} = e^{g(1-3f)}$, it is found that

$$\dot{w}(f) = -3g \exp\{g(1-3f)\}$$

So

$$w(\tfrac{1}{2}) = \exp(\tfrac{1}{2}g), \; w(\tfrac{1}{4}) = \exp(\tfrac{1}{4}g) \quad \text{and}$$

$$\dot{w}(\tfrac{1}{4}) = -3g \exp(\tfrac{1}{4}g)$$

Hence

$$\lambda_s = 2 \frac{\exp(\tfrac{1}{4}g) - \tfrac{3}{4}g \exp(\tfrac{1}{4}g)}{\exp(\tfrac{1}{4}g) + \exp(-\tfrac{1}{2}g)}$$

$$= 2 \frac{1 - \tfrac{3}{4}g}{1 + \exp(\tfrac{3}{4}g)}$$

When $g = 2$ we find $\lambda_s = -0.82$, but for $g = 2\tfrac{1}{6}$, $\lambda_s = -1.04$ so as g increases stability gives place to oscillations at a value a little higher than was found for the asexual population.

Location of the break points where permanent oscillation appears as frequency dependence becomes more sensitive is not, however, the main point of the model: it is enough to have shown that when once the fitness function enters a certain range of steepness oscillations of some kind are almost certain to occur in any mixed population. It is assumed for a mixed population that fitness depends on the joint frequency of the sexual geno-type and its asexual counterpart. Regarding a possible advan-tage to the asexual population in a mixture, interest centres on the separate long-term geometric mean fitness (LGMF) of the sexual strain versus the best such mean achieved by an asexual when all asexuals are given a two-fold fitness advantage, corresponding to the worst case of wastage due to unproductive-ness of males (Williams 1975, Maynard Smith 1978). I have not attempted formal analysis of the dynamics of mixtures but instead have studied the situation by computer simulation. Results indicate that analysis would certainly have to be com-plex: various oscillatory patterns were observed including 6-point cycles and also seemingly chaotic fluctuations. Often both sexuals and asexuals persisted together indefinitely. Some-times just one asexual strain went extinct, sometimes two did so while one persisted. But in general the advantage which the sexual strain gets from having, each generation, the arithmetic mean of a concave fitness set (Hamilton et al. 1980) insures that if g is made large enough all asexual strains go extinct, or

are at least kept at such low frequencies that, in nature,
extinction would be probable. For example, if g = 4.67 (fitness
function illustrated in Fig. 1a), total frequency of the persist-
ing asexuals was kept below 0.0001. Polymorphism here was
apparently chaotic. With this value of g the maximum fitness
possible in the model (given by $r = e^g$) is 106.3 and the minimum is 0.00009. The maximum fitness proves less important for
predominance of the sexual strain than the form of the lower
part of the curve; it was found that with g slightly higher than
the minimum needed to give predominance of the sexuals a "plateau fitness" could be imposed which was much less than the natural maximum and yet still high enough to enable the sexual
strain to drive out the asexual. For example, this happens when
g is 5.33 (giving r = 207.1) and a plateau fitness is imposed at
w = 7 (Fig. 1b). In this case a steady 6-point cycle occurred.
Using a different fitness function,

$$w_i = \{\frac{3}{2}(1 - f_i)\}^g$$

success with an even lower plateau was shown: with g=10 asexuals
could be kept below one per thousand when maximum fitness is
only 4.

   Such low maximum fitnesses are of interest because of the
difficulty previous authors have noted of finding any models
where the two-fold effective fecundity advantage of an asexual
can be overcome unless the maximum fecundity is set
rather high, roughly in hundreds or thousands (Williams 1975,
Maynard Smith 1978). However, the "plateau" models just mentioned have not really evaded this difficulty as regards origin
of sex, although they may possibly reveal an aspect of the
strength of sex to defend itself once it is well established.
This is because in the plateau models the asexuals on their own
cannot even constitute a viable population. In the last mentioned model if the sexual strain is absent the asexuals fluctuate wildly and go effectively to extinction in a few generations. In the preceding exponential model the three strains
enter a stable three-point cycle. When without plateau, the
fitness function dictates that the LGMF of each strain must be
at two (twofold fecundity advantage of asexuality being already
entered); but imposing the plateau causes this mean fitness to
drop. In the case where g = 5.33 and the plateau is at 7, the
LGMF is 0.228. Obviously such a population is inviable. But
the model does show that once sex is established it can evolve
into regions of stable coevolved fluctuation with its parasites
that are uninhabitable by any mixtures of parthenogenetic lines
that the sexual could give rise to. The sexual species in the
last case is viable, with LGMF at 1.407. In summary, artificial
as it is this simple one-locus model may be claimed to be a
little more realistic and relevant to sex than that model which

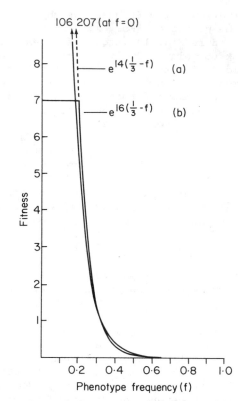

Fig. 1   Two examples of frequency-dependent fitness functions
         that permit a sexual species to preponderate against its
         set of asexual emergent strains despite effectively
         doubled fecundity in the latter.
In case (a) the limiting fitness of a very rare phenotype is 106.
This case gives rise to chaotically changing polymorphism in
which asexual strains go to very low frequencies (below 10^{-20}
for homozygous strains; below 10^{-3} for heterozygous strain).
Maximum and minimum fitnesses observed are about 3.0 and 1.7,
and the overall LGMF is 2.6.

In case (b) a maximum fitness of 7 is imposed on a function
otherwise going to 207 at f = 0.   This case gives rise to a
6-point cycle with highest mean fitness at 2.03, lowest at 0.88,
and LGMF at 1.41.   Here asexual genotypes reduce to very low
frequencies and may be going to zero: in the simulation cycle
preceding generation 200 none is above 10^{-5} and the heterozygotes are below 10^{-33}.

appears to be its only one-locus predecessor in the literature
so far (Hamilton et al. 1980).

3.   TWO-LOCUS HAPLOID SELECTION MODEL

Close to a model already outlined, without formal analysis,
by Jaenike (1978), I next consider a system with two loci each
with two alleles. For simplicity selection will be supposed to
operate only in the haploid phase. This is an unwished for
assumption from the present point of view because elaborate
multicelled sexual organisms that we aim to explain are mostly
diploid. But if viable haploid-selection models can be found,
it is to be expected that diploid-selection versions can likewise be devised (Hamilton et al. 1980), although so far, it has
to be admitted, it has been easier to make haploid ones realistic.

There are now four haplotypes, AB, Ab, aB, ab, and each is
supposed to confront a corresponding pathotype in the parasite
species. We assume that asexual variants of each haplotype
exist, each as before of twice the effective fecundity of its
sexual counterpart.

The following picture of the life cycle can be suggested.
After gamete fusion diploids persist only briefly and undergo
no selection in this stage (they might be resting eggs, say).
Then after meiosis haploid unicells are formed which multiply by
division and then initiate the multicellular bodies to whose
parasitism and selective elimination our previous story applies.
Once past a certain stage of development parasite infection no
longer kills them but the infected survivors can still harbour
and multiply parasites. Thus each haplotype breeds up the clone
to which it is susceptible. From among these clones, that corresponding to the most numerous genotype among current adults
decimates the young of the same genotype next season. So a high
fitness one season tends to be followed by low fitness next
season and so on. Alternatively, with probably little difference to the behaviour of the model, it could be supposed that
the young haploid hosts support infectious epidemics such that
each host genotype suffers as a function of its density which is
directly dependent on frequency. However strictly it is only
the first of the above alternatives that has been investigated
so far.

Fitness in the model is assumed to be frequency-dependent as
before but a frequency of 1/4 instead of 1/3 now plays the crucial role. Corresponding as closely as possible to the last
model although more general (see also Hamilton et al. 1980 for
the rationale) the following fitness function is chosen

$$w_{11} = \exp\left[-\delta\{(1-z)P_{11} + zP_{12} + zP_{21} + (-1-z)P_{22}\}\right]$$

$$= \exp\left[-\delta\{v_{11} - v_{22} - 2z(v_{11} + v_{22})\}\right]$$

where P_{ij} are frequencies of haplotypes, and $v_{ij} = P_{ij} - \frac{1}{4}$.
Likewise $w_{12} = \exp\left[-\delta\{v_{11} - v_{22} - 2z(v_{12} + v_{21})\}\right]$, and likewise
for the others.

These functions have the property that when all four are
present and persist and a sexual strain is absent the LGMF of
every strain is 1 (or 2 after two-fold fecundity advantage of
asexuals has been applied). However, if a sexual strain is present with asexuals or is present alone then the situation is
more complicated. Whatever the case a haplotype, whether sexual
or asexual, is to have its fitness formulated from the above
expressions using the total frequency of the haplotype (i.e.
sexual-type frequency + asexual-type frequency). We consider a
pure sexual population; analysis of this case covers that of a
pure mixture of asexuals if the parameter for linkage, c, is set
to zero.

Let P_{11}, P_{12}, P_{21}, P_{22} be frequencies of adult haplotypes
just after a round of selection. Then after meiosis and ferti-
lization corresponding frequencies among offspring are $P_{11}-cD$,
$P_{12}+cD$, $P_{21}+cD$, $P_{22}-cD$ where c is linkage and D is initial linkage disequilibrium, $D = P_{11}P_{21} - P_{12}P_{22}$.

The transformation of the system from one generation of
adults to the next is given by a system of four equations of
which the following is typical

$$P'_{11} = (P_{11} - cD)w_{11}/\bar{w}$$

where $\bar{w}$, the mean fitness, is the sum of the four products of
frequency and fitness like the product shown.

When all the v are small all w approach to 1. Thus $\bar{w}$ can be
ignored and using the linear approximation to the exponential
function, the above equation becomes approximately

$$\frac{1}{4} + v'_{11} = (\frac{1}{4} + v_{11} - cD) \times [1 - \delta\{v_{11} - v_{22} - 2z(v_{11} + v_{22})\}]$$

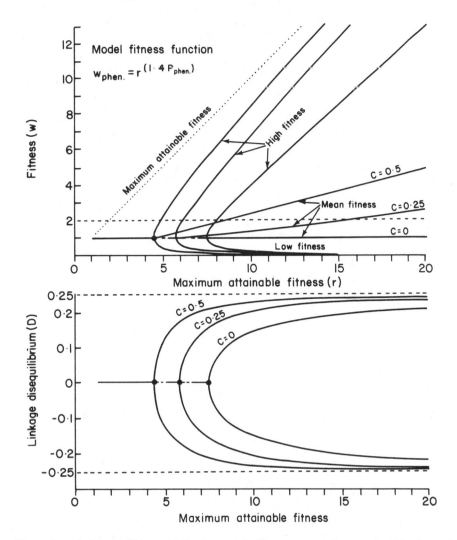

Fig. 2 Linkage disequilibrium and fitness performance displayed
as functions of maximum attainable fitness (r) for a model of
haploid selection on two alleles at each of two loci. At a
bifurcation point depending on the linkage parameter (c), increasing r renders a stable equilibrium for four constant equi-
frequent genotypes unstable and a two-point cycle supervenes.
Unless there is no recombination (c=0), almost linearly rising
geometric mean fitness in the cycles indicates that from some r
upwards the sexual species will out-compete the set of its emer-
gent asexual strains. The critical r occurs where the mean fitness rises through w=2 (dashed line; 2 represents effectively
doubled fecundity of the asexual strains).High and low fitness of
a particular genotype in the cycle are also shown.

Again ignoring terms in v^2, this is

$$v'_{11} = v_{11} - cD - \frac{1}{4}\delta\{v_{11} - v_{22} - 2z(v_{11} + v_{22})\}$$

D can be approximated by $\frac{1}{2}(v_{11} + v_{22})$; hence we obtain the system of four linear transition equations of which the above is the first. This linear system can be analyzed for stability, and its eigenvalues prove to be $1 - \frac{1}{2}\delta$ and $1 - c + \delta z$.

We are interested only in the positive range of the parameter δ, which roughly specifies the severity of selection. The first eigenvalue shows that $\delta > 4$ is a sufficient condition for instability at the fixed point, tending to specify an oscillatory departure. Independence of this eigenvalue of c indicates that both pure sexual and pure asexual populations will show cycles in this range of δ. However, instability due to the second eigenvalue can occur at lower values: assuming z to be in the range $-1/2$, $1/2$ instability can start as low as $\delta > 3$ if $c = 1/2$ and $z = -1/2$ (oscillatory departure), and occurs at every positive value of δ if $c = 0$ and $z > 0$ (non-oscillatory departure).

Non-oscillatory departure does not imply extinction or that, once far from the fixed point, cyclical patterns cannot occur. In fact $z > 0$ can give cycles and these in turn can lead to stability of sex if δ is high enough. But much easier conditions for stability of sex are obtained in the cases where $z < 0$. Since in this range $z = -1/2$ (assuming this to be the lower limit) is both best for sex and gives the simplest equations and closest similarity to the previous one-locus model (giving

$w_{11} = \exp\{2\delta \ (\frac{1}{4} - P_{11})\}$, etc.), I will now confine attention to this case.

Numerical simulation of the system in this case for $3 < \delta < 4$ shows that a stable 2-point cycle develops.

In this cycle allele frequency does not vary at all at either locus; instead each locus has frequencies constant at $1/2$. As to absolute values, all v's are also identical and constant but cycle in the following way: in one generation v_{11} and v_{22} are positive while v_{12} and v_{21} are negative, then v_{11} and v_{22} are negative while v_{12} and v_{21} are positive, and so on.

Knowing that this cycle existed, it was possible to locate the equilibrium absolute value of D analytically. In the briefest form I could obtain, the equilibrium equation is

$$\cosh \{\ln(4\sqrt{bD})\} - \cosh (\ln \sqrt{b}) \times \coth 2\delta D = 0$$

where $b = 1 - c$.

Treating the LHS expression as $f(D)$ we obtain, in preparation for a Newton method approximation to the solution for D,

$$f'(D) = 1/D \sinh \{ \ln(4 \sqrt{b}D) \} + 2\delta \cosh (\ln \sqrt{b}) \operatorname{cosech}^2(2\delta D)$$

Using this I obtained the results graphed in Fig. 2. As can be seen, the 2-point cycle described above potentially occurs at all $\delta > 3$. But when δ rises through 4 a further pair of stable cycles is potentiated. These are actually homologous to the case already implied in the figure where $c=0$: if loci are completely linked the system becomes equivalent to one of four independent asexual strains. The figure shows that there is a stable cycle where $c=0$ and D alternates. D is $P_{11}P_{22} - P_{12}P_{21}$: thus considering the other ways of pairing among four independent asexual strains there must also exist stable cycles for $D' = P_{11}P_{12} - P_{22}P_{21}$ and for $D'' = P_{11}P_{21} - P_{12}P_{22}$. As is implied in the graph and easily confirmed by simulation experiments, cycles for D' and D'' exist as attractors for all $\delta > 4$, whether or not $c = 0$. A little thought based on what has been said about the cycle already analyzed shows that these two new cycles, respectively, must arrange that $P_{11} = P_{12}$ and $P_{21} = P_{22}$, or else that $P_{11} = P_{21}$, and $P_{12} = P_{22}$; in other words, either gene frequency of A goes to 0.5 while that of B alternates, or vice versa. As apparent from the $c=0$ case in Fig. 1 (and as designed for in construction of the fitness function) cycles of this kind give no advantage to sexual reproduction for any magnitude of δ. Thus when $c>0$ and there is some hope for sex from the cycle and circumstances mentioned previously, the possibility that the system enters the domain of the alternative type of cycle must be considered a danger for sex, for as soon as the alternative cycle occurs the system is likely to be invadable by asexual mutants. Unfortunately, there is little that can be reported here on the sizes of the domains of "good" and "bad" cycles. When $c=0$ and $\delta > 4$ it is obvious from symmetry that all three cycles have equal domains; but then all three are equally bad. Since the inception of the cycle favourable to sex "grows" back to $\delta = 3$ as c increases to 0.5, it seems conjecturable that this cycle will have the largest domain at all $\delta > 3$ for all $c>0$. But one finding suggesting this may not be true is that in one set of simulation runs a certain fixed starting point was observed to pass out of the attractance of the good cycle into that of the bad as δ increased from 6 to 7.

Having given cautionary outline concerning the existence of cycles unsatisfactory for sex, I now resume consideration of the hopeful two-point cycle.

For the purpose of displaying results Fig. 2 does not use δ
itself as abscissa but instead that highest fitness which a
given δ makes possible. This highest fitness occurs when the
frequency of a type is zero and is given by $r = \exp(\tfrac{1}{2}\delta)$. Here
r is equivalent to what Williams (1975) called the ZZI ("zygote-
to-zygote increase") of a species. Its interest for the theory
of sexuality, arising from the difficulty of devising successful
models when r is low, has already been mentioned.

In the case of the present model values of r capable of
making sex succeed against parthenogenesis are satisfyingly low.
It can be seen from the figure that the changes accompanying the
onset of instability as r increases are quite dramatic. Most
relevant here, in best case, c=1/2, the mean fitness of the sexual begins a very nearly linear ascent at the bifurcation and
passes 2 when r≈8.6. The fecundity of a sexual species with a
1:1 sex ratio corresponding to this is 17.2. The actual highest
fitness expressed in the cycle at this point is about 6.8,
corresponding to fecundity 13.6.

There are hardly any sexual species - if any at all - whose
normal potential fecundity is less than this. Even for man, for
example, an expressed birth fecundity of 14 would not be extreme.
Of course a severe caution has to accompany such an example, for
even foetal selection in man is on diploids: for man and most
other sexual species only wastage of gametes could be strictly
relevant to the model. A previous model (Hamilton et al. 1980),
however, gave some ground for expectation that similar models
with diploid selection can be produced. Work on this is in
progress.

Another cause for caution in applying the above results lies
in the fact that the model studied so far covers a sexual species alone, or the set of four parthenogenetic strains alone
(the case c = O) but does not cover the behaviour of a mixed
sexual-asexual population. Thus it is not clear that as soon as
the LGMF of a pure sexual species rises above 2, the same species in a mixed population will be able to shed its asexual competitors. However, it is clear that the sexual population with
LGMF>2 is an ESS (evolutionarily stable strategy) with regard to
low frequency invasion by asexuals, and it will be surprising
if results suggested in Fig. 2 are not also robust against high
frequency invasions.

As Fig. 2 shows and as all the foregoing discussion has led
to expect, the best result for sex comes when c is maximal (i.e.
there is independent assortment of loci). For the benefit of
sex as in these models, different syllables of a password are
best coded in different chromosomes. While I am not aware that
contributions to self-identifying antigens can come from unlinked

loci, there is evidence, again for mice, that such loci may contribute to competence of antibodies against complex artificial
antigens (Caldwell 1976: 135). This and other recent evidence
that recognition of foreign substances is not wholly dependent
on a single short region of chromosome (Rosenstreich 1980) perhaps adds plausibility to the recombinant password idea.

Again we have not strictly shown that a high recombination
population beats a low recombination one, still less that a
linkage modifying locus is selected to cause high values of c,
but these outcomes seem probable. The demand for high recombination values in models like these which assume fluctuating environments is in contrast to the requirements on linkage found in
other broad classes of models concerned with sex, where usually
the puzzle is to see why selection for closer linkage doesn't
make the genotype "congeal"   (Turner 1967, Maynard Smith 1978).

Attempting to resolve this puzzle, Charlesworth (1976) has
shown that alleles causing higher rates of recombination can be
selected when linkage disequilibrium is made to fluctuate; and
very recently Graham Bell (pers. comm.) has shown this also in
a model where the changes in linkage disequilibrium result from
spontaneous cycling. Bell's model is frequency dependent and
coevolutionary like the present one but uses different fitness
functions. His analysis is focused on length of time lag
rather than selection intensity in the induction of cycling, and
on the selection for degree of linkage rather than ability of
sexuals to beat a doubled effective fecundity of asexuals.

In the present model lowest possible fitnesses are very low
$\exp\left(-\frac{3}{2}\delta\right)$. Low fitnesses in the stable cycles are less low -
in fact merely reciprocals of the high fitnesses - but their
contrast to the high fitnesses still implies an intensity of
selection that may seem very implausible. However, bearing in
mind another feature, that all this selective elimination goes
on with both mean fitness and gene frequencies remaining constant, it seems that the occurrence of such intense selection
might easily escape notice. Ideally, to reveal the kind of process envisioned, mortality statistics are needed classified both
for genotype and for major biotic causes. Lacking such data the
most hopeful simple sign would be linkage disequilibrium observed
to fluctuate radically from one generation to another. Hitherto
there have been too few genetic surveys of natural populations
that both cover enough loci to make likely the detection of
polymorphism loci that are at least close to "password syllable
loci, and at the same time cover enough generations. Data for
the same natural population over many generations are particularly lacking.

4. CONCLUSIONS

Of course the above model is bound to be an extreme oversim-
plification of any real situation. However this model, plus
some simple modifications and extensions which cannot be detailed here, plus also the even more artificial one-locus system
described earlier, can be summarized as having made certain
possibly useful points about what might be expected in nature if
biotic interactions (Glesener and Tilman 1978), and especially
interactions with short-lived parasites, are responsible for
maintenance of sexuality. The points emerging from the model
are:

1) Frequency dependent selection acting hardest against the most
common genotype easily sets up cyclical processes (Jaenike 1978).
2) In such processes population size may remain relatively constant and so fail to suggest intensity of selection.
3) When more than one locus is involved gene frequencies also
may remain relatively constant; but intense fluctuating selection then remains reflected by fluctuating linkage disequilibria.
4) In a two-locus model cyclical or fluctuating processes tend
to onset at lower intensities of selection for sexuals than for
asexuals.
5) As selection intensity increases there comes a point, usually
achievable at moderate levels of fecundity, where a sexual species has an advantage over any asexual strain even when the latter
are given a two-fold advantage in effective fecundity. Asexuals
then die out or are maintained only at very low frequency.
6) High levels of recombination facilitate such exclusion of
asexuals by sexuals.
7) Pressures on a host species by a set of varieties, or of
species, of parasites seems particularly likely to engender the
cycling discussed. In particular, shortness of life-cycle of
parasites relative to hosts gives their populations the kind of
over-reactive frequency dependence that is particularly favourable to sex.
8) Success of sex due to the frequency-dependent selection processes described does not require competition between sibs or
other relatives.

5. ACKNOWLEDGEMENTS

I would like to thank P.A. Henderson and N. Moran for encouragement and specifically for the ground work on related models
and literature (see reference below) which underlies this paper.

6. REFERENCES

Caldwell, J.L. (1976) Genetic regulation of immune responses, *In*
"Basic and clinical immunology", (H.H. Fudenberg et al. ed.),
Lange, Los Altos, pp. 130-139.

Charlesworth, B. (1976) Recombination modification in a fluctuating environment, *Genetics* **83**, pp. 181-195.

Clarke, B. (1976) The ecological genetics of host-parasite relationships, *In* "Genetic aspects of host-parasite relationships", (A.E.R. Taylor and R. Muller eds), Blackwell, London, pp. 87-103.

Fisher, R.A. (1934) Randomisation and an old enigma of card play, *Math. Gazette* **18**, pp. 294-297.

Glesener, R.R. and Tilman, D. (1978) Sexuality and the components of environmental uncertainty: Clues from geographical parthenogenesis in terrestrial animals, *Am. Nat.* **112**, pp. 659-673.

Haldane, J.B.S. (1949) Disease and evolution, *La Ricerca Sci. Suppl.* **19**, pp. 68-76.

Hamilton, W.D. (1975) Gamblers since life began: barnacles, aphids, elms., *Quart. Rev. Biol.* **50**, pp. 175-180.

Hamilton, W.D., Henderson, P.A. and Moran, N. (1980) Fluctuation of environment and coevolved antagonist polymorphism as factors in the maintenance of sex, *In* "Natural Selection and Social Behaviour: recent research and theory", (R.D. Alexander and D.W. Tinkle eds), Chiron Press, New York.

Hatchett, J.H. and Gallun, R.L. (1970) Genetics of the ability of the Hessian fly, *Mayetiola destructor*, to survive on wheats having different genes for resistance, *Ann. ent. Soc. Am.* **63**, pp. 1400-1407.

Jaenike, J. (1978) An hypothesis to account for the maintenance of sex within populations, *Evol. Theory* **3**, 191-194.

Lilly, F. (1972) *In* Genetic control of immune responsiveness: relationship to disease susceptibility, (H.Q. McDevitt and M. Landy eds), Academic Press, New York.

Maynard Smith, J. (1978) The evolution of sex, Cambridge University Press, Cambridge.

Rosenstreich, D.L. (1980) Genetics of resistance to infection, *Nature*, **285**, pp. 436-437.

Turner, J.R.G. (1967) Why does the genome not congeal?, *Evolution* **21**, pp. 645-656.

Williams, G.C. (1975) Sex and evolution, Princeton University Press, Princeton, New Jersey.

SOME PROBLEMS OF HUMAN AND ANIMAL POPULATIONS

J. Gani

*(CSIRO Division of Mathematics and Statistics
Canberra, Australia)*

1. INTRODUCTION

When the first Conference on the Mathematical Theory of the
Dynamics of Biological Populations (MTDBP) was held in Oxford in
1972, I was an academic at the University of Sheffield. I spoke
at the time on age distributions, and presented some rather
theoretical results applicable to demographic analysis (see Gani
(1973)). Since September 1974, I have worked for the Division
of Mathematics and Statistics in CSIRO, the Australian govern-
ment's applied research organisation. For the past six years,
we have been involved with extremely practical problems of
mathematical modelling and statistical analysis, many of them
in biology. In 1979, for example, over one third of the Division's work was concerned with biological populations.

Yet, despite the widespread use of mathematical methods in
biology, occasional criticisms of population modelling are still
voiced by biologists. They hint that mathematicians and stat-
isticians enjoy playing with models, but cast doubt on the
practical relevance of their results. Such criticisms are not
justified. While one might agree that models are only rough
approximations to reality, they nevertheless offer, among other
benefits,

    a)   qualitative insight into the mechanisms of population
        processes,

    b)   discrimination between possible models based on the
        quantitative analysis of phenomena,
and

    c)   numerical prediction of trends, useful in decision making.

In order to illustrate the advantages of population analysis
and modelling, I propose to outline three problems which have
arisen over the past few years in CSIRO. One of them originated
in the Division of Mathematics and Statistics, while the other
two were referred to it. It would seem appropriate at this

second MTDBP Conference to start with the problem of variation
in bird clutch size, a topic considered by Mountford (1973) at
the first Conference in 1972. This offers qualitative insight
into the evolutionary process. We then proceed with a quantitative analysis of the progress of myxomatosis in a rabbit
population; here we discriminate between possible mechanisms for
the spread of the infection. Lastly, we present a predictive
model for the age structure of scientists in CSIRO; this is
designed to assist in decision making with regard to recruitment
policies in the organisation.

2. BIRD CLUTCH SIZE AND SURVIVAL PROBABILITIES: A QUALITATIVE INSIGHT

Many bird species are known to have clutch sizes of either a
fixed number k, or one of (k, k+1), where k is some appropriate
integer. One might expect such behaviour to result in some
evolutionary advantage; it is in fact possible to show that for
a single colony of birds, these clutch sizes correspond to
maximising probabilities of survival. This is precisely what
Heyde and Schuh (1978) have demonstrated in their paper on the
evolution of reproduction rates, using branching processes to
model bird populations. When clutch sizes are k, or one of
(k, k+1) as above, survival probabilities for a species are in
fact maximised at every time point.

The argument of Heyde and Schuh rests on two theorems about
offspring probability generating functions (p.g.f.'s) in
branching processes. Let $F(s) = \sum_{j=0}^{\infty} p_j s^j$ $(0 \le s \le 1)$ be such an
offspring p.g.f. for which

$$p_0 = F(0) \ge \delta , \qquad 0 < F'(1-) \le M = k(1-\delta) + \eta$$

where $0 \le \delta < 1$, $0 \le \eta < 1 - \delta$, and k is a positive integer.
The following theorem can then be proved.

Theorem 1. Suppose a new offspring p.g.f.

$$F^*(s) = \delta + (1 - \delta - \eta)s^k + \eta s^{k+1} \qquad (2.1)$$

is defined. Then $F(s) \ge F^*(s)$, with the inequality holding on
(0,1) if $F \ne F^*$.

We note that this theorem leads directly to a smaller probability of eventual extinction for the Galton-Watson process with
new offspring p.g.f., its mean offspring $F^{*'}(1-) = k(1-\delta) + \eta$
being greater than or equal to $F'(1-)$. The results carry over

to Bellman-Harris age-dependent processes, as the authors show in their second theorem.

Theorem 2. Consider a Bellman-Harris process with p.g.f. $H(s, t)$ whose offspring p.g.f. is $F(s)$. Then the offspring distribution with uniformly maximal survival probabilities subject to $p_O \geq \delta$ and $F'(1-) \leq M$ has the p.g.f. $F^*(s)$. When $F \neq F^*$, it follows that for all $t \geq 0$, the probability of extinction $H^*(0, t)$ for the process with offspring p.g.f. $F^*(s)$ is smaller than $H(0, t)$.

To illustrate these results in detail, the authors consider a bird population whose individuals have a life span of $I+1$ years. In the first age interval $j = 0$ which corresponds to the immature phase of the first year, the individual either survives with probability $\lambda_{01}(0)$ to enter the next age interval, or is removed with probability $\lambda_{02}(0)$. Removals consist of female birds who die, or male birds who have no further role in the description of the population. Thereafter, for $j = 1, 2, \ldots$, $I-1$, the female either (a) has no offspring and dies with probability $\lambda_O(j)$, or (b) has $i \geq 1$ offspring and survives into the next age interval with probability $\lambda_{i1}(j) = (1 - \Delta(j))\lambda_i(j)$ or dies with probability $\lambda_{i2}(j) = \Delta(j)\lambda_i(j)$. Here $\lambda_i(j)$ denotes the probability of an individual's producing i offspring in the age interval j. In the terminal age interval I, female birds die with probability $\lambda_{02}(I) = 1$ without producing offspring.

If m_{ij} is the mean number of individuals of age j at time t+1 arising from a single individual of age i at time t, then in the present case

$$m_{ij} = \begin{cases} \Lambda(i) = \Sigma_k \, k\lambda_k(i) & \text{for } j = 0, \\ 1 - \mu(i) = 1 - \Sigma_k \, \lambda_{k2}(i) & \text{for } j = i + 1 \\ 0 \text{ otherwise.} \end{cases} \qquad (2.2)$$

In general, for positive regular matrices of the type $\{m_{ij}\}$, the maximum positive eigenvalue ρ satisfying the conditions

$$\rho \stackrel{\leq}{>} 1 \text{ according as } \zeta = \sum_{i=0}^{I} \Lambda(i) \prod_{j=0}^{i-1} \{1-\mu(j)\} \stackrel{\leq}{>} 1, \qquad (2.3)$$

governs the asymptotic behaviour of the process.

In our case (2.2), the full matrix $\{m_{ij}\}_{i,\ j\ =\ 0,\ \ldots,\ I}$ is not positive regular, since no offspring is produced by females of age I. The truncated matrix $\{m_{ij}\}_{i,\ j\ =\ 0,\ \ldots,\ I-1}$, however, is and has a maximum eigenvalue denoted by ρ. The population becomes extinct with probability 1 if and only if $\rho \le 1$ ($\zeta \le 1$); and has a non-zero probability of growing arbitrarily large if $\rho > 1$($\zeta > 1$); it remains reasonably stable if ρ is close to 1.

Since clutch size is limited by the maximum number of young which parents can raise, an upper bound K can reasonably be imposed on the mean number of offspring per adult female, conditional on offspring being produced, so that

$$(1 - \lambda_0(j))^{-1} \sum_{i=1}^{\infty} i\lambda_i(j) \le K \ (1 \le j \le I - 1) . \qquad (2.4)$$

From this inequality (2.4), Theorem 1 gives for $s_0 \epsilon [0, 1]$,

$$(1 - \lambda_0(j))^{-1} \sum_{i=1}^{\infty} \lambda_i(j) s_0^j \ge F^*(s_0) = (1 - \eta) \ s_0^k + \eta s_0^{k+1} , (2.5)$$

where $k = [K]$ and $\eta = K - [K]$.

It can now be verified from some equations of Goodman (1967) that the extinction probabilities $p_n(j)$ at time $t = n$, given an initial female in the age interval j at time $t = 0$, are minimised by choosing for the probabilities $\lambda_i(j)$ ($i \ge 1$), the values

$$\lambda_k^*(j) = (1 - \eta)(1 - \lambda_0(j)), \ \lambda_{k+1}^*(j) = \eta \ (1 - \lambda_0(j)),$$

$$\lambda_i^*(j) = 0 \ \text{for} \ i \ne k, \ k + 1 . \qquad (2.6)$$

Here $\lambda_{01}(0)$, $\lambda_{02}(0)$ and $\lambda_0(j)$, ($1 \le j \le I - 1$) are taken as fixed. Thus, survival probability is maximised if, when female birds have offspring, these number precisely k if K is an integer, or one of (k, k+1) if K is not an integer.

For the distribution maximising survival probability as in (2.6), the authors find

$$\Lambda(0) = 0, \ \mu(0) = \lambda_{02}(0),$$

$$\Lambda(i) = K(1 - \lambda_0(i)), \ \mu(i) = \lambda_0(i) + \Delta(i) (1 - \lambda_0(i)) \ (1 \le i \le I - 1),$$

$$\Lambda(I) = 0, \ \mu(I) = 1,$$

so that

$$\zeta = K\lambda_{01}(0) \sum_{i=1}^{I-1} (1 - \lambda_0(i)) \prod_{j=1}^{i-1} (1 - \lambda_0(j)) (1 - \Delta(j)) . \tag{2.7}$$

If, for simplicity, $\Delta(j) = \Delta$ and $\lambda_0(j) = \lambda_0$, then

$$\zeta = \frac{K\lambda_{01}(0) (1 - \lambda_0)}{1 - (1 - \lambda_0)(1 - \Delta)} \{1 - ((1 - \lambda_0) (1 - \Delta))^{I-1}\} , \tag{2.8}$$

which provides a simple stability criterion for the population process.

A practical example of this process considered by the authors is the case of the European swift, which lays clutches of 2 or 3 eggs in the proportions 3:1. With the assumptions above,

$$\frac{\eta}{1 - \eta} = \frac{1}{3} \tag{2.9}$$

whence $\eta = \frac{1}{4}$, while $[K] = 2$ so that $K = \eta + [K] = 2.25$. Substituting the realistic value $\lambda_{01}(0) = 0.3$ in (2.8), and neglecting the term $\{(1-\lambda_0) (1-\Delta)\}^{I-1}$ for large I, the critical level $\zeta = 1$ is found to correspond to

$$(1 - \lambda_0) (1.675 - \Delta) = 1 .$$

If the values of λ_0 and Δ are set at $\lambda_0 = 0.1$, $\Delta = 0.5638$, the probability of extinction after 100 years starting from a single female bird is

$$P_{100}(1) = 0.9611269413 \tag{2.10}$$

for the maximal process.

Thus, starting with 600 females, the probability of extinction after 100 years would be less than 10^{-10}; this provides a qualitative insight into the evolutionary survival value of the k or (k, k+1) clutch size strategy. It would be interesting to work out under what conditions 2 or more intermixing bird groups of different genetic constitutions, each laying clutches of

different sizes, would eventually produce a uniform group with
a single optimal clutch strategy.

3. THE SPREAD OF MYXOMATOSIS: DISCRIMINATION THROUGH QUANTITATIVE ANALYSIS

The standard model for the spread of an epidemic is based on
the hypothesis of homogeneous mixing of susceptibles and infectives in a population. A quantitative analysis of data from an
epidemic outbreak of myxomatosis in a rabbit warren near
Canberra in 1971 led Saunders (1980) to doubt the validity of
this mixing hypothesis. He found that a better fit to the data
could be obtained with a modified version which allowed for
bunching.

Let us consider the model in which i_n rabbits contract the
disease on day n; the infection remains latent for ℓ days, but
the rabbits finally exhibit symptoms and become infective on
day $n+\ell+1$. They survive a further k days, dying at the end of
day $n+\ell+k$. Two versions of the model are studied: the first is
stochastic based on chain binomial methods, while the second is
deterministic. The data analysed consist of counts of the
numbers of rabbits first seen with symptoms on each day $n+\ell+j$ of
the epidemic. For purposes of simplicity, we shall concentrate
here on the deterministic case.

Suppose that p_n denotes the total rabbit population on day n,
s_n being the number of susceptibles and i_n the number first
becoming infective on day n. The total number of infectives on
day n will thus be

$$\bar{i}_n = i_n + i_{n-1} + \cdots + i_{n-k+1} \, , \tag{3.1}$$

while the latent infectives are

$$\bar{i}'_n = i_{n+1} + \cdots + i_{n+\ell} \, . \tag{3.2}$$

Clearly, the remaining susceptibles on day n are

$$s_n = s_0 - i_{\ell+1} - \cdots - i_{n+\ell} \, , \, . \tag{3.3}$$

while the total rabbit population is

$$p_n = s_n + \bar{i}_n + \bar{i}'_n \, . \tag{3.4}$$

The standard epidemic model with homogeneous mixing assumes that

$$i_{n+\ell+1} = \alpha \bar{i}_n s_n \quad , \tag{3.5}$$

where α is the infection parameter, and new infectives on day $n+\ell+1$ result from contact between susceptibles and the total number of infectives on day n. One could interpret (3.5) heuristically as indicating that each infective comes into close contact with and infects a proportion α of the susceptibles each day. In fact, it is thought that rabbits have a tendency to bunch more closely together as their numbers decrease. Each infective might then contact a certain number of other rabbits, of which a proportion s_n/p_n would be susceptible, so that

$$i_{n+\ell+1} = \alpha \bar{i}_n s_n/p_n \quad . \tag{3.6}$$

Here α denotes the number of contacts made by each infective. Both equations (3.5) and (3.6) can be thought of as special cases of the more general

$$i_{n+\ell+1} = \alpha \bar{i}_n s_n/f(p_n) \quad , \tag{3.7}$$

where f is a positive real-valued function of p_n, which represents the bunching tendency of the population.

Saunders proves two theorems. The first is a threshold result stating that the epidemic governed by (3.7) will grow only if $\alpha k p_0/f(p_0) > 1$. The second is more technical, and shows that for small initial populations for which $\alpha p_0/f(p_0) < 1$ the model will never result in negative population sizes. For a model similar to that outlined in (3.5), de Hoog, Gani and Gates (1979) have found that negative values of susceptibles could be obtained.

Several interesting results emerge which are concerned with the fitting of models to the data, and the determination of a realistic bunching function $f(p)$. The value of the survival period is known to be $k=9$ days, and the estimate of the latent period which gives the best data fit is $\ell=6$ days. There remains the parameter α to estimate for each bunching function $f(p)$. Saunders uses an appropriate maximum likelihood estimator for the stochastic case, based on a Poisson approximation to the binomial distribution for α, and given by

$$\tilde{\alpha}_n = \sum_{j=1}^{n} I_{j+\ell+1} \bigg/ \sum_{j=1}^{n} \frac{\bar{I}_j S_j}{f(P_j)} \;. \tag{3.8}$$

Here $I_{j+\ell+1}$, $\bar{I}_j$, S_j, P_j, respectively, denote numerical data for stochastic equivalents of new infectives $i_{j+\ell+1}$ on day $j+\ell+1$, and all infectives $\bar{i}_j$, susceptibles s_j and total survivors p_j on day j in the deterministic case.

Fig. 1 illustrates the fit of the three different α's in equations (3.5), (3.6) and (3.7) in which $f(p) = 1$, p and $\sqrt{p}$, respectively. The observed data for surviving susceptibles in the 57 days of the epidemic are compared with the deterministic curves obtained from equation (3.3) for the appropriate $f(p)$. Roughly speaking, in Model 1, the epidemic appears to end too quickly, while in Model 2 it starts too slowly. Model 3, however, with $f(p) = \sqrt{p}$ gives a reasonable fit throughout the epidemic.

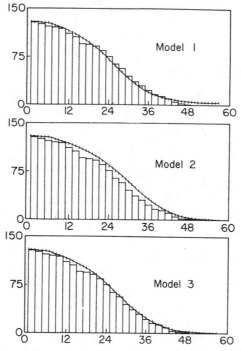

Fig. 1   Observed and predicted numbers of susceptibles for $f(p)=1$, p and $\sqrt{p}$.

Saunders concludes from this that rabbits tend to bunch together as their numbers decrease, though not sufficiently to maintain constant population density. The quantitative analysis in this example has allowed the author to discriminate between possible mechanisms of infection and decide on a more realistic mixing hypothesis than that commonly used in epidemic theory.

4. THE AGE STRUCTURE OF SCIENTISTS IN CSIRO

In an effort to predict the age structure of scientists in CSIRO over the next 40 years, the Division of Mathematics and Statistics was asked to set up a numerical prediction and decision making manpower model of the hierarchical type. Such models have been previously considered by Gani (1963), Bartholomew (1973) and Pollard (1973). In the present model, the details of which were worked out by R.I. Forrester in 1978-9, it was assumed that the ages of research scientists ranged from 25 to 65 years, 65 being the mandatory age of retirement. Scientists were subdivided into two categories, the first consisting of indefinite term (permanent), and the second of fixed term (temporary, usually 3-year) appointments.

Let us denote by $I_j(t)$ the number of indefinite term scientists of age j in year t; we write $T_j^{(1)}(t)$ for the number of fixed term scientists of age j recruited in year t in their first year of service, while $T_j^{(2)}(t)$ are those in their second and $T_j^{(3)}(t)$ those in their final year of the three-year term. Lastly, $N_j(t)$ is the number of new recruits to indefinite term appointments, aged j in year t; some of these (about a dozen each year) are assumed to have achieved translation from the ranks of experimental officer, the CSIRO classification partially overlapping that of research scientist, but with a lower salary ceiling.

Equations for the numbers of scientists in the different age ranges of the indefinite term category may be expressed in the form:

$$
\begin{bmatrix} I_{25}(t+1) \\ \cdots \\ I_{65}(t+1) \end{bmatrix} = \begin{bmatrix} N_{25}(t+1) \\ \cdots \\ N_{65}(t+1) \end{bmatrix} + \begin{bmatrix} \cdots & & \\ & 1-r_{j,j+1}-\pi_{j,j+1} & \\ & & \cdots \end{bmatrix} \begin{bmatrix} I_{25}(t) \\ \cdots \\ I_{65}(t) \end{bmatrix}
$$

$$
+ \begin{bmatrix} \cdots & & \\ & p_{j,j+1} & \\ & & \cdots \end{bmatrix} \begin{bmatrix} T_{25}^{(3)}(t) \\ \cdots \\ T_{65}^{(3)}(t) \end{bmatrix}
$$

with the matrix elements $1-r_{j,j+1}-\pi_{j,j+1}$ and $p_{j,j+1}$ in the positions $(j+1-24, j-24)$, all other elements being zero, or

$$I(t+1) = N(t+1) + K\,I(t) + P\,T^{(3)}(t) \quad . \tag{4.1}$$

This gives the numbers of indefinite term appointments $\{I_j(t+1)\}_{j=25}^{65}$ at time $t+1$; they consist of new recruits

$\{N_j(t+1)\}_{j=25}^{65}$, survivors after proportions $0 < \pi_{j,j+1} < 1$,

$0 < r_{j,j+1} < 1$ are removed for wastage (resignations and deaths) and retirement respectively, from among indefinite term appointees $\{I_j(t)\}_{j=25}^{65}$ at time t, and transfers of fixed term appointees $\{T_j^{(3)}(t)\}_{j=27}^{41}$ in their third year at time t to the indefinite term appointment category with transfer proportions $0 < p_{j,j+1} < 1$. It is assumed here that the ages of fixed term appointees lie between 25 and 39 years on recruitment; this is somewhat more restricted than the total age range of 25 to 65 for indefinite term appointments.

For fixed term appointees, following the number $T_j^{(1)}(t)$ of recruits of age j in year t entering their first year of service, we have in the second year

$$\begin{bmatrix} T_{25}^{(2)}(t+1) \\ \cdots \\ T_{65}^{(2)}(t+1) \end{bmatrix} = \begin{bmatrix} \cdots & & \\ & 1-w_{j,j+1}^{(1)} & \\ & & \cdots \end{bmatrix} \begin{bmatrix} T_{25}^{(1)}(t) \\ \cdots \\ T_{65}^{(1)}(t) \end{bmatrix}$$

where some of the $T_j^{(1)}(t)$, $T_j^{(2)}(t+1)$ are zero and $1-w_{j,j+1}^{(1)}$ is in position $(j+1-24, j-24)$ all other elements being zero, or

$$T^{(2)}(t+1) = M^{(1)}T^{(1)}(t) \quad . \tag{4.2}$$

This represents the number of term appointees in their second year of service where $w_{j,j+1}^{(1)}$ is the proportion of wastage among the fixed term appointees of age j in their first year of service. For appointees in their third year of service,

$$
\begin{bmatrix}
T_{25}^{(3)}(t+1) \\
\cdots \\
T_{65}^{(3)}(t+1)
\end{bmatrix}
=
\begin{bmatrix}
\cdots & & \\
& 1-w_{j,j+1}^{(2)} & \\
& & \cdots
\end{bmatrix}
\begin{bmatrix}
T_{25}^{(2)}(t) \\
\cdots \\
T_{65}^{(2)}(t)
\end{bmatrix}
$$

where again some $T_j^{(2)}(t)$, $T_j^{(3)}(t+1)$ are zero and $1-w_{j,j+1}^{(2)}$ is in position $(j+1-24, j-24)$, all other elements being zero or

$$
T^{(3)}(t+1) = M^{(2)}T^{(2)}(t). \tag{4.3}
$$

Here $w_{j,j+1}^{(2)}$ is now the proportion .of wastage among fixed term appointees of age j in the second year of service.

It is easy to calculate the vector $\underset{\sim}{S}(t)$ for the numbers of scientists in the various age ranges in CSIRO at any time t by summing

$$
S(t) = I(t) + T^{(1)}(t) + T^{(2)}(t) + T^{(3)}(t). \tag{4.4}
$$

This vector will depend essentially on the new recruits $\underset{\sim}{N}(t)$ and $\underset{\sim}{T}^{(1)}(t)$ in the indefinite and fixed term categories; in practice, these will be controlled in such a way that $\sum_j N_j(t) =$

$c \sum_j T_j^{(1)}(t)$. Here, c is some agreed constant whose value lies between $c = 1/9$ and $c = 1$ depending on the proportions 1:9 or 1:1 of indefinite to fixed term appointments decided upon in CSIRO's recruitment policies. Calculations illustrated in Fig. 2 were made on the assumption that the total population of research scientists remained stable at 1306, the current number; such an assumption reflects the present no-growth planning within CSIRO.

Other assumptions of the model were that the retirement rates $r_{j,j+1}$ lie between the following lower and higher estimates

$$
0 \leqslant r_{55,56} \leqslant 0.4, \quad 0 \leqslant r_{56+j,\ 57+j} \leqslant 0.1 \ (j=0,1,2,3),
$$

$$
0.4 \leqslant r_{60,61} \leqslant 0.8,
$$

$$
0.1 \leqslant r_{61,62} \leqslant 0.2, \quad 0.15 \leqslant r_{62,63} \leqslant 0.3,
$$

$$
0.2 \leqslant r_{63+j,\ 64+j} \leqslant 0.4 \ (j=0,1), \quad r_{65,66} = 1.
$$

The wastage rates $\pi_{j,j+1}$ for indefinite term appointments were taken as

$$\pi_{29,30} = 0.033, \quad \pi_{30+j,31+j} = 0.024 \ (j=0,1,2,3,4),$$

$$\pi_{35+j,36+j} = 0.008 \ (j=0,1,\ldots,9),$$

$$\pi_{45+j,46+j} = 0.018 \ (j=0,1,2,3,4), \pi_{50+j,51+j} = 0.006 (j=0,1,2,3,4),$$

$$\pi_{55+j,56+j} = 0.008 (j=0,1,\ldots9).$$

Recruitment ages of fixed term appointees have already been assumed to be in the range 25-39, and wastage rates $w_{j,j+1}^{(1)}$ for $25 \leqslant j \leqslant 39$ are of the order 0.003, while the $w_{j,j+1}^{(2)}$ have similar values for $26 \leqslant j \leqslant 40$. In the worked example, since term appointments are of short duration, the $w_{j,j+1}^{(k)}$ were taken to be 0 for simplicity. Transfer rates $p_{j,j+1}$ to indefinite term appointments for third year fixed term appointees were taken to lie in the range $0.0066 \leqslant p_{j,j+1} \leqslant 0.02$ so that, all together, only a small proportion of this group achieves permanency.

The age distributions of recruits, for indefinite and fixed term appointments based on empirical observations were taken as:

Age	Indefinite Term % of recruits	Fixed Term % of recruits
25	4.8	5.7
26	5.9	6.9
27	9.1	10.7
28	7.0	8.2
29	6.4	7.5
30+j (j=0,...,4)	7.48	8.8
35+j (j=0,...,4)	2.88	3.4
40+j (j=0,...,4)	1.40	0
45+j (j=0,...,4)	0.64	0
50+j (j=0,...,4)	0.42	0
55+j (j=0,1,...,4)	0.32	0
60+j (j=0,1,...,4)	0.22	0

As noted earlier, the population of scientists remained stable throughout at its 1978-9 value of 1306, and the initial vector $\underset{\sim}{I}$ (0) was taken as the age distribution for that year.

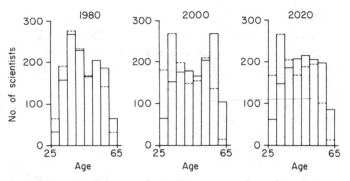

Fig. 2   Age distributions of CSIRO research scientists. Case 1: 1, Case 2:---.

The range of results for the age structure of the scientists in the two extreme cases 1 and 2 can be seen from the graphs in Fig. 2 for the years 1980, 2000, 2020.   In case 1, c = 1 so that equal numbers of indefinite and fixed term appointments are made, and the lower retirement and higher transfer rates obtain; we note that the age distribution becomes roughly evenly distributed as time progresses, with a decidedly greater proportion of older scientists.   In case 2, c = 1/9 so that 9 times as many fixed term appointments are made as indefinite term ones, and the higher retirement and lower transfer rates are used.   We see that the age distribution becomes more peaked in the lower age range, tailing off more rapidly as the scientists' ages increase. The average ages of scientists in these 2 cases is summarised below.

Average Age of Scientists

	1980	2000	2020
Case 1	44.96	46.11	45.55
Case 2	42.97	41.53	41.30

It will be noted that the average age difference for scientists in CSIRO ranges between 1.99 and 4.58 years, depending on which of the two extreme policies is adopted.   Clearly case 2, with its larger proportion of fixed term appointees at intake, its higher retirement rates, and lower transfer rates to the indefinite term stream, maintains the scientific personnel at a lower average age.   Whether the policies leading to this result (or some policy intermediate between cases 1 and 2) are adopted remains to be seen.

5. CONCLUSIONS

The three examples of population models outlined in this paper all arose from practical problems posed to scientists in the CSIRO Division of Mathematics and Statistics. The first used a branching process model for bird populations to reach a qualitative insight into the function of clutch size on optimal probabilities of survival. The second discriminated between mechanisms for the spread of infection in rabbit populations on the basis of a quantitative analysis of survivors over a period of 57 days. The last model provided numerical predictions on the age structure of scientists in CSIRO which should prove useful in decision making. None but the most sceptical biologist could deny the value of such analyses: I remain confident that the usefulness of population models will become increasingly clear to all our scientific colleagues.

6. ACKNOWLEDGEMENTS

I should like to thank Drs. C.C. Heyde, H.-J. Schuh and I.W. Saunders for allowing me to use their results as examples of the use of population and epidemic models, and Mr. R.I. Forrester for the detailed work on the CSIRO age-structure calculations. My thanks are also due to Dr. P.J. Brockwell who kindly read a draft of the paper and made suggestions for its improvement. I am grateful to the Statistics Secretaries at Colorado State University, Fort Collins, who typed the draft.

7. REFERENCES

Bartholomew, D.J. (1973) Stochastic Models for Social Processes, (2nd Edn), John Wiley, New York.

de Hoog, F., Gani, J. and Gates, D.J. (1979) A threshold theorem for the general epidemic in discrete time, *J. Math. Biology*, **8**, pp. 113-121.

Gani J. (1963) Formulae for projecting enrolments and degrees in universities, *J.R. Statist. Soc. A*, **126**, pp. 400-409.

Gani, J. (1973) Stochastic formulations for life tables, age distributions and mortality curves, *In* "The Mathematical Theory of the Dynamics of Biological Populations", (M.S. Bartlett and R.W. Hiorns, eds), Academic Press, London, pp. 291-302.

Goodman, L.A. (1967) The probabilities of extinction for birth-and-death processes that are age-dependent or phase dependent, *Biometrika*, **54**, pp. 579-596.

Heyde, C.C. and Schuh, H.-J. (1978) Uniform bounding of probability generating functions and the evolution of reproduction rates in birds, *J. Appl. Prob.*, **15**, pp. 243-250.

Mountford, M.D. (1973) The significance of clutch size, *In* "The Mathematical Theory of the Dynamics of Biological Populations", (M.S Bartlett and R.W. Hiorns, eds), Academic Press, London, pp. 315-323.

Pollard, J.H. (1973) Mathematical Models for the Growth of Human Populations, Cambridge U.P.

Saunders, I.W. (1980) A model for myxomatosis, *Math. Biosciences*, **48**, pp. 1-15.

MECHANISMS FOR THE GENERATION AND MAINTENANCE OF DIVERSITY IN ECOLOGICAL COMMUNITIES

S.A. Levin

(Section of Ecology and Systematics, Cornell University, USA)

1. INTRODUCTION

A central problem in ecological theory is how large numbers of species are able to coexist within a single habitat, ostensibly sharing the same small number of resources (Hutchinson, 1959). Attention to this question, crystallized in Hutchinson's classic (1959) paper, has arisen time and again and with fresh interest among ecologists studying a wide variety of systems. Hutchinson (1961, 1965) discussed possible causes of the coexistence of large numbers of planktonic species, bringing focus on a problem which is still not resolved (Hulburt 1977); similar puzzles are posed by communities of corals (Connell 1978) and by their associated fish fauna (Sale 1977, Talbot et al, 1978, Chesson and Warner, 1980), by intertidal sessile invertebrates and macroscopic algae (Levin and Paine, 1974, Paine and Levin, 1976, 1981), and by the rich associations of annuals found in some desert and semidesert communities (A. Shmida and R.H. Whittaker, pers. comm.). The list could easily be extended. Fascinating readings of a general nature may be found in the recent symposium of the British Ecological Society (Mound and Waloff, 1978) on the diversity of insect faunas.

A closely related problem is how morph diversity within a species is maintained. Several different reviews which approach this problem from different perspectives exist, but noteworthy among them are Karlin and McGregor (1972a), Endler (1978), and Clarke (1979). Endler, in studying the diverse colour polymorphisms of guppies (Poecilia reticulata) and cases of aspect diversity in other species, focuses attention on the relative roles of sexual selection and predation-induced effects, in particular crypsis and apostasis. These are ecological mechanisms which can lead to frequency-dependent selection, because of competition for mates, background, or predator avoidance. The importance of such effects is emphasised by Clarke (1979), who discusses both ecological and genetical factors. Karlin and McGregor (1972a), whose interest is primarily in

genetic mechanisms, summarize the ways in which natural selection may lead to stable polymorphism:

   (i) Heterozygote advantage

  (ii) Mutation-selection balance

 (iii) Migration-selection balance

  (iv) Temporal variation in selection

   (v) Haploid-diploid selection balance (selection tending to
      favour different genes during the haploid versus diploid
      phases)

  (vi) Selection varying between sexes

 (vii) Frequency-dependent selection

(viii) General selection balance (resulting from the balance of
      fertility, viability, and segregation distortion forces)

  (ix) Multi-locus selection balance

   (x) Multi-locus mutation-selection balance

  (xi) Negative assortative mating

 (xii) Incompatibility and self-sterility mechanisms

In addition to this list, they discuss in great detail the
importance of spatial structure in maintaining polymorphisms,
even when there is no underlying pattern of environmental variation. Their fundamental paper, although necessarily mathematical in the discussion of the effects of weak coupling of systems,
should be read by anyone interested in the general question of
the maintenance of polymorphism.

   The approach taken in the present paper draws heavily on the
ideas of these and other authors. Although a few new twists
are introduced, all of the mechanisms have been identified previously. The principal differences from the other works will be
a shift in emphasis, and an attempt to interpret mechanisms from
a primarily ecological perspective.

   I distinguish four major categories of mechanisms which
enhance coexistence within a single habitat: the openness of the
system, niche and microhabitat differentiation, temporal
partitioning, and frequency-dependent mechanisms (which include
some mechanisms for niche and habitat partitioning). Although
the categories overlap with one another, they provide a convenient skeleton about which to organise ideas. The primary
focus of this paper will be frequency-dependent mechanisms.
There is no suggestion that these are any more or less important
than the others; it is simply that they constitute a grab bag of

processes which require further distinction. A mechanism for
coexistence will be termed frequency-dependent if coexistence
results from the sensitivity of the growth rates of types to the
relative frequencies of types. This should be distinguished
from the sensitivity of the growth rate of a type to its own
density alone, which is an example of density dependence. Many
examples of coexistence through resource partitioning can be
explained by density dependence alone, without resort to frequency dependence. In other situations, both are of importance.

Gilbert and Singer (1975), in considering diversity and segregation among butterflies, distinguish six categories of mechanisms. Four of these—speciali ation on host plant species, partitioning of host plant parts, habitat partitioning, and adult
resource partitioning—fall in the general category of niche,
habitat, or microhabitat partitioning, although to some extent
frequency dependence will be involved. A fifth, phenology and
voltinism, involves temporal partitioning. The sixth broad category, including interactions with predators, parasites, and
mutualists, primarily deals with frequency-dependent mechanisms.

2. SYSTEM OPENNESS

The importance of system openness depends on how inclusive
the system definition is. For example, in the middle range of
the rocky intertidal of the United States Northwest coast, a
major reason why most the primary space occupiers are able to
coexist with the dominant competitor Mytilus californianus is
that they have refugia at tidal heights where the mussel does
not do well, or in other habitat types (Paine and Levin, 1981).
Thus their survival in the system of study is because that
system is open, and because therefore new propagules arrive from
outside the system. Indeed, this is only part of the story; one
must also recognise the importance of high levels of wave disturbance, the force which continually opens up space for colonization. But the high diversity of the system is in large part due
to the existence of refuge areas outside. The results of
Simberloff and Wilson (1969) and others who have studied the
colonization of islands following disturbance provide other
examples of the importance of external source areas in maintaining the fauna (and flora) of particular habitats.

3. NICHE AND MICROHABITAT DIFFERENTIATION

As suggested above, whether or not a source is external to a
system is a matter of definition: one can often eliminate the
problem of external factors by enlarging the scale of the system
to include them. However, this simply transfers the diversity-
enhancing factors from the external category to that of niche or
microhabitat differentiation within the habitat. Microhabitat

differentiation is a catchall term used to include all ways in
which within-habitat heterogeneity may contribute to coexistence
of species. In many systems of interest, niche differentiation
(including resource partitioning) and microhabitat heterogeneity
are the major causes of high diversity, and their importance
should be assessed before other sources are examined.

4. TEMPORAL PARTITIONING

Temporal partitioning is of at least three types: synchronized and simultaneous over the habitat, synchronized but not
simultaneous, and non-synchronized. In the first category are
diurnal and seasonal patterns of activity, in which certain
species are favoured during different times of the cycle; these
constitute forms of temporal microhabitat differentiation.
Other temporal sharing, for example through successional partitioning, may involve different sites experiencing more or less
the same sequence of species, but out of phase with one another.
Under some circumstances, as with the travelling waves of death
and regeneration in balsam fir forests (Sprugel, 1976), the phase
difference between sites will be constant over time and sites
may be thought of as synchronous in the sense that the local
cycles have the same period. Under other circumstances (e.g.
Watt, 1947, Paine and Levin, 1981), random factors intervene,
changing the phase relationships between sites and lowering the
degree of synchrony. Sharing of resources through spatio-
temporal partitioning can be an important contribution to diversity. Feinsinger (1980) showed that large numbers of short-
billed hummingbird species could coexist by asynchronous migration patterns over a mosaic of habitat patches; in each patch
the local population of each species "fluctuated in a unique
temporal pattern".

Finally, random factors may be so important that they swamp
any regularity in local pattern or environmental change so
rapidly that the system never achieves an asymptotic pattern.
Hutchinson (1953) advanced the latter nonequilibrium hypothesis
as a major contributing factor to the coexistence of large
numbers of phyto- and zooplankton, and coral reef fish communities may exhibit similar properties (Talbot et al, 1978).
Hutchinson's suggestion was of a shifting competitive balance,
on the average presumably neutral. Hence it bears close relationship to neutral gene theory (Kimura 1968) in which a large
number of types are always present, but through a balance between
mutation and extinction. Individual types do not reach equilibrium frequencies; extinctions of types are frequent, but these
are more or less balanced by new mutants which enter the system.
This general nonequilibrium view applies equally if new types
are "created" by immigration rather than mutation, and this is
the basic idea which underlies the work of May and MacArthur

(1972) in which an order-of-magnitude estimate of the number of species in a community is derived by consideration of extinction rates. Implicit in their approach is the notion that species turnover is high, but that there is a rough (order-of-magnitude) balance between extinctions and new establishments of species.

5. NEGATIVE FREQUENCY DEPENDENCE

In the classical Lotka-Volterra metaphor for two competing species (of densities N_1, N_2),

$$\frac{dN_1}{dt} = r_1 N_1 (1 - (N_1 + \alpha_{12}N_2)/K_1),$$

$$\frac{dN_2}{dt} = r_2 N_2 (1 - (N_2 + \alpha_{21}N_1)/K_2), \tag{5.1}$$

both species can coexist indefinitely provided

$$K_1 > \alpha_{12}K_2, \; K_2 > \alpha_{21}K_1. \tag{5.2}$$

These conditions work because they guarantee that either species will increase when rare, provided that the numerically dominant species is close to its "carrying capacity" K. In other words, they assure a competitive advantage to the rare type. Such an advantage could become manifest either through exploitation or through interference. In the former case, implicit in this formulation of the equations is the notion that either through microhabitat differentiation or through clumping, individuals of one species intrude more upon the resources of their conspecifics than upon the resources of the other species. In the case of interference, the idea is that individuals actually interfere more with individuals of their own type than with those of other types. Again, this could be due to proximity, but there are cases where disproportionate interference which is independent of the proximity effect has been suggested. For example (F.E. Smith, unpubl.; Forcier, 1975; Whittaker and Levin, 1977; Woods, 1980), data suggest that at some sites saplings of beech and sugar maple fare better under canopy trees of the other species; whether this occurs by direct effects or by increased competition for resources among conspecifics is unclear. Effects of predators associated with the parent type provide yet another possible mechanism (Janzen, 1970, Connell, 1971).

Negative frequency-dependent selection is a frequently suggested mechanism for the maintenance of diversity over evolutionary time (Clarke, 1979, Karlin and Campbell, 1981).

Pimentel et al.(1965) and Ayala (1966), reviving an idea due to
Park and Lloyd (1955), argued that in competitive systems, rare
types will be selected for interspecific competitive ability
while common types will primarily evolve to become better at
intraspecific competition. Pimentel et al.(1965) provided
experimental support for this idea, although their laboratory
system did not result in the coexistence of species. In their
experiment, a population of blowflies driven close to extinction
through competition with houseflies recovered, apparently due to
selection for interspecific competitive ability, and eventually
eliminated the houseflies; similar results were obtained by
Seaton and Antonovics (1967) working with Drosophila. Levin
and Pimentel (1981), in considering the evolution of avirulence
in parasite populations, show the potential importance of frequency dependence in host parasite systems. For one form of
their model, selection can favour the virulent type when it is
rare because it can invade hosts which have been colonized by the
less virulent form. However, if the virulent type is relatively
common, there will be few new sites to invade but serious losses
due to the deaths of hosts associated with the virulent form.
Under these conditions, the avirulent type will be selected;
the overall result is coexistence between the virulent and
avirulent viruses.

Balanced polymorphisms, which result from heterozygote over-
dominance, may be thought of as due to frequency dependence,
although in the classical formulation genotype fitnesses are
constant. However, if one views micro-evolution as competition
between alleles (Dawkins, 1976), then (Levin, 1978) one finds
that even with constant genotypic fitnesses the mean fitnesses
of the various alleles do depend on the relative frequencies of
those alleles, and that this is what is responsible for coexistence. Similarly, several of the other genetic mechanisms
suggested by Karlin and McGregor (1972a) can be thought of as
due to frequency dependence; for example, the overall mutation
rate to the rare type increases as the frequency of the other
type increases, and this can result in mutation-selection
balance.

Frequency dependence can also operate through spatial, age,
or other structures, or through and upon the sex ratio. Indeed,
the classical argument for the stability of the sex ratio
(Fisher, 1930) is simply a variant on the above frequency-
dependent arguments; that is, it rests upon the selective advantage of the rare type.

  Predation (and disturbance) can operate in a number of ways
to enhance coexistence through frequency-dependent mechanisms.
Although it is true that a perfectly generalized predator,
attacking all prey impartially, makes no difference to

competitive coexistence among prey whose intrinsic rates of increase are identical (May, 1977), this is not true when prey differ in those rates of increase (Slobodkin, 1961, May, 1977). When indiscriminate predation (or rarefaction) is superimposed on the system (1), yielding the new system

$$\frac{dN_1}{dt} = r_1 N_1 (1 - (N_1 + \alpha_{12}N_2)/K_1) - \varepsilon N_1$$

$$(5.3)$$

$$\frac{dN_2}{dt} = r_2 N_2 (1 - (N_2 + \alpha_{21}N_2)/K_2) - \varepsilon N_2,$$

the conditions for coexistence become

$$K_1 (1 - \varepsilon/r_1) > \alpha_{12} K_2 (1 - \varepsilon/r_2); \quad K_2 (1 - \varepsilon/r_2) > \alpha_{21} K_1 (1 - \varepsilon/r_1),$$

$$(5.4)$$

where $\varepsilon < r_1$, r_2 (Slobodkin, 1961). When $\varepsilon = 0$, these reduce to (5.2); but clearly if $r_1 \neq r_2$, varying ε varies the ratio $K_1 (1 - \varepsilon/r_1)/K_2 (1 - \varepsilon/r_2)$ and can make coexistence possible. For example, if $K_1 > \alpha_{12} K_2$ but $K_2 < \alpha_{21} K_1$, then species 1 is the competitively superior species in that it will always win in competition in (5.1). However, provided $\alpha_{12} \alpha_{21} < 1$, $r_1 < r_2$, and

$$(K_1 - \alpha_{12} K_2)/(K_1/r_1 - \alpha_{12} K_2/r_2) > \varepsilon$$

$$(5.5)$$

$$> (\alpha_{21} K_1 - K_2)/(\alpha_{21} K_1/r_1 - K_2/r_2),$$

coexistence becomes possible. Thus under some conditions, $\varepsilon > 0$ will lead to coexistence of species which could not coexist when $\varepsilon = 0$. However, under other conditions, $\varepsilon > 0$ can destroy coexistence. In general (see equations (5.4)), increasing ε will serve to decrease the potential for survival of the species with the smaller intrinsic rate of increase r, while increasing it for the species with the larger rate. Thus (Harper, 1969) it is not possible to draw a priori conclusions of a general nature about the effects of indiscriminate predation; one can only point out possibilities. Because (5.3) is appropriate to the description of the interaction between species in a chemostat, (5.5) may be thought of as defining the range of flushing rates which will

allow the opportunistic species 2 to survive without displacing
species 1.

The preceding demonstrates that, at least in principle, indiscriminate predation can enhance coexistence. In a related work,
Roughgarden and Feldman (1975) study theoretically the effects
of predation pressure on species packing along gradients.
However, in many natural situations, the effects of predation
or disturbance are felt most by competitive dominants (Paine,
1966, Harper, 1969), either because of direct effects or because
the dominants enter only at the end of a successional sequence.
Under such conditions, it is generally easier to establish
coexistence. In a common scenario, as for example in the intertidal system described by Levin and Paine (1974; see also Paine
and Levin, 1981) or in forests (see Watt, 1947, Sprugel, 1976,
Runkle, 1979), disturbance affects disproportionately a competitive dominant, thereby initiating a replacement sequence of
"successional" species eventually leading back to the dominant.
Coexistence thereby occurs through a spatio-temporal partitioning of the community mosaic into a variety of successional
stages.

The notion of diffusive instability (Turing, 1952) leads to
another view of how predation can affect the structure of prey
communities. In the simplest version (see Segel and Jackson,
1972, Levin, 1974, Levin and Segel, 1976, Segel and Levin, 1976),
one assumes that prey-predator (victim (v)-exploiter (e)) dynamics are governed (in the absence of movement) by equations of
the form

$$\frac{dv}{dt} = vA(v) - B(v,e) = f(v,e)$$

$$\tag{5.6}$$

$$\frac{de}{dt} = cB(v,e) - D(e) = g(v,e),$$

where A and D dictate the population dynamics in the absence of
interaction. B is a consumption rate, and c a conversion efficiency. Assume that for e fixed, the per capita rate of predation f/v is, at least at low density, an increasing function of
v. This reflects decreasing predator capture efficiency.
Holling (1965) suggested such an effect in his study of
functional responses, and identified handling time of prey as
potentially responsible. A recent study by Calvert et al, (1979)
notes similar effects concerning bird predation on monarch
butterflies, and suggests that this is due to the fact that bird
predation is concentrated on the periphery of the colonies:
larger aggregations of butterflies have smaller ratios of surface
area to volume. Assuming $f(0,e) > 0$, $\partial f/\partial v$ will therefore be
positive for small v. At higher densities, f/v will be

decreasing, as the effects of increased competition become over-riding; for v sufficiently large, it is assumed that f and $\partial f/\partial v$ will both be negative. Further, f is assumed to be a decreasing function of e, g an increasing function of v, and g/e a decreasing function of e. For e large enough (for fixed v), it is assumed that g and $\partial g/\partial e$ will be negative.

Under suitable conditions this model can admit steady-state solutions $(\bar{v}, \bar{e})$ in the region in which $\partial f/\partial v$ is positive but small enough that the steady state is stable; this requires that $\partial f/\partial v + \partial g/\partial e < 0$. If these conditions prevail, and if one allows the organisms to move about by diffusion, then the system which describes the dynamics,

$$\frac{\partial v}{\partial t} = f(v,e) + D_v \nabla^2 v$$

$$(5.7)$$

$$\frac{\partial e}{\partial t} = g(v,e) + D_e \nabla^2 e$$

admits a steady-state and spatially uniform solution $v \equiv \bar{v}$, $e \equiv \bar{e}$. However, although with $D_v = D_e = 0$ this solution was stable as a solution of (5.6), it may become unstable as a solution of (5.7) if the ratio D_e/D_v is sufficiently large. A possible result of this is that non-uniform stationary solutions will result, stable at least up to a translation (Levin and Segel, 1976, Segel and Levin, 1976). In a bounded region under zero flux conditions, these solutions will be locally stable.

The existence of non-uniform stationary solutions creates a heterogeneous spatial environment which can result in the survival of an increased number of species: inferior competitors may be able to survive through reduced competition in the areas where the prey in (5.7) is at low density.

The system (5.7) can also be thought of as a metaphor for movement of a predator among different prey types at different locations, or less literally as the shifting of the search image of a switching predator among prey of different aspects. In this interpretation, the clumping which results actually corresponds to a reduction in diversity as measured by equitability. However, if predators hunt apostatically by concentrating upon the most prevalent prey, then this reduces the potential for destabilization and serves to increase diversity. Indeed (Harper, 1969, Murdoch and Oaten, 1975, Murdoch, 1977, Tansky, 1978), switching can stabilize systems of one predator and two prey in which neither prey species could survive without the other.

The notion that apostatic selection is an important frequency-dependent mechanism has been advanced by several authors (Clarke, 1962, 1969; Murdoch, 1969; Comins and Hassell, 1979; see also Curio, 1976). Clarke (1979) cites numerous cases of apostatic selection of prey; to this list should be added recent studies by Rausher (1978) of search image for leaf shape in butterflies, and by Pietrewicz and Kamil (1979) of search image formation in the blue jay. Rand (1967), Ricklefs and O'Rourke (1975), and other authors have devoted special attention to the role of apostatic selection in maintaining aspect diversity, and suggest that "predators and prey evolve a balance in which the degree of nearest similarity of prey species" in different areas is roughly equilibrated. Endler (1978) provides a fascinating review of the whole issue of predator interaction with animal colour patterns. His principal organisms of interest, wild populations of guppies (Poecilia reticulata Peters), exhibit a great diversity of colour and spot patterns. However, in his studies colour pattern variation and patch size variation decrease at high levels of predation, suggesting that apostatic selection is not the most important factor in the maintenance of pattern diversity (Endler, 1980).

With Lee Segel (Levin and Segel, 1980), I have begun an investigation of mathematical models for the evolution of aspect diversity using a phenotypic model for quantitative inheritance; these models in principle can include the effects of crypsis and sexual selection as well as apostatic selection, although special cases may ignore or downgrade the importance of particular features. For example, if one assumes perfect heritability (this can be weakened; see Slatkin and Lande, 1976) and that the patterns of interest may be ranked by the single aspect variable z (e.g. mean spot size, position on a colour spectrum, etc.), and ignores the problem of background matching (which as already mentioned could be included), the equations describing the change in the victims' aspect distribution v(z,t) and the exploiters' search image distribution e(z,t) take the form

$$\frac{\partial v(z,t)}{\partial t} = -f(v(z,t))e(z,t) + \iint v(\eta,t)v(\xi,t)\alpha(\eta,\xi)$$

$$\frac{r(\eta,W(\eta,t))}{W(\eta,t)} \; \phi \left(\frac{\eta+\xi}{2},z\right)d\xi$$

$$(5.8)$$

$$\frac{\partial e(z,t)}{\partial t} = -e(z,t)m(V(z,t)) + c(z,t) - s(v(z,t))e(z,t) +$$

$$\int \Psi(z,\eta)e(\eta,t)s(v(\eta,t))d\eta$$

$$(5.9)$$

where

$$W(z,t) = \int \alpha(z,\eta) v(\eta,t) d\eta,$$

$$(5.10)$$

$$V(z,t) = \int \theta(z,\xi) v(\xi,t) d\xi,$$

and

$$\int \alpha(x,y) dy = \int \phi(x,y) dy = \int \psi(x,y) dy = \int \theta(x,y) dy = 1 \quad (5.11)$$

for all x. The first term on the right of (5.8) represents the loss due to predation, and incorporates a functional response; the second term, the mating term, includes a mate preference function $\alpha(\eta,\xi)$ and a fecundity $r(\eta,W(\eta,t))$ for females of type η; r is dependent upon the number W of available mates, weighted by their desirability. (For a general discussion of sexual selection and assortative mating, see Karlin, 1978.) Such an approach is reasonable if the trait in question is metric and controlled by many alleles at a single locus; moreover, implicit in the modelling of phenotypic dynamics via the offspring distribution kernel ϕ is that that distribution can be predicted if the parental types are known.

The first two terms on the right of (5.9) represent switching by the predators to prey other than those under explicit consideration; the latter two terms represent direct switching of search image among the various aspect values. Both types of switching are assumed to be controlled by the relative desirabilities of particular search images as represented by the densities of prey having those aspects. However, the presumably more dramatic decision to abandon the class of prey entirely, as reflected in the first term, is allowed to depend on a weighted average $V(z,t)$ of prey likely to be encountered under "short range" switching, rather than on simply the local density $v(z,t)$. V and v become identical if θ is taken to be the δ-function. A more general form of the model applies such a weighted measure to both types of switching.

In Levin and Segel (1980), our interest is in which asymptotic distributions of aspect will result from the system (5.8)-(5.9). Under what conditions will spikes develop in which one or a few aspect types are selected? When the spike solutions may be shown to be unstable, how much diversity in aspect will evolve? When will stationary distributions develop, and when spatio-temporal ones? When will a uniform distribution, in which all

possible types are equally represented, emerge? What are the
effects of boundary conditions?

We have begun study of these questions for certain special
cases of (5.8)-(5.9) by analyzing the stability of uniform solutions. It may be shown that as the controlling parameters are
varied, uniform solutions become unstable and non-uniform ones
bifurcate from these, analogously to the diffusive instabilities
discussed earlier. These bifurcating solutions may be either
time-varying or time-invariant. Because we are interested in
questions of limiting similarity, it is not sufficient to study
only this linear problem, but we must be concerned with the non-
linear behaviour as well. Here, extensive numerical work is
necessary because of the limitations of analytic methods.

In summary then, and as Endler (1978) has summarized more
effectively, predation interacts with other factors to contribute to diversity in morph types in several ways, but including
both crypsis and apostatic selection. Both of these may be frequency dependent, because of competition for backgrounds in
escaping from predation.

6. POSITIVE FREQUENCY DEPENDENCE

Although it is obvious how negative frequency dependence,
which favours the rare type, will enhance coexistence, it would
seem that positive frequency dependence, which favours the
common type, should work to reduce diversity. This of course
is true if the frequencies in question are overall frequencies
in the community. However, in a spatially structured environment local positive frequency dependence (e.g. through allelo-
pathy or plant pollinator or other mutualistic associations)
serves to enable local isolates of species to withstand the
"mass effect" (Shmida and Whittaker, 1981); that is, it allows
them to survive in the face of invasion by colonists from other
species established elsewhere. Positive frequency dependence in
population dynamics contributes to a situation in which multiple
stable states are possible; which stable state will result in a
particular subcommunity will depend upon initial conditions and
chance events. Under these conditions, founder effects combined
with the multiple stable states can result in greatly increased
diversity (Levin, 1974); multiple successional pathways and
transient effects or cyclical local dynamics can magnify the
importance. In the latter case, the community may be similar in
structure to a collection of nonlinear oscillators, coupled
through diffusion (see Winfree, 1980).

The simplest model system in which such behaviour can be
observed was discussed in detail in Levin (1974), and is based
on the Lotka-Volterra dynamics (5.1), but with the inequalities

(5.2) reversed. Levin (1974) discusses the consequences of such dynamics, but within a more general framework.

   Following Levin (1974), consider an environment subdivided into m subenvironments (patches), numbered $\mu = 1, \ldots, k$. Let u^μ be the vector of species densities in patch μ, and assume that the system dynamics are defined by

$$\frac{du^\mu}{dt} = f^\mu(u^\mu) + \sum_{\nu=1}^{k} D^{\nu\mu}(u^\nu - u^\mu), \qquad (6.1)$$

in which $D^{\nu\mu}$ is a diagonal matrix of non-negative diffusion coefficients. The functions f_i^μ are arbitrary except that they are continuously differentiable on the non-negative orthant, and $f_i^\mu \geq 0$ if $u_i^\mu = 0$ and all other components of u^μ are non-negative.

Using a continuous version of the method of small parameters (Karlin and McGregor, 1972b), Levin (1974) proves the following result.

Theorem: If when $D = 0$ (6.1) admits multiple stable states, then when $D = 0$ but is close to 0 (6.1) admits multiple stable spatially non-uniform stationary solutions as well as spatially uniform ones.

This means that if local environments can be in different stable states from one another, then sufficiently small coupling through diffusion will not upset that non-uniform pattern.

   Considerable interest has recently been focused upon continuous versions of this result. In particular, for a bounded domain $A \subset R^n$, under what conditions can the system

$$\frac{\partial u_i}{\partial t} = f_i(u,x) + \nabla \cdot (D_i \nabla u_i) \text{ in } A,$$

$$\frac{\partial u_i}{\partial \eta} = 0 \text{ on } \partial A, \ i = 1, \ldots, m \qquad (6.2)$$

admit stable spatially non-uniform stationary solutions? Here η denotes the outward normal to ∂A. It is not surprising that such solutions can exist if f_i depends in a suitable way upon x (see for example Namba and Mimura, 1980); but the harder problem

occurs when f_i is independent of x. A review of this question was
given in Levin (1979), but recent advances require an updating.

Assume that ∂A is smooth and that f_i is independent of x.
Then (Chafee, 1975), when m = 1 and n = 1, there are no such
stable non-uniform stationary solutions, and Casten and Holland
(1978) prove that this result extends to higher dimensions
(n > 1) provided the region A is convex. (Technically, they
prove that $C^3(A)$ non-uniform solutions are unstable in the
Sobolev norm.) However, still for m = 1 and n > 1, Matano (1980)
shows that for suitably non-convex regions, stable non-uniform
solutions may be maintained provided the function f admits multiple stable states. An example of such a region would be a
dumbbell-shaped region with a narrow middle portion.

Such a region works because it approximates a discrete patchy
region consisting of two patches with some flow between them, a
situation covered by the theorem given earlier. This led Levin
(1978) to conjecture that similar results would hold even for
convex regions if the diffusion coefficients were permitted to
depend upon spatial position in such a way as to restrict flow
in certain portions sufficiently that the region became effectively patchy. A proof of this, or at least of a closely
related result, has been given by Fife and Peletier (1980).
Actually, Fife and Peletier (1980) examine solutions on the
(infinite) real line, and demonstrate the existence of clines
(solutions attaining different values at $\pm \infty$, and which are
stable in some sense) for the equation whose steady states are
defined by

$$\frac{d}{dx} (D(x)\frac{du}{dx}) + s(x)f(u) = 0; \qquad (6.3)$$

however, they state that similar results hold for finite intervals (presumably with no-flux boundary conditions). In particular, if s(x) is allowed to vary subject to certain restrictions, then clines can exist if the equation is bistable (admits
two stable states). Further, they point out that the equation
(6.3) can be reduced to a canonical form with $D(x) \equiv 1$ by the
rescaling $\hat{x} = \int_0^x d\xi/D(\xi)$, and hence even if $s \equiv 1$ in (6.3), variation in D(x) can be sufficient to permit coexistence. This
result is important not only in providing a formal justification
for the intuitive claims made in Levin (1979), but also in demon-
strating the equivalence of models with spatially variable diffusion with a class of constant diffusion models with spatially
varying growth. Similar results can also be obtained if

diffusion depends on space only through its dependence on population density (Mimura, pers. comm.).

In the consideration of systems of interacting species, the situation is more complex. It was demonstrated earlier that for some predator-prey systems in which predator and prey have sufficiently different diffusion rates, such patterns are possible; in systems with m < 2, less restrictive conditions apply than are necessary with two species. However, if the diffusion rates are the same for all species, then (for any m) the uniform solution cannot be destablized by diffusion, and so small-amplitude non-uniform solutions cannot bifurcate from the uniform ones as with diffusive instabilities. However, for suitable non-convex regions large-amplitude non-uniform stationary solutions may be stable; trivial examples may be constructed using Matano's results for scalar equations by considering systems of non-interacting such scalar equations.

The hardest problem occurs for convex regions, with diffusion coefficients identical. Here the conjecture still is that non-uniform solutions cannot be stable, but the problem is not completely settled. Kishimoto (1981) examines the problem for rectangular parallelopiped domains and under periodic boundary conditions, and shows that the competitive system

$$\frac{\partial u_1}{\partial t} = u_1 f_1(u_1, u_2) + D_1 \nabla^2 u_1,$$

$$\frac{\partial u_2}{\partial t} = u_2 f_2(u_1, u_2) + D_2 \nabla^2 u_2,$$

(6.4)

where the C'' functions f_i are strictly decreasing in u_1 and u_2 does not admit stable non-uniform solutions. For more general systems, the problem is to my knowledge still open.

Mimura and Kawasaki (1979) and Mimura (1980) study competition systems in which either the diffusion coefficients are density dependent, or in which movement is density dependent. Although these are similar situations, they do not result in the same equations (see Shigesada et al, 1979, Okubo, 1980): in the latter case, the appropriate form is

$$\frac{\partial u_i}{\partial t} = \Delta(D_i(u)u_i) + f_i(u), \quad i = 1, \ldots, m$$

(6.5)

rather than the familiar form

$$\frac{\partial u_i}{\partial t} = \nabla \cdot (D_i(u) \nabla u_i) + f_i(u), \quad i = 1, \ldots, m \qquad (6.6)$$

In particular, Mimura (1980) considers the system (6.5) with
m = 2 and

$$f_1 = (R_1 - a_1 u_1 - b_1 u_2) u_1, \quad f_2 = (R_2 - a_2 u_2 - b_2 u_1) u_2, \qquad (6.7)$$

the Lotka-Volterra system, and

$$D_1 = d_1(1 + k_1 u_2), \quad D_2 = d_2(1 + k_2 u_1), \qquad (6.8)$$

and shows that subject to appropriate conditions on the parameters, non-uniform solutions are possible "spatially segregat-
gating" the two competing species. Shigesada et al, (1979) had
demonstrated such spatial segregation by computer simulations
for a complementary case involving environmental heterogeneity
and density-dependent dispersal.

7. CONCLUSIONS

This paper began by asking how large numbers of species of
morphs could coexist within a single habitat, and followed with
a litany of candidate mechanisms, including external influences,
niche and microhabitat differentiation, temporal partitioning,
and frequency dependence. That there are so many possible
mechanisms makes somewhat less surprising the coexistence of
large numbers of species when a naive interpretation of the competitive exclusion principle would seem to dictate otherwise;
but it hardly solves the problem, which is to determine the relative importances of the various mechanisms and to explain species
diversity. The central challenge facing both theoreticians and
field biologists is not the further elaboration of the list of
possible causes, but the development of methodologies to assign
relative importances to particular factors in specific situations. It seems unlikely that this can be achieved with pencil
and paper alone; what are needed are controlled experimental
manipulations of natural systems specifically designed to test
conjectures. Mathematical theory can serve a role by suggesting
and directing experimentation, but without data theories remains
pie-in-the-sky.

8. ACKNOWLEDGEMENTS

It is a pleasure to acknowledge the support of the John Simon
Guggenheim Memorial Foundation, and of the National Science
Foundation under grants MCS7701076 and MCS8001618. Dan Cohen
read the manuscript and provided numerous helpful comments.

9. REFERENCES

Ayala, F.J. (1966) Reversal of dominance in competing species of Drosophila, *Amer. Natur.*, **100**, pp. 81-83.

Calvert, W.H., Hedrick, L.E. and Brower, L.P. (1979) Mortality of the monarch butterfly (Danaus plexippus L.): avian predation at five overwintering sites in Mexico, *Science,* **204**, pp. 847-851.

Casten, R.G. and Holland, C.J. (1978) Instability results for reaction diffusion equations with Neumann boundary conditions, *J. Diff. Eq.,* **27**, pp. 266-273.

Chafee, N. (1975) Asymptotic behaviour for solutions of a one-dimensional parabolic equation with homogeneous Neumann boundary conditions, *J. Diff. Eq.,* **18**, pp. 111-135.

Chesson, P.L. and Warner, R. (1980) Environmental variability promotes coexistence in lottery competitive systems, Manuscript.

Clarke, B.C. (1962) Balanced polymorphism and the divergence of sympatric species, *In* "Taxonomy and Geography", (D. Nichols, ed.), Systematics Association, Oxford, pp. 47-70.

Clarke, B.C. (1969) The evidence for apostatic selection, *Heredity,* **24**, pp. 347-352.

Clarke, B.C. (1979) The evolution of genetic diversity, *Proc. R. Soc. London,* **B205**, pp. 453-474.

Comins, H.N. and Hassell, M.P. (1979) The dynamics of optimally foraging predators and parasitoids, *J. Anim. Ecol.,* **48**, pp. 335-351.

Connell, J.H. (1971) On the role of natural enemies in preventing competitive exclusion in some marine animals and in rain forest trees, *In* "Dynamics of Populations", (P.J. Den Boer and G.R. Gradwell, eds), Proc. Adv. Study Inst. Oosterbeek, 1970, Pudoc, Wageningen, pp. 298-312.

Connell, J.H. (1978) Diversity in tropical rain forests and coral reefs, *Science,* **199**, pp. 1302-1310.

Curio, E. (1976) The Ethology of Behaviour, Springer-Verlag, New York.

Dawkins, R. (1976) The Selfish Gene, Oxford Univ. Press.

Endler, J.A. (1978) A predator's view of animal colour patterns, *Evol. Biol.,* **11**, pp. 319-364.

Endler, J.A. (1980) Natural selection on colour patterns in
Poecilia reticulata, *Evolution*, **34**, pp. 76-91.

Feinsinger, P. (1980) Asynchronous migration patterns and the
coexistence of tropical hummingbirds, *In* "Migrant Birds in the
Neotropics: Ecology, Behaviour, Distribution, and Conservation",
(A. Keast and E.S. Morton, eds), Smithsonian Inst. Press,
Washington, D.C., pp. 411-419.

Fife, P.C. and Peletier, L.A. (1980) Clines induced by variable
migration, *In* "Biological Growth and Spread. Mathematical
Theories and Applications", (W. Jager, H. Rost, and P. Tautu,
eds), Lecture Notes in Biomathematics 38, Springer-Verlag,
Berlin-Heidelberg-New York.

Fisher, R.A. (1930) The Genetical Theory of Natural Selection,
Dover Reprint (1958), New York.

Forcier, L.K. (1975) Reproductive strategies and the co-
occurrence of climax tree species, *Science,* **189**, pp. 808-810.

Gilbert, L.E. and Singer, M.C. (1975) Butterfly ecology, *Annu.
Rev. Ecol. Syst.,* **6**, pp. 365-397.

Harper, J.L. (1969) The role of predation in vegatational diversity, *In* "Diversity and Stability in Ecological Systems", (G.M.
Woodwell and H.H. Smith, eds), *Brookhaven Symp. Biol.,* **22**,
pp. 48-62.

Holling, C.S. (1965) The functional response of predators to
prey density and its role in mimicry and population regulation,
Mem. Entomol. Soc. Can., **45**, pp. 1-60.

Hulburt, E.M. (1977) Coexistence, equilibrium, and nutrient
sharing among phytoplankton species of the Gulf of Maine, *Amer.
Natur.,* **111**, pp. 967-980.

Hutchinson, G.E. (1953) The concept of pattern in ecology, *Proc.
Acad. Natural Sciences (Philadelphia),* **105**, pp. 1-12.

Hutchinson, G.E. (1959) Homage to Santa Rosalia or why are there
so many kinds of animals?, *Amer. Natur.,* **93**, pp. 145-159.

Hutchinson, G.E. (1961) The paradox of the plankton, *Amer.
Natur.,* **95**, pp. 137-145.

Hutchinson, G.E. (1965) The Ecological Theater and the Evolutionary Play, Yale Univ. Press, New Haven.

Janzen, D.H. (1970) Herbivores and the number of tree species in tropical forests, *Amer. Natur.*, **104**, pp. 501-528.

Karlin, S. (1978) Comparison of positive assortative mating and sexual selection models, *Theor. Pop. Biol.*, **14**, pp. 281-312.

Karlin, S. and Campbell, R.B. (1981) The existence of a protected polymorphism under conditions of soft as against hard selection in a multideme population system, *Amer. Natur.*, In press.

Karlin, S. and McGregor, J. (1972a) Polymorphisms for genetic and ecological systems with weak coupling, *Theor. Pop. Biol.*, **3**, pp. 210-238.

Karlin, S. and McGregor, J. (1972b) Application of methods of small parameters to multi-niche population genetic models, *Theor. Pop. Biol.*, **3**, pp. 186-209.

Kimura, M. (1968) Genetic variability maintained in a finite population due to mutational production of neutral and nearly neutral isoalleles, *Genet. Res.*, **11**, pp. 247-269.

Kishimoto, K. (1981) Instability of non-constant equilibrium solutions of a system of competition-diffusion equations, *J. Math. Biol.*, In print.

Levin, S.A. (1974) Dispersion and population interactions, *Amer. Natur.*, **108**, pp. 207-228.

Levin, S.A. (1978) On the evolution of ecological parameters, *In* "Ecological Genetics: The Interface", (P.F. Brussard, ed.), Springer-Verlag, Berlin-Heidelberg-New York, pp. 3-26.

Levin, S.A. (1979) Non-uniform stable solutions to reaction-diffusion equations: applications to ecological pattern formulation, *In* "Pattern Formation by Dynamic Systems and Pattern Recognition", (H. Haken, ed.), Springer-Verlag, Berlin-Heidelberg-New York, pp. 210-222.

Levin, S.A. and Paine, R.T. (1974) Disturbance, patch formation, and community structure, *Proc. Nat. Acad. Sci. USA* **71**, pp. 2744-2747.

Levin, S.A. and Pimentel, D. (1981) Selection of intermediate rates of increase in parasite-host systems, *Amer. Natur.*, In press.

Levin, S.A. and Segel, L.A. (1976) Hypothesis for origin of planktonic patchiness, *Nature*, **259**, p. 659.

Levin, S.A. and Segel, L.A. (1980) Models of the influence of predation on aspect diversity in prey populations, Manuscript.

Matano, H. (1979) Asymptotic behaviour and stability of solutions of semilinear diffusion equations, *publ. RIMS Kyoto Univ.*, **15**, pp. 401-451.

May, R.M. (1977) Predators that switch, *Nature*, **269**, pp. 103-104.

May, R.M. and MacArthur, R.H. (1972) Niche overlap as a function of environmental variability, *Proc. Nat. Acad. Sci. USA*, **69**, pp. 1109-1113.

Mimura, M. (1980) Stationary patterns of some density-dependent diffusion systems with competitive dynamics (ms).

Mimura, M. and Kawasaki, K. (1979) Spatial segregation in competitive interaction-diffusion equations, *J. Math. Biol.*, **9**, pp. 49-64.

Mound, L. and Waloff, N. (1978) Diversity of Insect Faunas, Symposia of the Royal Entomological Society of London: Number 9, Blackwell, Oxford.

Murdoch, W.W. (1969) Switching in general predators; experiments on predator specificity and stability of prey populations, *Ecol. Monogr.*, **39**, pp. 335-354.

Murdoch, W.W. (1977) Stabilizing effects of spatial heterogeneity in predator-prey systems, *Theor. Pop. Biol.*, **11**, pp. 252-273.

Murdoch, W.W. and Oaten, A. (1975) Predation and population stability, *Adv. Ecol. Res.*, **9**, pp. 1-131.

Namba, T. and Mimura, M. (1980) Spatial distribution of competing populations, Manuscript.

Okubo, A. (1980) Diffusion and Ecological Problems: Mathematical Models, Springer-Verlag, Berlin-Heidelberg-New York.

Paine, R.T. (1966) Food web complexity and species diversity, *Amer. Natur.*, **100**, pp. 65-75.

Paine, R.T. and Levin, S.A. (1976) Responses to perturbation in the intertidal zone, *In* "The Study of Species Transients. Their Characteristics and Significance for Natural Resource Systems", (O.L. Loucks, ed.), The Institute of Ecology, Indianapolis, pp. 23-27.

Paine, R.T. and Levin, S.A. (1981) Intertidal landscapes: distur-bance and the dynamics of pattern, *Ecol. Monogr.*, In print.

Park, T. and Lloyd, M. (1955) Natural selection and the outcome of competition, *Amer. Natur.*, **96**, pp. 235 240.

Pietrewicz, A.T. and Ramil, A.C. (1979) Search image formation in the blue jay (Cyanocitta cristata), *Science*, **204**, pp. 1332-1333.

Pimentel, D., Feinberg, E.H., Wood, P.W. and Hayes, J.T. (1965) Selection, spatial distribution, and the coexistence of competing fly species, *Amer. Natur.*, **99**, pp. 97-109.

Rand, A.S. (1967) Predator-prey interactions and the evolution of aspect diversity, Atas. do Simposio sobra a Biota Amazonica 5 (Zoologia), pp. 73-83.

Rausher, M.D. (1978) Search image for leaf shape in a butterfly, *Science*, **200**, pp. 1071-1073.

Ricklefs, R.E. and O'Rourke, K.E. (1975) Aspect diversity in moths: a temperate-tropical comparison, *Evolution*, **29**, pp. 313-324.

Roughgarden, J. and Feldman, M. (1975) Species packing and pre-dation pressure, *Ecology*, **56**, pp. 489-492.

Runkle, J.R. (1979) Gap phase dynamics in climax mesic forests, Ph.D. Thesis, Cornell University, Ithaca, New York.

Sale, P.F. (1977) Maintenance of high diversity in coral reef fish communities, *Amer. Natur.*, **111**, pp. 337-359.

Seaton, A.P.C. and Antonovics, J. (1967) Population interrela-tionships. I. Evolution in mixtures of Drosophila mutants, *Heredity*, **22**, pp. 19-33.

Segel, L.A. and Jackson, J. (1972) Dissipative structure: an explanation and an ecological example, *J. Theor. Biol.*, **37**, pp. 545-559.

Segel, L.A. and Levin, S.A. (1976) Application of nonlinear stability theory to the study of the effects of diffusion on pre-dator-prey interactions, *In* "Topics in Statistical Mechanics and Biophysics: A Memorial to Julius L. Jackson, (R.A. Piccirelli ed.), Proc. AIP Conf. 27, pp. 123-152.

Shigesada, N., Kawasaki, K. and Teramoto, E. (1979) Spatial segregation of interacting species, *J. Theor. Biol.*, **79**, pp. 83-99.

Shmida, A. and Whittaker, R.H. (1981) Pattern and biological microsite differentiation in two shrub communities, southern California", *Ecology,* In press.

Simberloff, D.S. and Wilson, E.O. (1969) Experimental zoogeography of islands: the colonization of empty islands", *Ecology,* **50**, pp. 278-296.

Slatkin, M. and Lande, R. (1976) Niche width in a fluctuating environment-density independent model, *Amer. Natur.*, **110**, pp. 31-55.

Slobodkin, L.B. (1961) The Growth and Regulation of Animal Numbers, Holt, Rinehart, and Winston, New York.

Sprugel, D. (1976) Dynamic structure of wave-regenerated <u>Abies balsamea</u> forests in the northeastern United States, *J. Ecol.*, **64**, pp. 889-911.

Talbot, F.H., Russell, B.C. and Anderson, G.R.V. (1978) Coral reef fish communities: unstable, high-diversity systems?, *Ecol. Monogr.*, **48**, pp. 425-440.

Tansky, M. (1978) Switching effect in prey-predator systems, *J. Theor. Biol.*, **70**, pp. 263-271.

Turing, A. (1952) The chemical basis of morphogenesis, *Philos. Trans. R. Soc. London Ser. B*, **237**, pp. 37-72.

Watt, A.S. (1947) Pattern and process in the plant community, *J. Ecol.*, **35**, pp. 1-22.

Whittaker, R.H. and Levin, S.A. (1977) The role of mosaic phenomena in natural communities, *Theor. Pop. Biol.*, **12**, pp. 117-139.

Winfree, A. (1980) The Geometry of Biological Time, Springer-Verlag, Berlin-Heidelberg-New York.

Woods, K.D. (1980) Reciprocal replacement and the maintenance of codominance in a beech-maple forest, *Oikos*, **33**, pp. 31-39.

PART III

BIOMETRICAL ASPECTS OF THE DYNAMICS OF

BIOLOGICAL POPULATIONS

LOGLINEAR MODELS FOR CAPTURE-RECAPTURE EXPERIMENTS ON OPEN POPULATIONS

R.M. Cormack

(Department of Statistics, University of St. Andrews, St. Andrews, Scotland)

1. INTRODUCTION

Capture-recapture is one of the methods by which the biologist attempts to obtain numerical estimates for the basic parameters - population size, birth and immigration, death and emigration - of an animal population in the wild. Repeated samples are taken from the population, some at least of the sampled individuals being given an identifiable mark and returned to the population. The record of recaptured marks and captures of unmarked individuals then provides a set of statistics from which, under certain assumptions, information on population parameters can be deduced.

In the early use of capture-recapture methods, the population was assumed closed and subject to two samples, a marking sample and a recapture sample. If marked and unmarked animals are equally at risk to capture in the second sample, the simple Petersen estimate of population size is obtained by equating the unknown proportion of unmarked individuals caught in the second sample to the known proportion of marked individuals caught. More precise estimates are obtained from longer chains of samples as in the Schnabel census, but by then the dangers of postulating a closed population are too great to be ignored. The longer the time between samples the more likely is the requirement of random mixing of the population to be met, but the less likely is the postulated closure of the population.

Early work attempted to correct for such dynamics, but this quickly changed to a positive effort to use the data from an extended capture-recapture experiment to estimate the parameters of the dynamic population. These culminated in the model of Jolly (1965) and Seber (1965) which yields estimates of birth parameters, death rates and population size of a population. Certain assumptions need to be satisfied, and these remain the bugbear of most practical studies. There are three principal assumptions:

 (i)   that individuals who have been captured retain on average
the same parameters of survival and liability to capture as those
who have not been captured;
 (ii) that all individuals are homogeneous in their behaviour
as far as it affects their interaction with the sampling process;
(iii) that no individuals emigrate from the population during
one or more sampling periods and then return.

The third difficulty remains. Considerable progress has been
made with the first two, trap dependence and behavioural heterogeneity, for the study of closed populations (Otis, Burnham,
White and Anderson, 1978).

 There are further technical difficulties with the Jolly-Seber
model. A minor problem is that impossible estimates, negative
birth or death rates, often occur. A major difficulty is the
lack of parsimony in the form of the model which is usually
applied. Estimates are readily available only if different survival parameters ϕ_i, different birth parameters B_i, and different
catchability parameters p_i are postulated for each sampling
period. Lack of parsimony increases the variability of parameter
estimates. Again there has been recent progress, notably by
Jolly (1979).

 The conduct of such an experiment has been modelled by
statistical distributions in many different ways and the history
of these has been extensively documented (Cormack (1968, 1979);
Seber (1973)). The subject provides an excellent example of the
biological insight to be gained from different mathematical or
statistical models of the same situation.

 Many of these statistical methods, including the Jolly-Seber
method, utilize only information which is provided by a batch
mark; that is, one knows for each individual in the ith sample
only when that individual was last caught. If we are to try to
model individual behaviour, we cannot expect to progress very
far unless we know the complete capture history of each individual throughout the experiment. We assume henceforth that such
records are available.

 For such capture-recapture data we shall develop a sequence
of models representing a closed population, birth, death, trap
dependence, with variable or constant sampling effort, and show
how the GLIM computer package can readily be used to select the
model from among combinations of these factors most appropriate
for the data set.

2. LOGLINEAR MODELS FOR CONTINGENCY TABLES

The modern approach to the analysis of data on counts expresses the logarithm of the expected value of every count as a linear function of a set of parameters. The general theory and methodology is described by Bishop, Fienberg and Holland (1975). Consider a 2 × 2 contingency table with

Observations		Probabilities		Expectations	
n_{11}	n_{12}	π_{11}	π_{12}	m_{11}	m_{12}
n_{21}	n_{22}	π_{21}	π_{22}	m_{21}	m_{22}

where $\Sigma\Sigma n_{ab} = N$, $\Sigma\Sigma \pi_{ab} = 1$, $m_{ab} = N\pi_{ab}$. We model the expectations as:

$$\log m_{11} = u + u_1 + u_2 + u_{12}$$
$$\log m_{12} = u + u_1 - u_2 - u_{12}$$
$$\log m_{21} = u - u_1 + u_2 - u_{12}$$
$$\log m_{22} = u - u_1 - u_2 + u_{12}$$

$$(2.1)$$

If the four counts are from unrelated distributions, this is purely a reparameterization, the 4 m-parameters being replaced by 4 u-parameters. Any hypothesis about the m_{ab} generates a corresponding hypothesis about the u. Thus, for example, the usual contingency table hypothesis of independence of the row and column categorizations: $\pi_{11}\pi_{22} = \pi_{12}\pi_{21}$ corresponds to the hypothesis: $u_{12} = 0$. The parameter u_{12} represents the interaction between the two categorizations.

Denote by $m_{abc...s}$ the expected counts in a 2^s table, the suffices a,b,...,s taking values 1 or 2 for the two alternatives in each of the s categorizations. In our application the s categorizations are the s samples, $m_{abc...s}$ being the expected number of individuals with capture history abc...s, where, for example, a = 1 if these individuals were caught in the first sample and a = 2 if they were not caught. The complete, fully saturated, model reparameterizes log $(m_{abc...s})$ as a sum or difference of:

an overall mean   u

main effects u_i for the ith sample

two-factor interactions u_{ij} between the ith and jth samples

three-factor interactions u_{ijk} etc.

We may write $\underset{\sim}{m}$, the 2^s-vector of $m_{abc...s}$, in terms of $\underset{\sim}{u}$, the 2^s-vector of all the u's, as

$$\log \underset{\sim}{m} = A\underset{\sim}{u} \qquad (2.2)$$

where A is a $2^s \times 2^s$ orthogonal matrix with elements ± 1. The notation, and to a certain extent the interpretation, is the same as that for the analysis of variance of a 2^s factorial experiment. We adopt the convention of writing the elements of $\underset{\sim}{\ell} = \log \underset{\sim}{m}$ and of $\underset{\sim}{u}$ in the standard order of treatments and corresponding contrasts for the factorial experiment, as exemplified for the 3-sample experiment by:

$$
\begin{bmatrix} \ell_{111} \\ \ell_{211} \\ \ell_{121} \\ \ell_{221} \\ \ell_{112} \\ \ell_{212} \\ \ell_{122} \\ \ell_{222} \end{bmatrix}
=
\begin{bmatrix}
1 & 1 & 1 & 1 & 1 & 1 & 1 & 1 \\
1 & -1 & 1 & -1 & 1 & -1 & 1 & -1 \\
1 & 1 & -1 & -1 & 1 & 1 & -1 & -1 \\
1 & -1 & -1 & 1 & 1 & -1 & -1 & 1 \\
1 & 1 & 1 & 1 & -1 & -1 & -1 & -1 \\
1 & -1 & 1 & -1 & -1 & 1 & -1 & 1 \\
1 & 1 & -1 & -1 & -1 & -1 & 1 & 1 \\
1 & -1 & -1 & 1 & -1 & 1 & 1 & -1
\end{bmatrix}
\begin{bmatrix} u \\ u_1 \\ u_2 \\ u_{12} \\ u_3 \\ u_{13} \\ u_{23} \\ u_{123} \end{bmatrix}
\qquad (2.3)
$$

Fienberg (1972) presented the capture-recapture of a closed population in these terms. The observation $n_{22..2}$, the number of individuals not seen in any of the samples, is unknown, and it is the object of the study of a closed population to estimate this. For such an incomplete table a fully saturated model must have (2^s-1) parameters. We need to assume that (at least) the highest order interaction is identically zero to achieve

identifiability for the other parameters. In the simple 2-sample
case the samples must be assumed independent to permit estimation
of N, just as, dually, knowledge of N in the contingency table
permits testing of the hypothesis of independence. In the s-
sample case the usual model of independent samples is obtained
by setting all the interactions $u_{ij}, u_{ijk}, \ldots$ to be zero. The
advantage of the formulation (2.3) is in the exploration of
models in which some of the interaction terms are non-zero.
Interaction between sampling periods, in the form of trap-
happiness or trap-shyness, is one phenomenon likely to invalidate
seriously the classical closed-population estimates. Trap dependence lasting for one sampling period can be modelled by including in the model the neighbouring two-factor interaction terms
$u_{i,i+1}$. This intuitively reasonable result can be justified
rigorously by constructing appropriate matrices similar to those
given in Sections 3, 4 and 5. Heterogeneity between individuals
caused by different behaviour leads to an unpatterned set of
interactions. Different models can be explored and the simplest
acceptable model identified. This model is then extended to the
missing cell of unseen animals, and an estimate $\hat{n}_{22..2}$ obtained
from the chosen model.

The loglinear formulation provides a natural characterization
of dependences between different samples in a way which other
formulations of capture-recapture experiments do not provide.
Distributionally the N individuals in the population are thought
of as being multinomially allocated to the 2^s cells of different
capture histories with probabilities $m_{ab..s}/N$. The (2^s-1)
observed histories are also multinomial, index $(N-n_{22..2})$. The
details of the sampling scheme in a capture-recapture experiment
are usually not fixed in advance, since neither fixed sample
size nor fixed effort are usually adhered to; but the multinomial
should provide a good working distribution since statistically
it can arise from the product of binomial distributions or of
independent Poisson distributions conditioned on the observed
sample size.

Different sets of non-zero interactions in the model (2.3)
lead to different forms of estimator for the unknown population
size. Some yield estimators in closed form, others require
iterative solution. The details for hierarchical interaction
models, in which an interaction can be non-zero only if all
lower order interactions formed by a subset of the symbols are
non-zero, are given in Bishop, Fienberg and Holland (1975).

3. POPULATIONS WITH DEATH

With an open population, trap dependence will still be manifest simply in the interactions between successive samples. The
question is whether the natural dynamics of a population - birth,
death and migration - result in any characteristic pattern of
interaction. We can illustrate that they do by examining the
detail of the 3-sample experiment with death occurring (Cormack,
1979). We use the standard notation (referring to these as the
CR parameters):

ϕ_i : Probability (animal alive at (i+1)|alive at i)

p_i : Probability (animal caught at i|alive at i)

χ_i : Probability (animal not seen after i|alive at i)

noting that the set of χ_i is functionally dependent on the p_i,
ϕ_i:

$$\chi_i = 1 - \phi_i + \phi_i (1-p_{i+1}) \chi_{i+1}. \tag{3.1}$$

The N animals in the population are multinomially distributed
into the $8 = 2^3$ cells with expectations

$$m_{111} = Np_1 \phi_1 p_2 (1-\chi_2)$$

$$m_{211} = N(1-p_1) \phi_1 p_2 (1-\chi_2)$$

$$m_{121} = Np_1 \phi_1 (1-p_2) (1-\chi_2)$$

$$m_{221} = N(1-p_1) \phi_1 (1-p_2) (1-\chi_2)$$

$$m_{112} = Np_1 \phi_1 p_2 \chi_2 \tag{3.2}$$

$$m_{212} = N(1-p_1) \phi_1 p_2 \chi_2$$

$$m_{122} = Np_1 \chi_1$$

$$m_{222} = N(1-p_1) \chi_1.$$

Since all expectations are products of parametric functions, a
linear model exists for $\ell = \log m$ in terms of β, the vector of
parameters:

$(\log N, \log p_1, \log (1-p_1), \log \phi_1, \log p_2, \log (1-p_2), \log (1-\chi_2),$

$$\log \chi_2, \log \chi_1)'$$

as $\ell = D\beta$ where D is a matrix with elements 0 or 1, readily obtainable from the expectations above. We can transfer from ℓ to the loglinear parameterization u, since $\ell = Au$ and

$$A^{-1} = \frac{1}{2^s} A \quad \text{imply}$$

$$u = \frac{1}{2^s} A\ell = \frac{1}{2^s} AD\beta = T\beta. \tag{3.3}$$

The full relationship for a 3-sample experiment, which reveals the interactions which death imposes on the model, is:

$$
\begin{bmatrix} u \\ u_1 \\ u_2 \\ u_{12} \\ u_3 \\ u_{13} \\ u_{23} \\ u_{123} \end{bmatrix}
= \frac{1}{2^3}
\begin{bmatrix}
8 & 4 & 4 & 6 & 4 & 2 & 4 & 2 & 2 \\
0 & 4 & -4 & 0 & 0 & 0 & 0 & 0 & 0 \\
0 & 0 & 0 & 2 & 4 & -2 & 0 & 2 & -2 \\
0 & 0 & 0 & 0 & 0 & 0 & 0 & 0 & 0 \\
0 & 0 & 0 & 2 & 0 & 2 & 4 & -2 & -2 \\
0 & 0 & 0 & 0 & 0 & 0 & 0 & 0 & 0 \\
0 & 0 & 0 & -2 & 0 & -2 & 0 & -2 & 2 \\
0 & 0 & 0 & 0 & 0 & 0 & 0 & 0 & 0
\end{bmatrix}
\begin{bmatrix} \log N \\ \log p_1 \\ \log (1-p_1) \\ \log \phi_1 \\ \log p_2 \\ \log (1-p_2) \\ \log (1-\chi_2) \\ \log \chi_2 \\ \log \chi_1 \end{bmatrix}
$$

$$\tag{3.4}$$

In this parameterization the only interaction induced by death is u_{23}. The interactions u_{12}, u_{13}, u_{123} remain identically zero. Five loglinear parameters correspond to five estimable CR parameters N, p_1, p_2, ϕ_1, χ_2. Unfortunately, with a longer chain of samples this correspondence fails. Only those interactions including the first sample are identically zero in this parameterization, and the number of loglinear parameters required in the model becomes greater than the number of CR parameters.

4. THE GLIM PARAMETERIZATION

GLIM is a program, developed by the Working Party on Statistical Computing of the Royal Statistical Society, which provides a framework for fitting generalized linear models to data. It is widely available throughout the world. The underlying theory is given by Nelder and Wedderburn (1972) and the operation is described in the NAG Manual (1978). The distributional assumptions for contingency tables are that the counts in all cells have independent Poisson distributions whose means are exp ($\beta \cdot x$) for some known x and unknown β, a formulation which accords perfectly with the capture-recapture models above.

For a 2^s factorial structure the GLIM parameterization differs from the loglinear vector u displayed in (2.3). The representation for the 2^3 experiment is:

$$
\begin{bmatrix} \ell_{111} \\ \ell_{211} \\ \ell_{121} \\ \ell_{221} \\ \ell_{112} \\ \ell_{212} \\ \ell_{122} \\ \ell_{222} \end{bmatrix}
=
\begin{bmatrix}
1 & 0 & 0 & 0 & 0 & 0 & 0 & 0 \\
1 & 1 & 0 & 0 & 0 & 0 & 0 & 0 \\
1 & 0 & 1 & 0 & 0 & 0 & 0 & 0 \\
1 & 1 & 1 & 1 & 0 & 0 & 0 & 0 \\
1 & 0 & 0 & 0 & 1 & 0 & 0 & 0 \\
1 & 1 & 0 & 0 & 1 & 1 & 0 & 0 \\
1 & 0 & 1 & 0 & 1 & 0 & 1 & 0 \\
1 & 1 & 1 & 1 & 1 & 1 & 1 & 1
\end{bmatrix}
\begin{bmatrix} GM \\ A \\ B \\ AB \\ C \\ AC \\ BC \\ ABC \end{bmatrix}
\qquad (4.1)
$$

of which the inverse is:

$$
\begin{bmatrix} GM \\ A \\ B \\ AB \\ C \\ AC \\ BC \\ ABC \end{bmatrix}
=
\begin{bmatrix}
1 & 0 & 0 & 0 & 0 & 0 & 0 & 0 \\
-1 & 1 & 0 & 0 & 0 & 0 & 0 & 0 \\
-1 & 0 & 1 & 0 & 0 & 0 & 0 & 0 \\
1 & -1 & -1 & 1 & 0 & 0 & 0 & 0 \\
-1 & 0 & 0 & 0 & 1 & 0 & 0 & 0 \\
1 & -1 & 0 & 0 & -1 & 1 & 0 & 0 \\
1 & 0 & -1 & 0 & -1 & 0 & 1 & 0 \\
-1 & 1 & 1 & -1 & 1 & -1 & -1 & 1
\end{bmatrix}
\begin{bmatrix} \ell_{111} \\ \ell_{211} \\ \ell_{121} \\ \ell_{221} \\ \ell_{112} \\ \ell_{212} \\ \ell_{122} \\ \ell_{222} \end{bmatrix} .
\qquad (4.2)
$$

In this parameterization "main effects" and "interactions" are not evaluated from all observations, but only from those in which every other factor is at level 1. Since level 1 in our notation represents a set of animals which are seen in that sample and are therefore known, this form is particularly advantageous for modelling capture-recapture experiments. The unobserved $n_{22...2}$ is the only observation whose expectation depends on the highest order interaction AB··S. Thus, analysis of the observed counts is unaffected by the value of AB··S. and can be carried out even when, as in the case of birth and death, this interaction is known to be non-zero and non-estimable.

Multiplication of the appropriate matrices to obtain the vector of GLIM parameters in terms of the vector of CR parameters β shows that the only interactions induced by the occurrence of death are those with consecutive factors ending in the final one: BCD···S, CD···S, ···, RS. The correspondence between GLIM inter-action parameters and CR survival parameters is then 1 to 1 for any number of sample periods - $(2s-1)$ parameters of each type. In the loglinear formulation (3.4) extended to a longer series of samples the extra constraints take the form of equality of sets of non-zero interactions. The form of the transforming matrix is also much simpler than in the loglinear parameteriza-tion, its elements all being ± 1 or 0 (see Table 2).

5. BIRTH AND DEATH

The usual description of birth or immigration in CR studies is as an unknown, fixed or random, addition to the population prior to each sampling period. Thus Seber (1973) defines the unknown random variable B_i as the number of new animals joining the population in the interval from time t_i to time t_{i+1} which are still alive and in the population at time t_{i+1}. To incor-porate birth into the loglinear model we need to represent it by a multiplicative parameter. To this end we define parameters:

$$\psi_1 = 1 + B_1/N(1-p_1)\phi_1$$

$$\psi_2 = 1 + B_2/N(1-p_1)\phi_1\psi_1(1-p_2)\phi_2 \tag{5.1}$$

etc.

such that the population of unmarked individuals immediately before the (i+1)th sample is increased by a factor ψ_i. We may interpret $1/\psi_i$ as the probability that an unmarked individual alive at the ith sample was also alive in the population at the preceding sample.

TABLE 1

Expectations of numbers of animals with different capture
histories in a 4-sample CR experiment with birth and death

$$m_{1111} = Np_1\phi_1p_2\phi_2p_3(1-\chi_3)$$

$$m_{2111} = N(1-p_1)\phi_1\psi_1p_2\phi_2p_3(1-\chi_3)$$

$$m_{1211} = Np_1\phi_1(1-p_2)\phi_2p_3(1-\chi_3)$$

$$m_{2211} = N(1-p_1)\phi_1\psi_1(1-p_2)\phi_2\psi_2p_3(1-\chi_3)$$

$$m_{1121} = Np_1\phi_1p_2\phi_2(1-p_3)(1-\chi_3)$$

$$m_{2121} = N(1-p_1)\phi_1\psi_1p_2\phi_2(1-p_3)(1-\chi_3)$$

$$m_{1221} = Np_1\phi_1(1-p_2)\phi_2(1-p_3)(1-\chi_3)$$

$$m_{2221} = N(1-p_1)\phi_1\psi_1(1-p_2)\phi_2\psi_2(1-p_3)(1-\chi_3)\psi_3$$

$$m_{1112} = Np_1\phi_1p_2\phi_2p_3\chi_3$$

$$m_{2112} = N(1-p_1)\phi_1\psi_1p_2\phi_2p_3\chi_3$$

$$m_{1212} = Np_1\phi_1(1-p_2)\phi_2p_3\chi_3$$

$$m_{2212} = N(1-p_1)\phi_1\psi_1(1-p_2)\phi_2\psi_2p_3\chi_3$$

$$m_{1122} = Np_1\phi_1p_2\chi_2$$

$$m_{2122} = N(1-p_1)\phi_1\psi_1p_2\chi_2$$

$$m_{1222} = Np_1\chi_1$$

$$m_{2222} = N(1-p_1)\xi_1$$

TABLE 2

Transformation $g = T\beta$ for 4-sample experiment with birth and death

$$
\begin{bmatrix}
\text{GM} \\ \text{A} \\ \text{B} \\ \text{AB} \\ \text{C} \\ \text{AC} \\ \text{BC} \\ \text{ABC} \\ \text{D} \\ \text{AD} \\ \text{BD} \\ \text{ABD} \\ \text{CD} \\ \text{ACD} \\ \text{BCD}
\end{bmatrix}
=
\begin{bmatrix}
 & & & & & & & & & & & & & & & \\
 & & & & & & & & & & & & & & & \\
\end{bmatrix}
\begin{bmatrix}
\log N \\ \log p_1 \\ \log(1-p_1) \\ \log \phi_1 \\ \log \chi_1 \\ \log \psi_1 \\ \log p_2 \\ \log(1-p_2) \\ \log \phi_2 \\ \log \chi_2 \\ \log \psi_2 \\ \log p_3 \\ \log(1-p_3) \\ \log(1-\chi_3) \\ \log \chi_3 \\ \log \psi_3
\end{bmatrix}
$$

	$\log N$	$\log p_1$	$\log(1-p_1)$	$\log \phi_1$	$\log \chi_1$	$\log \psi_1$	$\log p_2$	$\log(1-p_2)$	$\log \phi_2$	$\log \chi_2$	$\log \psi_2$	$\log p_3$	$\log(1-p_3)$	$\log(1-\chi_3)$	$\log \chi_3$	$\log \psi_3$
GM	1	0	0	0	0	0	0	0	0	0	0	0	0	0	0	0
A	0	1	0	0	0	0	0	0	0	0	0	0	0	0	0	0
B	0	0	1	0	0	0	0	0	0	0	0	0	0	0	0	0
AB	0	0	0	1	0	0	0	0	0	0	0	0	0	0	0	0
C	0	0	0	0	1	0	0	0	0	0	0	0	0	0	0	0
AC	0	0	0	0	0	0	0	0	0	0	0	0	0	0	0	0
BC	0	0	0	0	0	0	0	0	0	0	0	0	0	0	0	0
ABC	0	0	0	0	0	0	0	0	0	0	0	0	0	0	0	0
D	0	0	0	0	0	0	1	0	0	0	0	0	0	0	0	0
AD	0	0	0	0	0	0	0	1	0	0	0	0	0	0	0	0
BD	0	0	0	0	0	0	0	0	1	0	0	0	0	0	0	0
ABD	0	0	0	0	0	0	0	0	0	1	0	0	0	0	0	0
CD	0	0	0	0	0	0	0	0	0	0	-1	0	0	0	0	-1
ACD	0	0	0	0	0	0	0	0	0	0	0	0	0	1	0	0
BCD	0	0	0	0	0	0	0	0	0	0	-1	0	0	0	0	-1

With this description of birth, and N remaining as the population size at the start of the experiment, the expectations of the
numbers of animals having the 16 different capture histories in
a 4-sample CR experiment are given in Table 1.

The parameter ξ_1 is a thoroughly untidy function of the ϕ, p
and ψ, best defined by the recurrence

$$\xi_i = 1 - \phi_i + \phi_i \psi_i (1-p_{i+1}) \xi_{i+1} \tag{5.2}$$

with boundary condition $\xi_s = 1$. Since only m_{222} (and analogously
in longer experiments only $m_{22..2}$) depends on ξ_1, and since the
GLIM model does not represent m_{2222}, it need not concern us
further. The CR parameters appear in 16 different forms to represent the 15 observable classes. The transformation is shown in
Table 2. This reveals that the GLIM interactions

$$AC, \ BC, \ AD, \ BD, \ ABD \ \text{and} \ ACD$$

are identically zero. In general, birth induces, in a way
exactly symmetrical to death, only those interactions with consecutive factors starting from the first: AB, ABC, ..., ABC..S.
The remaining 9 effects stand in 1 to 1 correspondence with 9
estimable CR parametric functions as shown in Table 3.

TABLE 3

Equivalence of GLIM and CR parameters

$$GM = \log \left[Np_1 \phi_1 p_2 \phi_2 p_3 (1-\chi_3) \right]$$

$$A = \log \left[(1-p_1) \psi_1 / p_1 \right]$$

$$B = \log \left[(1-p_2) / p_2 \right]$$

$$AB = \log \psi_2$$

$$C = \log \left[(1-p_3) / p_3 \right]$$

$$ABC = \log \psi_3$$

$$D = \log \left[\chi_3 / (1-\chi_3) \right]$$

$$CD = \log \left[\chi_2 / \phi_2 (1-p_3) \chi_3 \right]$$

$$BCD = \log \left[\chi_1 / \phi_1 (1-p_2) \chi_2 \right]$$

If this model is selected as appropriate these equations, with estimators replacing parameters, yield the estimates of these parametric functions. Of course not all the basic parameters are expressible in terms of these functions: for example, p_1 and ψ_1 are not separately estimable. Nor is N, the initial population size. But the population size N_2 at the time of the second sample can be expressed as $Np_1\phi_1[1 + (1-p_1)\psi_1/p]$, which is estimable.

   The structure of the estimating relationships is important for the choice of model. Models with death only and birth only are sub-models of that shown in Table 3. With no birth $\psi_i = 1$ for all i so that the interactions AB and ABC are identically zero, and the main effect A takes on the same form as the main effects B and C, representing the log odds against a live individual being captured in the corresponding sample. The death parameters look, but are not, slightly more complicated: $\phi_i(1-p_{i+1})\chi_{i+1}/\chi_i$ is the conditional probability that an individual alive at i but not seen thereafter survives at least until (i+1) - the precise dual of the birth parameter $1/\psi_i$. With no death, $\phi_i = 1$ and $(1-p_{i+1})\chi_{i+1}/\chi_i = 1$, so that the interactions CD and BCD are identically zero, and the main effect D becomes $\log[(1-p_4)/p_4]$.

   Direct justification of the multinomial model used by Fienberg (1972) for the closed population is no longer possible, since the multiplicative birth parameters ψ_i are not probabilities (but are the inverses of probabilities). However, it seems a priori reasonable to postulate that each observed $n_{ab\cdots s}$ is an independent observation from a Poisson distribution with mean $m_{ab\cdots s}$. This distributional assumption can be tested by the analysis. Under this assumption the estimates derived above for the parametric functions are maximum likelihood estimates, and hence estimates of the basic CR parameters such as ϕ_i, p_i, N_i (where estimable) calculated from these functions are also maximum likelihood estimates. Details of the estimates will be published elsewhere, but it is worth noting here that, for an open population with different birth, death and capture probabilities for each sample period, the estimates obtained are the usual Jolly-Seber ones.

6. CHOICE OF MODEL

   When a capture-recapture study is to be carried out, the experimenter may attempt by careful attention to the detail of

the design to restrict the type of change and behavioural interaction to which the population is subject during the study. He
knows that, if trap dependence and heterogeneity can be eliminated but birth and death and/or migration are occurring, the
Jolly-Seber estimates are valid. If he can restrict the study
to a closed population, his estimate of population size will have
a much smaller error than that obtained from an open population,
but the estimate may be severely biased if the closure and other
assumptions are unjustified. Within the assumption of closed
populations and the hypergeometric sampling model a family of
tests of different assumptions has been provided by Otis et al
(1978). Tests of closure have been given by Pollock et al.
(1974). A general goodness-of-fit of the Jolly-Seber model is
discussed in Seber (1973).

The loglinear model provides a unification of a number of
previously disparate models, though by no means all previously
considered models. The analysis of any model by the GLIM package yields a deviance, measuring the lack of fit of the model,
which for Poisson variables has asymptotically a χ^2 distribution.
Study of these deviances may allow identification of the best
fitting, most parsimonious model. The importance of parsimony
in reducing estimate variability in loglinear models is stressed
by Bishop, Fienberg and Holland (1975).

The interaction patterns induced by birth and death were
developed in the previous section. Constant sampling intensity
will result in the equality of certain of the main effects.
Trap dependence which lasts for one sampling period only will be
reflected in the need for all interactions of the type R,R+1:
it should be noted, however, that AB is also induced by birth
and S-1,S by death. Heterogeneity, in the form of varying
behaviour of groups or of individuals with respect to the population dynamics or interaction with the sampling scheme, induces
all interactions, and thus will yield an analysis in which no
reduced (unsaturated) model is found to fit: typically when
individuals have different capture probabilities all simpler
models are found to have equally bad fits.

The complete range of patterns for a 4-sample experiment is
given in Table 4. (Interpretation of the constant effort models
accompanies Table 5.)

One further advantage of this analysis is its ability to
force out-of-range estimates back within the limits of biological reality, at least when trap dependence is absent. Frequently
a Jolly-Seber analysis yields survival estimates $\hat{\phi}_i > 1$ or birth
estimates $\hat{B}_i < 0$, a problem of analysis for which a solution has

TABLE 4

GLIM models for 4-sample experiment

Closed	A + B + C + D
Birth only	A + B + C + D + AB + ABC
Death only	A + B + C + D + CD + BCD
Birth and death	A + B + C + D + AB + CD + ABC + BCD
Trap dependence	A + B + C + D + AB + BC + CD
Birth with dependence	A + B + C + D + AB + BC + CD + ABC
Death with dependence	A + B + C + D + AB + BC + CD + BCD
Birth, death, dependence	A + B + C + D + AB + BC + CD + ABC + BCD
Constant effort: closed	GM
Constant effort with birth	As birth with B = C = D i.e., A + PB + AB + ABC
Constant effort with death	As death with A = B = C i.e., PD + D + CD + BCD
Constant effort with birth and death	As birth and death with B = C i.e., A + PBD + D + AB + CD + ABC + BCD

recently been proposed by Buckland (1980). Within the GLIM
analysis such out-of-range estimates will show up as negative
estimates for the corresponding birth or death interactions,
since these represent the logarithms of the inverse of a conditional probability of birth or death. Thus, if trap dependence
is not found to be necessary, no birth or death interaction terms
should be negative in the final chosen model, and models with
such interactions set to zero should be explored for the final
choice.

7. THE GLIM PROGRAM

If variables are declared as factors within GLIM, interactions
must be hierarchical in the sense that if an interaction PQ is
zero, all higher order interactions including PQ must be zero.
Since birth and death induce patterns of interactions defying
this rule the factor levels must be converted to vectors of independent regression variables. These vectors are the columns of
$2^s \times 2^s$ matrices in the pattern of (4.1). The complete program
allowing exploration of all the models described for a 4-sample
experiment is given in Table 5. The three factors with labels
starting with P are for models with constant effort: in GLIM one
forces two parameters to be identical by constructing the sum of
the corresponding explanatory variables and fitting that instead
of the separate vectors. We read in a fictitious value for
$n_{22..2}$ and then give it zero weight W in the analysis.

TABLE 5

GLIM program for analysis of 4-sample experiment

```
$UNITS  16              $DATA N              $READ
31  9  19  5  5  7  12  20  9  7  13  8  6  5  16  100

$CAL A=%GL(2,1)-1 : B=%GL(2,2)-1 :
    C=%GL(2,4)-1 : D=%GL(2,8)-1 :
   AB=A*B : BC=B*C : CD=C*D:
   ABC=AB*C : BCD=BC*D : W=1
   PBD=B+C : PB=PBD+D : PD=PBD+A
$EDIT 16 W O   $YVAR N   $ERR P   $WEI W
$FIT    a selection of interesting models from Table 4
```

The data used in the above example were extracted from a long-term study of the fulmar petrel Fulmarus glacialis (see, for example, Dunnet and Ollason (1978), Cormack (1973)). They represent records from 1955-58 of all birds sighted during that period. Death is occurring, although the survival rate is high; "birth" occurs, since new marked birds were added to the population in each year; trap dependence will be limited since most birds are sighted without being caught or handled; heterogeneity is expected since the two sexes have different behaviour patterns which affect their probabilities of being observed by the experimenters. This pattern is revealed by the deviances from selected models given in Table 6, none of which gives an acceptable fit.

TABLE 6

Selected deviances from analysis of all birds

Closed $\qquad \chi^2_{10} = 35.5$

Birth only $\qquad \chi^2_8 = 20.5$

Birth and death $\qquad \chi^2_6 = 13.3$

Birth, death and dependence $\qquad \chi^2_5 = 11.8$

By contrast, when males alone were analyzed and the new birds added during these years excluded by restricting attention only to birds marked prior to 1955, so that death should be the only effective parameter, the deviances are given in Table 7.

TABLE 7

Selected deviances from analysis of males with no births

Closed $\qquad \chi^2_{10} = 18.1$

Death only $\qquad \chi^2_8 = 10.4$

Birth and death $\qquad \chi^2_6 = 8.8$

Birth, death and dependence $\qquad \chi^2_5 = 8.0$

Death with constant effort $\qquad \chi^2_{10} = 12.4$

The final model is a parsimonious, well-fitting model which
accords with the effort expended by the experimenter.

8. CONCLUSIONS

   Loglinear models form a natural way of representing dependence
between different sampling occasions of a capture-recapture
study. Developed hitherto only for closed populations, they can
be applied with the appropriate parameterization to dynamic populations, different patterns of interaction revealing different
aspects of the population dynamics and the sampling behaviour.
They are readily analyzed by GLIM, a widely available computer
package, at least for a limited number of sampling periods.
Inappropriate models can be immediately identified and evidence
obtained for the most appropriate parsimonious model.

9. ACKNOWLEDGEMENTS

   This work was completed during an extended visit to the Biometrics Unit of Cornell University, financed by Grant No. 1393
from NATO Scientific Affairs Division.

   Discussions with colleagues C.D. Sinclair and I.F. West at
St. Andrews and D.S. Robson at Cornell helped in the development
of these models.

10. REFERENCES

Baker, R.J. and Nelder, J.A. (1978) The GLIM System Manual -
Release 3, Numerical Algorithms Group, Oxford.

Bishop, Y.M.M., Fienberg, S.E. and Holland, P.W. (1975) Discrete
Multivariate Analysis: Theory and Practice, MIT Press, Cambridge,
Massachusetts.

Buckland, S.T. (1980) A modified analysis of the Jolly-Seber
capture-recapture model, *Biometrics,* **36**, pp. 419-435.

Cormack, R.M. (1968) The statistics of capture-recapture, *Oceano-
graphy and Marine Biology Annual Review,* **6**, pp. 455-506.

Cormack, R.M. (1973) Commonsense estimates from capture-recapture
studies, *In* "The Mathematical Theory of the Dynamics of Biological
Populations",(M.S. Bartlett and R.W. Hiorns, eds), Academic Press,
London, pp. 225-235.

Cormack, R.M. (1979) Models for capture-recapture, *In* "Sampling
Biological Populations", (R.M. Cormack, G.P. Patil and D.S. Robson,
eds), International Co-operative Publishing House, Fairland,
Maryland, pp. 217-255.

Dunnet, G.M. and Ollason, J.C. (1978) The estimation of survival rate in the fulmar Fulmarus glacialis, *J. Anim. Ecol.*, **47**, pp. 507-520.

Fienberg, S.E. (1972) The multiple recapture census for closed populations and incomplete 2^k contingency tables, *Biometrika*, **59**, pp. 591-603.

Jolly, G.M. (1965) Explicit estimates from capture-recapture data with both death and immigration - stochastic model, *Biometrika*, **52**, pp. 225-247.

Jolly, G.M. (1979) A unified approach to mark-recapture stochastic models exemplified by a constant survival rate model, *In* "Sampling Biological Populations", (R.M. Cormack, G.P. Patil and D.S. Robson, eds), International Co-operative Publishing House, Fairland, Maryland, pp. 277-282.

Nelder, J.A. and Wedderburn, R.W.M. Generalised linear models, *J. Roy. Statist. Soc. A*, **135**, pp. 370-384.

Otis, D.L., Burnham, K.P., White, G.C. and Anderson, D.R. (1978) Statistical inference from capture data on closed animal populations, Wildlife Monograph No. 62.

Pollock, K.H., Solomon, D.L. and Robson, D.S. (1974) Tests for mortality and recruitment in a K-sample tag-recapture experiment, *Biometrics*, **30**, pp. 77-87.

Seber, G.A.F. (1965) A note on the multiple-recapture census, *Biometrika*, **52**, 249-259.

Seber, G.A.F. (1973) The Estimation of Animal Abundance, Griffin, London.

THE STABILITY OF SITE ORDINATIONS IN ECOLOGICAL SURVEYS

R.A. Kempton

*(Statistics Department, Plant Breeding Institute,
Cambridge, England)*

1.   INTRODUCTION

While methods for modelling spatial pattern in biological
populations have primarily been developed from the point of view
of populations developing over time (Skellam, 1952), the temporal element is almost invariably missing from any statistical
analysis. This is partly due to the fact that appropriate techniques for spatio-temporal analysis are of only recent origin
(see Bennett, 1979, for a review), but also because biologists
do not always seem to appreciate the dynamic nature of the
spatial patterns they observe and fail to collect data which are
replicated in time as well as space.

The paper is concerned with the patterns of abundances in
multi-species communities occupying a range of possibly widely
dispersed environments. The summarization of these patterns to
allow an overall comparison of communities frequently involves
the multivariate techniques of ordination and classification.
However most ecological surveys are of a single year's duration
and the longer term validity of any observed association between
communities is never verified. Among plant communities, the
relative biomass of different species may show large fluctuations
from year to year even in undisturbed environments (see for
example changes in abundance of different herbage species on
unmanured plots of Park Grass, Rothamsted (Williams, 1978)).
Among animal populations Taylor and Taylor (1977) have stressed
the importance of migration in population dynamics, and found
that individual moth species show large and independent changes
in their geographical distributions throughout Great Britain
from year to year. These observations raise the question of
the stability of inter-site comparisons based on species
abundances.

We have investigated the stability of site ordinations based
on samples of moths taken in light traps operating at 14 sites
from the Rothamsted Insect Survey (Taylor, 1974) for the six
years 1969-74 (Fig. 1). The traps were all located in or close
to woodland, with the exception of site I which was situated in
the intensive agricultural environment of an arable research
station. A total of 285 000 individuals comprising 510 species
was sampled and the average number of individuals and species
caught per year at each site is shown in Table 1. Comparisons
between moth communities at the different sites were based on
the actual abundances of the species in each sample, the simple
list of species present, and finally the structure of sample
abundances disregarding species names.

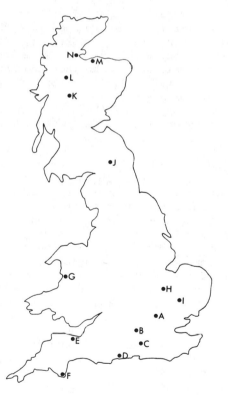

Fig. 1   Location of sites from the Rothamsted Insect Survey used
         in this study. Site names are given in Table 1.

TABLE 1

Population statistics for the 14 sites in Survey. The final two columns represent the contribution of each site to the total residual sum of squares of the individual yearly ordinations about a common centroid ordination.

Code	Site number and name	Mean Individuals	Mean Species	RSS about centroid	
				Manhattan	Jaccard
A	22 Rothamsted	7095	188	1.5	0.4
B	16 Stratfield	2560	189	1.1	0.3
C	46 Alice Holt	2957	239	0.3	0.4
D	78 Ringwood	2412	206	0.3	0.4
E	92 Nettlecombe	3913	196	0.3	0.4
F	67 Slapton Ley	2097	147	0.9	2.0
G	126 Aberystwyth	1838	172	0.4	0.5
H	94 Monks Wood	1849	151	1.4	1.0
I	88 Brooms Barn	1139	125	0.7	0.8
J	127 Kielder	6948	148	0.2	0.4
K	29 Rannoch	4827	119	0.2	0.7
L	49 Fort Augustus	3934	146	4.3	0.7
M	58 Elgin	2172	140	0.7	1.4
N	57 Ardross	3711	134	4.6	0.1
	RSS as % total sum of squares about origin			17.0	9.1

2.   COMPARISONS OF ORDINATIONS

Gower (1975) and Sibson (1978) have described the technique
of Procrustes rotation for fitting several configurations of
points in multidimensional space to a common centroid configuration.   The operations on each configuration are restricted to
translation, rotation, reflection and scaling so that the relative inter-point distances remain unchanged.   If P_{uv} represents
the position of the uth point (site) for the vth configuration
(year) after transformation and G_u is the centroid of
$P_{uv}(v = 1,2..)$,   then the sum of squared distances $\Sigma_v \Delta^2 (P_{uv}, G_u)$
represents the contribution of site u to the total residual sum
of squares, RSS $= \Sigma_u \Sigma_v \Delta^2 (P_{uv}, G_u)$, about the fitted configuration.
RSS expressed as a proportion of the total sum of squares about
the origin, can then be used as a measure of year to year consistency of the set of ordinations.

2.1   *Ordinations based on species abundances*

A standard method for obtaining an ordination of a set of n
sites classified by m variates - termed principal coordinate
analysis (Gower, 1966) - is based on an n x n symmetric matrix
with elements defining the similarity between each pair of sites.
The technique involves reducing the multi-dimensional sample to
a small number of dimensions - usually two or three principal
coordinates - which continue to reflect as far as possible the
inter-site distances.

An important aspect of this type of analysis is the suitable
choice of similarity measure.   Since differences in population
density between sites may most simply be studied by comparison
of sample sizes (Table 1), it would seem appropriate for any
measure of similarity to be based on the relative rather than
absolute species abundances.   A commonly used measure, the
Manhattan metric, defines the similarity between two communities
C and C' as

$$\phi(CC') = 1 - \Sigma |\pi_i - \pi'_i|/r,$$

where π_i, π'_i are the relative abundances of species i in communities C, C', r is the total number of species which occur in
the two communities, and the summation is over all such species.

Ordinations of the 14 sites based on the first two principal
coordinate axes are illustrated for successive years in Fig. 2.
Each ordination accounted for only 25-30% of the total variation

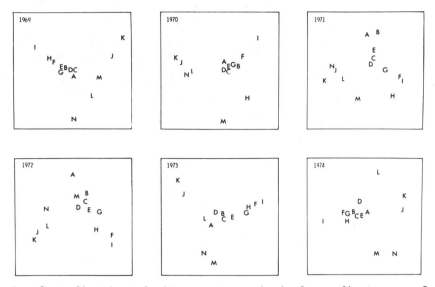

Fig. 2   Ordination of sites on two principal coordinate axes for
          each of six years using Manhattan metric similarity
          measure.

between sites, which was disappointing but perhaps not
unexpected since the sites formed a fairly heterogeneous group
and were not associated with any single dominant environmental
gradient. However, the ordinations still showed some
consistency in separating northern from southern sites, and also
sites F, H, I among the southerly group of sites; but separation
within the northern sites was inconsistent.

     Because of the complexity of the pattern, the ordinations
were extended to include the third principal axis and then compared by the rotation technique. The average of the three-
dimensional ordinations for the 6 years is shown in Fig. 3a, and
Table 1 shows the residual sums of squares of the individual
yearly site values about the fitted average value for each site.
Sites L and N are seen to contribute more than 50% of the total
residual sum of squares. This implies that these two sites
are atypical in the sense that they contribute most to the site
by year interaction, but not that their moth populations are
necessarily more temporally variable than the others. Note
that if only a common 3-dimensional ordination is required, it
is more efficient to transform the complete 13-dimensional configurations, and take the first three principal coordinate axes
of their average configuration: this ordination was found to be
very similar to Fig. 3a.

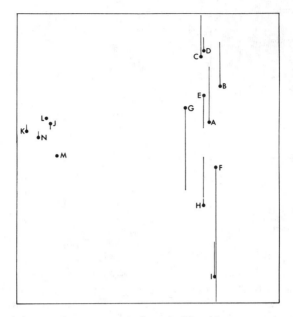

(a)   Manhattan metric similarity measure

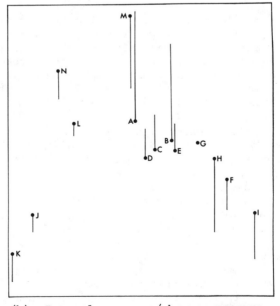

(b)   Jaccard presence/absence measure

Fig. 3   Common configuration of the three-dimensional ordinations
for the six years. The position on the third axis is
indicated by the length and direction of the vertical
line drawn from each site.

2.2 *Ordinations based on presence/absence*

   Much discussion has taken place in the literature of the
relative merits of using a measure of intra-site similarity
based on quantitative species scores compared with one based on
presence/absence information, which is often easier to collect.
On the one hand Greig-Smith (1964) has argued that "the important
difference between stands (of vegetation) lies in the amount of
different species ...... of which presence and absence are only
a crude expression", whereas Lambert and Dale (1964) hold to the
contrary view, that "in large-scale phytosociological work any
increase in information gained by using quantitative instead of
qualitative methods is likely to be extremely small".

   The presence/absence similarity measure equivalent to $\phi(CC')$
is

(number of species occurring in both communities C and C')/r,

sometimes known as Jaccard's coefficient. The average of the
three-dimensional ordinations (Fig. 3b) is seen to be somewhat
different from that using quantitative data. In contrast to
Fig. 3a the ordinations of sites on the three axes appear to be
largely independent separating respectively northern from
southern sites, sites F, H, I from the remaining southern sites,
and sites in the south-west, E, F and G from the rest. It is
notable that the northern sites are not separated on the three
principal axes. Table 1 shows that the individual yearly
ordinations based on presence/absence information are much more
consistent than those based on the Manhattan metric measure.
The separation of the northern sites based on quantitative information is not reliable.

   It might appear that the abundances contain no useful information for discriminating between sites, but this is an over-
simplication. The Manhattan similarity measure is very much
dominated by the most abundant species and these will inevitably
show greater intra-site variability on an absolute scale than
rarer species. This effect can be reduced either by standardis-
ing the absolute difference of each species by say its overall
range, or what in this author's view is preferable, applying an
initial transformation to the π_i. Using, for example, the pth

power of π_i, the Manhattan metric measure becomes more sensitive

to rare species as p → 0, with this limiting value corresponding
to the Jaccard coefficient. With p = 0.5, the overall residual
sum of squares of the individual year ordinations about the
common configuration is 6.7% of the total sum of squares, an
improvement over that achieved using presence/absence information
alone; hence the actual species abundances do contain some
reliable information.

One disadvantage in using a similarity measure that is more
sensitive to the rarer species is that it is also sensitive to
sample size. Indeed when a wider range of sample sizes occurs
than in this study, the primary axis may simply reflect differences in population density between communities. This is a
problem more commonly met in describing species abundance distributions which we consider in the following section.

3.   ORDINATION BASED ON THE STRUCTURE OF SPECIES ABUNDANCES

An alternative basis for classifying communities is the
distribution of relative abundances of the species, independent
of any reference to species names. Here the patterns are simpler
and generally allow a more efficient summarization. Solomon
(1979) has defined a partial ordering on a set of communities
which relies on the principle of majorization. Suppose two
communities, C and C', have <u>ordered</u> species abundance vectors
$(\pi_1, \pi_2, \ldots, \pi_s)$, $(\pi'_1, \pi'_2, \ldots, \pi'_s)$, where $\pi_i \geq \pi_j \geq 0$,
$\pi'_i \geq \pi'_j \geq 0$ for $i < j$, and s represents the maximum number of
species at any site. Then π' majorizes π ($\pi' > \pi$) implies
$\Sigma_{i \geq k}(\pi'_i - \pi_i) \geq 0$ for all $k = 1 \ldots s$.

Another criterion for ordering communities, proposed by Patil
and Taillie (1979), involves the operation of forward transfer of
abundance. π is defined to lead to π' by a forward transfer of
abundance if there are integers i and j, $i<j$, and quantity h,
$0 \leq h \leq \pi_i - \pi_j$, such that

$$
\pi'_k = \begin{cases}
\pi_k & \text{if } k \neq i,j \\
\pi_i - h & \text{if } k = i \\
\pi_j + h & \text{if } k = j
\end{cases}
$$

with the elements of π' reordered as necessary. Such an operation increases species richness when $\pi_j = 0$ and increases evenness when $\pi_j \neq 0$. C' is then defined to be intrinsically more
diverse than C if π leads to π' by a finite sequence of forward
transfers of abundance. It is easy to show that the two partial
orderings are equivalent, viz. that C' is intrinsically more
diverse than C if and only if $\Sigma_{i \geq k}(\pi'_i - \pi_i) \geq 0$ for all
$k = 1 \ldots s$. This latter inequality implies that for a set of
communities to be capable of an ordering the curves of <u>cumula-
tive</u> proportional abundance plotted against rank should not
intersect; plots of this kind are thus likely to be more informative in comparing species abundance vectors than the

traditional plots of species proportional abundance against
rank (see e.g. Williamson, 1973).

One disadvantage of comparing communities by their empirical
rank-cumulative size plots is that these will be affected by
sample size: the rarer species in the community will be missing
from small samples. To circumvent this problem we might charac-
terize the species abundance vector by the expected number of
species in a sub-sample of size m, $S_m = \sum_1^S \{1 - (1 - \pi_i)^m\}$, for
which unbiased estimators exist (Hurlbert, 1971; Smith and
Grassle, 1977). $S'_m \geq S_m$ for all m is a necessary condition for
$\pi' > \pi$ (Patil and Taillie, 1979) so it would seem that non-
intersection of the expected species curves forms a somewhat
weaker ordering condition than majorization.

Expected species curves were derived for the 14 study sites
for each year, using the unbiased estimator for S_m given a
sample of size N with individual species abundances
$N_1, N_2, \ldots N_s, \hat{S}_m = \sum_1^S \{1 - (N-N_i)! (N-m)!/(N-N_i-m)! N!\}$.
Values of $\hat{S}_m$ were obtained for m = 2,4,8, .. and mean values for
each site were calculated from the yearly values and standar-
dised by dividing by the overall within-site root mean square
for each m. Fig. 4 shows the standardized estimates plotted as
deviations about site A (Rothamsted) which caught the largest
samples. Two things are immediately apparent. First, for any
m there are differences in species numbers between sites and
these differences are fairly consistent from year to year,
particularly for large m. Secondly the ordering of sites is not
consistent for all m, particularly the comparisons of northern
with southern sites. The different forms of the curves are
related to the distributions of species abundances in the different communities and the different emphasis members of $\{S_m\}$ give
to different parts of the distribution. In small sub-samples,
only the most abundant species are likely to be included, and
hence the ordering of S_m for small m is most dependent on the
relative abundance of the commonest species in the community,
while for large m, S_m is more closely related to the total
species complement. Thus comparison of the species abundance
vectors for the arable site I with the woodland site A indicates
that the former is dominated by a few abundant species but
has a similar species complement to A because of its large
number of rare species. In contrast most northern sites had a
smaller species complement than A but species were distributed
more evenly and hence S_m estimates were larger in small sub-
samples. Not surprisingly, community comparisons based mainly

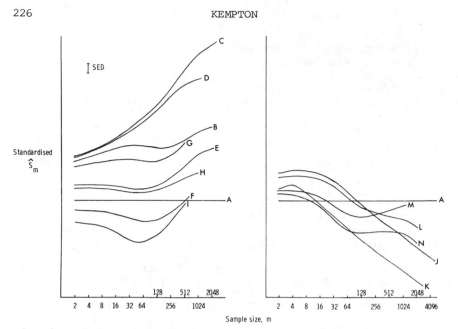

Fig. 4 Standardized expected species numbers for each site for
        different sub-sample size m. The standard error of site
        differences, SED, is obtained from the within-site sum
        of squares between years.

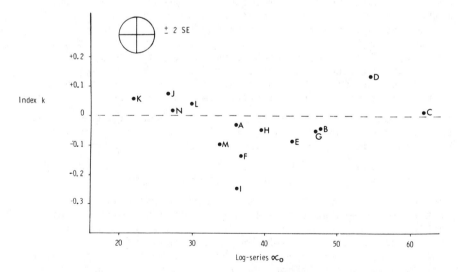

Fig. 5 Ordination of sites based on parameters of the gamma
        species abundance model.

on the small number of commonest species ($\hat{S}_m$ with m small) are less consistent from year to year than those giving greater emphasis to the full species complement.

The above argument may be neatly summarized by adopting a theoretical distribution for the species abundances and characterizing the communities by the parameter estimates.   Much theoretical development has surrounded the gamma abundance model (Engen, 1978, 1979; Engen and Taillie, 1979), which has been shown generally to give a good fit to moth data in this Survey (Kempton, 1975). For this model the probability a randomly chosen individual has abundance λ in the population

$$g(\lambda) = \frac{(\alpha/\mu)^{k+1}}{\Gamma(k+1)} \lambda^k e^{-(\alpha/\mu)\lambda}$$

where μ is the mean species density and α and k are density independent parameters. Note the function is defined for all $k \geq -1$, in contrast to the density function of the gamma distribution which is only defined for positive index k. The expected number of species in sub-sample size m is given by

$$S_m = \frac{\alpha}{k} \{1 - \frac{\Gamma(\alpha)\ \Gamma(m+\alpha-k)}{\Gamma(\alpha+m)\ \Gamma(\alpha-k)}\},$$

and a necessary and sufficient condition for $C'(\alpha', k')$ to be intrinsically more diverse than $C(\alpha, k)$ is that either $k' \geq k > 0$ and $\alpha'/k' \geq \alpha/k$ or $k' \leq k$ and $\alpha' \geq \alpha$ (Patil and Taillie, 1979). A slightly weaker condition is given by Kempton (1979) for a consistent ordering on S_m for all $m \geq 2$. For models with fixed k (e.g. $k = 0$, the log-series model) a complete ordering of the communities exists and is specified by the parameter α.

The gamma model was fitted to all site-year samples. Estimates of α and k for different years at the same site were highly correlated, and the major separation of sites was achieved by estimating $\alpha = \alpha_0$ with k set to zero - the preferred one-parameter model for species frequency data. The two-dimensional ordination of sites based on $\hat{\alpha}_0$ and $\hat{k}$ is shown in Figure 5. Once again the Scottish sites are separated on the primary axis, an example of the well documented observation that diversity decreases with latitude, but this axis also discriminates between the southern woodland sites A,B,C,D and E which formed quite a cohesive group relative to other sites from the point of view of their species lists. The distinctive form of the S_m curves for the Scottish sites is explained by the higher values of the index k, which indicates the evenness of the abundance distribution. In contrast, the intensive agricultural site I has a very low index of evenness; we find this to be characteristic of urban and other environmentally unstable sites.

4. DISCUSSION AND CONCLUSIONS

The main purpose of this paper has been to stress the importance of recognising the dynamic nature of multi-species populations, and of any ordination based on the structure of these populations. It is not concerned with accounting for the temporal changes in species abundance that do occur: this is altogether too daunting a task and requires longer term observation than the 15 years so far achieved by the Rothamsted Insect Survey. However, comparison of ordinations of a group of sites over several years does serve to identify those patterns which are of long term standing, and do not relate, for example, to the particular weather conditions experienced in one year.

Most published investigations comparing different methods of site ordination from vegetation or faunal surveys base their recommendation on how well the methods mimic known environmental gradients. If an ordination method provides the expected result it is accepted - if not it is discarded. This leads to the criticism that the methods only assert the obvious. The current suggestion of using temporal consistency as a criterion is more objective: if an unexpected ordination is repeated year after year it might shed new light on the working of the ecosystem.

May (1976) points to many examples "where the world appears chaotic and vagarious at the level of individual species but nonetheless constant and predictable at the level of community organisation". This suggests that an ordination of the multi-species communities at different sites, whether based on an overall species similarity measure or the structure of species abundance, may be more stable than comparisons based on the individual component species, or a divisive ordination method based on a small group of indicator species (Hill, Bunce and Shaw, 1975).

5. ACKNOWLEDGEMENT

I am grateful to Dr. L.R. Taylor for allowing the use of data from the Rothamsted Insect Survey in this study.

6. REFERENCES

Bennett, R.J. (1979) Spatial time series, Pion, London.

Engen, S. (1978) Stochastic Abundance Models, Chapman Hall, London.

Engen, S. (1979) Abundance models: sampling and estimation, *In* "Statistical Distributions in Ecological Work", (J.K. Ord, G.P. Patil and C. Taillie, eds), International Co-operative Publishing House, Fairland, Maryland, pp. 313-332.

Engen, S. and Taillie, C. (1979) A basic development of abundance models: community description, *In* "Statistical Distributions in Ecological Work", (J.K. Ord, G.P. Patil and C. Taillie, eds), International Co-operative Publishing House, Fairland, Maryland, pp. 289-312.

Gower, J.C. (1966) Some distance properties of latent root and vector methods used in multivariate analysis, *Biometrika,* **53**, pp. 325-338.

Gower, J.C. (1975) Generalized Procrustes analysis, *Psychometrika,* **40**, pp. 33-51.

Greig-Smith, P. (1964) Quantitative Plant Ecology, 2nd ed., Butterworth, London.

Hill, M.O., Bunce, R.G.H. and Shaw, M.W. (1975) Indicator species analysis, a divisive polythetic method of classification, and its application to a survey of native pinewoods in Scotland, *Journal of Ecology,* **63**, pp. 597-613.

Hurlbert, S.H. (1971) The non-concept of species diversity: a critique and alternative parameters, *Ecology,* **52**, pp. 577-586.

Kempton, R.A. (1975) A generalized form of Fisher's logarithmic series, *Biometrika,* **62**, pp. 29-38.

Kempton, R.A. (1979) The structure of species abundance and the measurement of diversity, *Biometrics,* **35**, pp. 307-321.

Lambert, J.M. and Dale, M.B. (1964) The use of statistics in phytosociology, *Advance in Ecological Research,* **2**, pp. 59-100.

May, R.M. (1976) Patterns in multi-species communities, *In* "Theoretical Ecology", (R.M. May, ed.), Blackwell, Oxford, pp. 142-162.

Patil, G.P. and Taillie, C. (1979) An overview of diversity, *In* "Ecological Diversity in Theory and Practice", (J.F. Grassle, G.P. Patil, W.K. Smith and C. Taillie, eds), International Co-operative Publishing House, Fairland, Maryland, pp. 3-28.

Sibson, R. (1978) Studies in the robustness of multidimensional scaling, *Journal of the Royal Statistical Society,* **40**, pp. 234-238.

Skellam, J.G. (1952) Studies in statistical ecology, (I) Spatial pattern, *Biometrika,* **39**, pp. 246-362.

Smith, W. and Grassle, J.F. (1977) Sampling properties of a family of diversity indices, *Biometrics,* **33**, pp. 283-292.

Solomon, D.L. (1979) A comparative approach to species diversity, *In* "Ecological Diversity in Theory and Practice", (J.F. Grassle, G.P. Patil, W.K. Smith and C. Taillie, eds), International Co-operative Publishing House, Fairland, Maryland, pp. 29-36.

Taylor, L.R. (1974) Monitoring change in the distribution and abundance of insects, Report of the Rothamsted Experimental Station for 1973, Part 2, pp. 202-239.

Taylor, L.R. and Taylor, R.A.J. (1977) Aggregation, migration and population mechanics, *Nature,* **265**, pp. 415-421.

Williams, E.D. (1978) Botanical composition of the Park Grass Plots at Rothamsted, 1856-1976, Rothamsted Experimental Station, Harpenden.

Williamson, M. (1973) Species diversity in ecological communities, *In* "The Mathematical Theory of the Dynamics of Biological Populations", (M.S. Bartlett and R.W. Hiorns, eds), Academic Press, London, pp. 325-335.

A MARKOV CHAIN MODEL OF PLANT SUCCESSION

D. Cooke

*(School of Mathematical and Physical Sciences,
University of Sussex, Brighton, England)*

1. INTRODUCTION

Plant succession may be defined as the process of change in
vegetation. Although succession has been, and remains, a
subject of lively debate, commonly held ideas are that vegetation passes through stages to a state of equilibrium, or
relative equilibrium, called a climax, and that varying initial
stages tend to the same climax. Markov chain models can exhibit
similar behaviour. It is therefore tempting to try to use these
models to describe and analyse succession.

In this paper I begin with a brief review of the use that has
been made of Markov chain models to describe plant succession
and then describe in detail a Markov model based on plant-by-
plant replacement. This model assumes that an area of land may
be divided into sites, each occupied by a single plant. The
state of a site is the species occupying the site. Over time,
as plant replaces plant, the state of each site changes and the
assumption is that this process is a Markov chain with stationary transition probabilities. If the individual sites cannot
be observed, their behaviour may be inferred from the percentage
of sites in each state at regular time intervals. A least
squares method of deriving estimates of the transition probabilities from this type of data is given.

Estimates of transition probabilities are found from herbaceous data of percentage cover on plots where the dominant
species is Festuca ovina. Six states are used in the model.
The model has some success but is not entirely satisfactory;
nonetheless it would make a good starting point for a better
model. Some simple forms that the transition matrix might take
are proposed.

2. SELECTIVE REVIEW OF PREVIOUS WORK

The major step in setting up a Markov chain model is the definition of states. Two main approaches have been used in plant succession studies: in one, individual communities are taken as units; in the other, plants are taken as units. The two approaches may be illustrated by examples.

Williams et al., (1969) worked in a tropical rain forest. They cleared ten sites in the forest and recorded the presence and absence of more than a hundred species on twelve occasions. The 120 (i.e. 10 sites × 12 occasions) records were classified into seven states labelled A to G. Thus the states corresponded to communities of differing composition. The records of each site were interpreted as specifying a sequence of states (e.g. AABCCC...) through which the site passed. By counting the frequency with which one state followed another, the transition probabilities of the chain were estimated.

Another example of specifying states by community properties is the investigation of Waggoner and Stephens (1970). Their units were tracts of forests and they defined five states (maple, oak, birch, other major species, minor species) according to which species had most stems on a tract. They made a test of the model in the following way. The transition matrices A for 1927-37 and B for 1927-67 were estimated from observed transitions. The authors argued that if a stationary Markov chain were being followed over the 40 - year period 1927-67 then the A matrix raised to the fourth power should equal the B matrix. They found that the two matrices, A^4 and B, were broadly similar except for transitions involving Oak.

Horn (1975a and 1975b) investigated succession in a temperate deciduous forest. He considered the forest as being, to use his own words, a honeycomb of independent cells, each occupied by a tree, and that all trees were replaced synchronously by a new generation that rose from their understory. Thus an area of land occupied by a single tree formed a unit; the species of the tree determined the state of the unit. Horn defined eleven states (including red maple, grey birch, red oak and sweet gum) according to the species present. He used an interesting method of estimating transition probabilities: he assumed that the probability that a given species would be replaced by another given species was proportional to the number of saplings of the latter in the understory of the former. He determined the equilibrium vector from the matrix of estimated transition probabilities and compared it with the proportion of each species in a long-established and undisturbed forest. He found a broad agreement between the two sets of proportions.

Both the main approaches to defining states allow us to model
a climax - either as an absorbing state (community level) or as
an equilibrium composition (plant level) - and to model the
arrival of new species and the extinction of species. The
attraction of the definition at the plant level, i.e. the use of
a plant-by-plant replacement model, is that, if it is true, one
can argue from the life-history of individual plants to the
behaviour of the whole community. The method of reproduction of
species, the length of life and the interactions with other
species will imply certain transition probabilities which will
in turn imply certain types of community behaviour. Also, as
will be shown in this paper, records of community behaviour
allow the estimation of transition probabilities and hence give
information on the behaviour of individual species.

Trees have been the favourite type of organism to which
Markov chain models have been applied, as will be seen from the
references above. But the time scale is long; a reasonable time
interval for a transition is many decades. Thus it is difficult
to collect data on such systems and there are not enough data to
make really critical tests of the model. In this paper I consider the application of the Markov model to communities of
herbaceous plants. Data on the species composition of a herbaceous community at regular intervals of a year, say, are relatively easy to collect though observation of the transitions of
individual small areas would be very time-consuming.

Van Hulst (1979) has written about Markov chains as models of
succession. He considered, in particular, statistical methods
of testing the assumptions of the model when data are available
on the transitions made by individual units. He commented that
appropriate data were hard to find.

Some authors (e.g. Bledsoe and Van Dyne, 1971, and Shugart et
al., 1973) have used compartmental and differential equation
models for succession. These are closely related to the Markov
chain models considered in this paper.

3. A MODEL OF PLANT-BY-PLANT REPLACEMENT

Assume that an area of land is divided into a large number of
sites each of which is occupied by a single plant. If a site is
occupied by a plant of species i we shall say that the site is
in State i. We imagine that each site is observed after a fixed
interval (e.g. a year), when the same plant may be occupying the
site or the plant may be replaced by another plant. If the
species of the plant occupying a site is unchanged we say that
the site is in the same state; otherwise we say the state has
changed. Thus, over a period of time, as plant replaces plant,

each site will make transitions between states. We may therefore consider each site as changing according to a Markov chain.

Let the probability that a site be in State i in year t be
$p_i(t)$ where i may equal 1,2, ...,k corresponding to the k distinct states (species) that are recognised. Also assume that
there is a fixed probability p_{ij} that a site which is in State
i one year will be in State j (where j = 1,2,...,k) in the
following year. We may then relate the probability that a site
is in a given state in year t to the probability that it was in
any of the states in year t - 1 by the equations:

$$p_1(t) = p_{11} p_1(t-1) + p_{21} p_2(t-1) + \ldots + p_{k1} p_k(t-1)$$

$$p_2(t) = p_{12} p_1(t-1) + p_{22} p_2(t-1) + \ldots + p_{k2} p_k(t-1)$$

$$\cdots \cdots \cdots \cdots \cdots$$

$$p_k(t) = p_{1k} p_1(t-1) + p_{2k} p_2(t-1) + \ldots + p_{kk} p_k(t-1).$$

We denote the (column) vector of probabilities at time t by
$\underline{p}(t)$, and the matrix of transition probabilities by

$$\underline{P} = \begin{bmatrix} p_{11} & p_{12} & \cdots & p_{1k} \\ p_{21} & p_{22} & \cdots & p_{2k} \\ \cdots & \cdots & \cdots & \cdots \\ p_{k1} & p_{k2} & \cdots & p_{kk} \end{bmatrix}$$

The system of equations may be summarised by the matrix equation

$$\underline{p}(t) = \underline{P}^T \underline{p}(t-1),$$

where the index T denotes a transpose. Alternatively, the
equation may be written

$$\underline{p}^T(t) = \underline{p}^T(t-1) \underline{P}.$$

If individual sites can be observed the transitions can be
counted and the transition probabilities estimated directly.
But if, as is likely to be the case with herbaceous data, only

overall behaviour can be observed, then the estimation problem
is more complex. A method of estimation is proposed in the next
section.

4. THE ESTIMATION OF TRANSITION PROBABILITIES FROM AGGREGATE DATA

Consider a system, or large collection, of units each of which
is changing independently according to a given Markov process.
The *proportion* of units in State i at time t is $n_i(t)$. The state
of the system as a whole is described by the vector of proportions
$(n_1(t), n_2(t), \ldots, n_k(t))$, assuming each chain has k possible
states. This vector is known at a number of times, and perhaps
for a number of systems, but there is no information on the
sequence of states through which individual units pass. In this
situation it is said that one has aggregate data, or information,
on the chain.

Two types of data may be distinguished: (a) time series data,
when there is information on a single system for a regular
sequence of times, (b) replicate data, when there is information
at only two successive times for many replicate systems; there
may be data which combine these two extreme situations.

Time Series Data

The data are the proportions in each of k states on T + 1
recording times spaced at equal intervals. They may be set out
in a table:

Time	0	$n_1(0)$	$n_2(0)$	$\ldots$	$n_k(0)$
	1	$n_1(1)$	$n_2(1)$	$\ldots$	$n_k(1)$
		$\ldots$	$\ldots$	$\ldots$	$\ldots$
	t-1	$n_1(t-1)$	$n_2(t-1)$	$\ldots$	$n_k(t-1)$
	t	$n_1(t)$	$n_2(t)$	$\ldots$	$n_k(t)$
		$\ldots$	$\ldots$	$\ldots$	$\ldots$
	T	$n_1(T)$	$n_2(T)$	$\ldots$	$n_k(T)$

In the Markov chain model the probability that a unit makes a
transition from State i to State j is p_{ij} (i,j = 1,2,...,k).

If we consider the proportions in the states to be fixed at time
t - 1 then, conditional on this situation, the Markov chain
model allows us to write:

$$E[n_i(t)] = p_{1i} \, n_1(t-1) + p_{2i} \, n_2(t-1) + \ldots + p_{ki} \, n_k(t-1) \quad .$$

Writing similar equations for all possible times, we obtain the
matrix equation:

$$E \begin{bmatrix} n_i(1) \\ n_i(2) \\ \vdots \\ n_i(T) \end{bmatrix} = \begin{bmatrix} n_1(0) & n_2(0) & \ldots & n_k(0) \\ n_1(1) & n_2(1) & \ldots & n_k(1) \\ & & \\ n_1(T-1) & n_2(T-1) & \ldots & n_k(T-1) \end{bmatrix} \begin{bmatrix} p_{1i} \\ p_{2i} \\ \vdots \\ p_{ki} \end{bmatrix}$$

which may be written as

$$E[\underline{y}_i] = \underline{X} \, \underline{p}_i \quad . \tag{4.1}$$

There are similar matrix equations for all values of i. Note
that the $\underline{X}$ matrix is identical in all these equations.

Replicate data

Let the proportion in State i at time 0 on Replicate A be
$n_{iA}(0)$. Using a notation of this form the data may be set out
in a table as follows:

Replicate	Proportion at time 0	Proportion at time 1
A	$n_{1A}(0) \; n_{2A}(0) \; \ldots \; n_{kA}(0)$	$n_{1A}(1) \; n_{2A}(1) \; \ldots \; n_{kA}(1)$
B	$n_{1B}(0) \; n_{2B}(0) \; \ldots \; n_{kB}(0)$	$n_{1B}(1) \; n_{2B}(1) \; \ldots \; n_{kB}(1)$
. . . .		
R	$n_{1R}(0) \; n_{2R}(0) \; \ldots \; n_{kR}(0)$	$n_{1R}(1) \; n_{2R}(1) \; \ldots \; n_{kR}(1)$

From the Markov chain model, in a similar way to that shown
above, we obtain the matrix equation

$$
\begin{bmatrix} n_{iA}(1) \\ n_{iB}(1) \\ \vdots \\ n_{iR}(i) \end{bmatrix} = \begin{bmatrix} n_{1A}(0) & n_{2A}(0) & \cdots & n_{kA}(0) \\ n_{1B}(0) & n_{2B}(0) & \cdots & n_{kB}(0) \\ \cdot & \cdot & \cdots & \cdot \\ n_{1R}(0) & n_{2R}(0) & \cdots & n_{kR}(0) \end{bmatrix} \begin{bmatrix} p_{1i} \\ p_{2i} \\ \vdots \\ p_{ki} \end{bmatrix}
$$

which, with a slight modification in the interpretation of the symbols, may be written in a matrix equation of the same form as in equation (4.1):

$$
E\,[\underline{y}_i] = \underline{X}\,\underline{p}_i \quad .
$$

Unconstrained least squares solution

An alternative way of writing equation (4.1) that makes the random disturbance explicit is

$$
\underline{y}_i = \underline{X}\,\underline{p}_i + \underline{u}_i \tag{4.2}
$$

where $\underline{u}_i$ is assumed to be a random disturbance vector such that $E[\underline{u}_i] = 0$ and $E[\underline{u}_i \underline{u}_i^{T}] = \sigma^2\,I$, where I is the indentity matrix. This is the specification of a conventional linear statistical model. Using least squares we obtain the estimation equations

$$
\underline{X}^T \underline{X}\,\underline{\hat{p}}_i = \underline{X}^T \underline{y}_i \quad . \tag{4.3}
$$

If we write $\underline{P}$ for the matrix $[\underline{p}_1,\ \underline{p}_2,\ \ldots,\ \underline{p}_k]$ with the vectors $\underline{p}_i$ for columns, and $\underline{Y}$ for the similar matrix $[\underline{y}_1, \underline{y}_2,\ \ldots,\ \underline{y}_k]$, the estimation equation may be summarised succinctly in the matrix equation:

$$
\underline{X}^T \underline{X}\,\underline{\hat{P}} = \underline{X}^T \underline{Y} \quad . \tag{4.4}
$$

The transition probabilities of a Markov chain are subject to the following contraints:

(i) $0 \le p_{ij} \le 1$ for all i, j ;

(ii) $\sum_j p_{ij} = 1$ for all i.

We wish the estimates $\hat{p}_{ij}$ to satisfy these constraints. It can be shown that the estimates $\hat{\underline{P}}$ obtained from equation (4.4) automatically satisfy the equality constraints (ii) but do not necessarily satisfy the inequality constraints (i). My experience with plant data suggests the inequality constraints are rarely satisfied; therefore it is necessary to introduce the constraints into the estimation procedure.

Constrained least squares

T.C. Lee et al., (1970) discuss the problem of estimating Markov transition probabilities from aggregate data. They recommend treating the constrained least squares problem as a quadratic programming problem in which one seeks to minimise

$$\sum_i (\underline{y}_i - \underline{X}\,\underline{p}_i)^T \,(\underline{y}_i - \underline{X}\,\underline{p}_i) ,$$

or a similar expression which includes weights, subject to the equality and inequality contstraints on the p_{ij}. I have preferred to adopt an alternative approach.

I have used a method of introducing prior information into a linear model. The idea appears to date from Theil, H. (1961). We consider the p_{ij} as having prior distributions. The statement that $0 \leq p_{ij} \leq 1$ is implied if we state that p_{ij} has a uniform distribution on $(0,1)$. This in turn is equivalent to the statement

$$\tfrac{1}{2} = p_{ij} + v \tag{4.5}$$

where v is a random variable with a uniform distribution on $(-\tfrac{1}{2},\tfrac{1}{2})$; let us write $V[v] = \sigma_1^2$. We can write k^2 equations similar to (4.5) corresponding to all values of i and j.

Equations of the form (4.2) and (4.5), when assembled, specify a linear statistical model which may be summarised in the matrix equation:

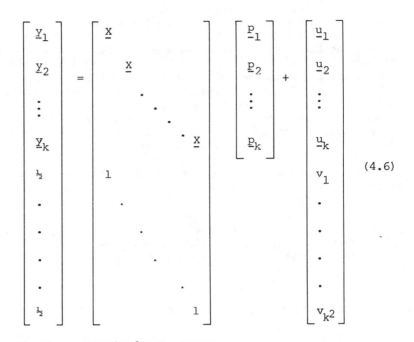

$$\begin{bmatrix} \underline{y}_1 \\ \underline{y}_2 \\ \vdots \\ \underline{y}_k \\ \tfrac{1}{2} \\ \cdot \\ \cdot \\ \cdot \\ \cdot \\ \tfrac{1}{2} \end{bmatrix} = \begin{bmatrix} \underline{x} \\ & \underline{x} \\ & & \ddots \\ & & & \underline{x} \\ 1 \\ & 1 \\ & & \ddots \\ & & & 1 \end{bmatrix} \begin{bmatrix} \underline{p}_1 \\ \underline{p}_2 \\ \vdots \\ \underline{p}_k \end{bmatrix} + \begin{bmatrix} \underline{u}_1 \\ \underline{u}_2 \\ \vdots \\ \underline{u}_k \\ v_1 \\ \cdot \\ \cdot \\ \cdot \\ v_{k^2} \end{bmatrix} \qquad (4.6)$$

Gaps in the large matrix denote zeros.

We treat the disturbance terms in the equations involving observations as independent and of variance σ^2. In fact the observations are proportions and would not have constant variance; the method given here may be refined by introducing weights in the least squares procedure, though experience so far suggests the improvement would not be great. The disturbance terms in the equations introducing the prior information we treat as independent and of variance σ_1^2. When minimising the sum of squares of residuals, weights of unity are used for expressions involving observations and weights of c (= σ^2/σ_1^2) are used for expressions deriving from prior information. The equality constraints are introduced by the use of Lagrangian multipliers, to give the following matrix equation for the estimates:

$$(\underline{x}^T \underline{x} + k\,\underline{I})\,\hat{\underline{P}} = \underline{x}^T \underline{y} + (c/r)\,\underline{1}\underline{1}^T , \qquad (4.7)$$

where $\underline{I}$ is the identity matrix and $\underline{1}$ denotes a vector whose elements all equal unity.

Since σ^2 is unknown, c is unknown. I have therefore used the
following procedure. Initially c is set equal to zero; (4.7)
then gives the ordinary least squares result. Usually some of
the estimates are out of range so c is increased by steps of
0.01 until the estimates of all the probabilities are within
range. When this happens the estimation procedure is stopped
unless any estimates are changing substantially at each iteration, in which case c is stepped on until the estimates change
only slightly from one iteration to the next. These estimates
closely resemble 'ridge regression' estimates.

I give an example based on artificially generated data to
illustrate the results of the method. Transition probabilities
were chosen for a system with one hundred units and three states.
The process was simulated and the proportion of units in each
state was found at each of twelve times. The estimates of the
probabilities, when unconstrained least squares was used, were
the following (the true transition probabilities are given in
brackets):

	A	B	C
A	.08 (.10)	1.10 (.80)	-.18 (.10)
B	.18 (.20)	.43 (.50)	.39 (.30)
C	.01 (0)	.08 (.10)	.91 (.90)

Using weighted least squares, with prior information, the estimates were:

	A	B	C
A	.16 (.10)	.82 (.80)	.02 (.10)
B	.16 (.20)	.51 (.50)	.33 (.30)
C	.02 (0)	.08 (.10)	.90 (.90)

5. FITTING MODEL TO DATA ON HERBACEOUS PLANTS

I obtained data from the research station of the Institute of
Terrestrial Ecology at Bangor, Wales. In a sheep grazing
experiment, supervised by Professor R.E. Hughes with the assist-
ance of Dr. J. Dale, certain of the plots were enclosed to pre-
vent grazing taking place. One site was at Crib Goch in
Snowdonia, and the data to be analysed are from the four ungrazed
plots at this site. Each summer, one hundred point quadrats were
selected at random from each plot and the species present at

each point were recorded. The percentage cover of each species
on each plot was determined. The experiment was first recorded
in 1960; annual recording continued until 1972.

The record from each point quadrat may be, and usually is, of
more than one species. One cannot therefore associate the sites
described in the model above with a particular piece of ground,
as one might if only one species was recorded from each quadrat.
I have assumed that, as the model requires, there exist a large
and fixed number of plant sites in each plot, even though it is
impossible to observe directly any one of them. I have taken
the percentage cover of species i, c_i, as proportional to the
number of sites occupied by species i. Hence the relative percentage cover $c_i/\Sigma c_i$ has been taken as the proportion of sites
occupied by species i.

The number of species that were observed on each plot exceeded
twenty. Some grouping of species is necessary if reasonable
estimates of the transition probabilities are to be obtained.
This may be appreciated when it is pointed out that if 20 states
are used there are 400 transition probabilities to estimate.
The species on the plots were divided into the following groups:

     (1)   F,   Festuca ovina;

     (2)   A,   Agrostis tenuis;

     (3)   E,   Ericaceous plants (Erica tetralix, E.cinerea,
                  Calluna vulgaris, Vaccinium myrtillus);

     (4)   G,   Galium saxatile;

     (5)   P,   Polytrichum spp. (P. communa, P. juniperum,
                  P. piliferum);

     (6)   R,   Remaining species.

The relative percentage cover of each of the six "species" was
found for each of the four blocks for each year. The mean values
over blocks for each year were found and were used as the basic
data of an analysis to determine estimates of the transition
probabilities.

TABLE I

Least square predictions (pre.) of each year's values from the
preceeding year's, together with observed values (ob.) and
residuals (res.).

	F			A			E		
	ob.	pre.	res.	ob.	pre.	res.	ob.	pre.	res.
1960	41.8			15.4			1.5		
61	39.9	39.6	0.3	20.3	18.8	1.4	0.6	5.5	-4.9
62	38.5	39.8	-1.3	29.1	20.3	8.8	0.7	5.2	-4.5
63	41.2	39.9	1.2	20.1	21.1	-0.9	3.0	5.2	-2.2
64	40.5	39.7	0.8	21.7	19.8	1.9	4.2	6.0	-1.7
65	40.2	39.5	0.6	28.9	19.8	9.1	5.4	6.1	-0.7
66	41.1	40.0	1.1	21.8	20.3	1.5	6.0	5.7	0.3
67	39.3	39.6	-0.3	12.9	19.3	-6.4	11.1	6.0	5.1
68	35.5	38.0	-2.5	18.4	17.2	1.2	5.9	7.7	-1.9
69	40.7	38.0	2.7	13.4	18.8	-5.4	8.2	6.8	1.5
1970	39.6	38.5	1.1	10.8	17.5	-6.8	8.9	7.2	1.7
71	39.8	38.1	1.7	12.9	17.6	-4.7	12.9	7.6	5.3

	G			P			R		
	ob.	pre.	res.	ob.	pre.	res.	ob.	pre.	res.
1960	17.9			5.3			18.1		
61	11.6	11.5	0.1	4.8	7.6	-2.9	22.8	16.8	6.0
62	11.6	11.6	0.1	8.7	7.8	0.9	11.3	15.3	-4.0
63	9.6	11.4	-1.8	9.9	7.8	2.1	16.2	14.6	1.6
64	9.2	11.4	-2.2	9.9	7.9	2.0	14.5	15.3	-0.8
65	11.7	11.5	0.2	5.5	8.0	-2.5	8.4	15.2	-6.8
66	12.4	11.5	0.9	5.0	7.5	-2.5	13.7	15.1	-1.4
67	12.3	11.6	0.7	7.4	7.7	-0.3	17.0	15.8	1.2
68	13.1	12.0	1.1	7.5	8.3	-0.8	19.6	16.7	2.9
69	14.7	12.0	2.6	8.5	6.7	1.8	14.4	15.8	-1.4
1970	9.9	11.7	-1.9	9.5	8.1	1.4	21.4	17.0	4.5
71	10.9	11.9	-1.0	9.0	8.5	0.5	14.5	16.3	-1.8

The estimates found, with c = 0.06, were:

	F	A	E	G	P	R
F	.52	.19	.02	.07	.02	.18
A	.37	.31	.04	.13	.10	.05
E	.20	.01	.27	.18	.14	.20
G	.28	.09	.08	.16	.10	.29
P	.26	.15	.16	.13	.16	.14
R	.30	.20	.09	.15	.14	.12

Using these estimates, predicted values were calculated for each data point. For example, the predicted value of F in 1962 was determined from the observed percentage values for the species in 1961 and the estimated probabilities for transitions from each species to species F. The observed and predicted values and their differences, the residuals, are listed in Table I.

The fit for the species labelled F, G, P, as demonstrated by Table I, may be regarded as satisfactory. With species A we see many large residuals (e.g. 8.8, 9.1, -6.8) while with species E the values of the residuals show a marked systematic shift over time from negative values to positive values. The introduction of probabilities that change with time, perhaps through density-dependence, would improve the fit with E; a similar introduction should improve the fit of A, though not all irregularities are likely to be removed in this way. The R category is associated with some large residuals but this is to be expected with this heterogeneous category.

An alternative method of assessing the model is to predict the mean percentages of each species each year and compare them with the observed percentages shown in Table I. We begin with the 1960 observed percentages and then, by using the estimated transition matrix to act on these and successively determined values, we generate the percentages for each year. Note that, except for 1960, these are mean values and observed values would fluctuate about them.

	F	A	E	G	P	R
1960	41.8	15.4	1.5	17.9	5.3	18.1
61	39.5	18.8	5.5	11.6	7.7	16.9
62	38.9	19.1	6.4	11.7	8.1	15.8
63	38.7	18.9	6.7	11.7	8.1	15.8
64	38.6	18.8	6.7	11.8	8.2	15.9
65	38.6	18.8	6.8	11.8	8.2	15.9
EQUIL.	38.6	18.8	6.8	11.8	8.2	15.9

Reaction is quick; within two years, values are close to the equilibrium values. (The second largest eigenvalue of the esti-mated transition matrix is 0.37.) The model fits well the data for F, for G (the rapid observed change from 17.9% in 1960 to 11.6% in 1961 and approximate constancy from then on is well mimicked), and the fit for P is reasonable. The mean values for A show an initial rise but their later decrease is much less than that of the observed values; the mean values for E show a more rapid rise than that observed and also do not continue to increase over time.

6. FORM OF THE TRANSITION MATRIX

It is useful to establish forms that the transition matrix might take in simple situations. We shall assume we are con-sidering four species A, B, C, D.

Suppose we are considering annual plants and that each site becomes vacant each year and is then occupied by another plant. Suppose also that there are fixed probabilities a, b, c, d that the species A, B, C, D, respectively, will occupy a vacant site. The transition matrix then takes the form

$$
\begin{bmatrix}
a & b & c & d \\
a & b & c & d \\
a & b & c & d \\
a & b & c & d
\end{bmatrix}
$$

Note that $a + b + c + d = 1$.

This supposition is too simple if there are perennial plants. We must allow for a plant to continue to occupy its site. Let us consider a site occupied by a plant of species A. We suppose the probability that the site is occupied by the same *plant* in the following year is α, and hence there is a probability $(1 - \alpha)$ that the site is occupied by another plant. In the latter case, we assume that the probability that the plant is replaced by one of the species A, B, C or D is a, b, c or d, respectively. The model may be summarised by a diagram:

Time t - 1   Time t

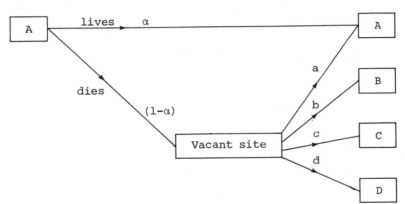

The probability of the transition A - A is $\alpha + (1 - \alpha)a$, of the transition A - B, $b(1 - \alpha)$, etc. Define probabilities similar to α for other species B, C, D and call them β, γ, δ, respectively. Note that $\alpha + \beta + \gamma + \delta$ is not necessarily equal to unity although $a + b + c + d = 1$ as before. Possible names for α, β, γ, δ are persistence parameters and for a, b, c, d replacement parameters.

The form of the transition matrix in this case is:

$$
\begin{bmatrix}
\alpha + (1-\alpha)a & (1-\alpha)b & (1-\alpha)c & (1-\alpha)d \\
(1-\beta)a & \beta + (1-\beta)b & (1-\beta)c & (1-\beta)d \\
(1-\gamma)a & (1-\gamma)b & \gamma + (1-\gamma)c & (1-\gamma)d \\
(1-\delta)a & (1-\delta)b & (1-\delta)c & \delta + (1-\delta)d
\end{bmatrix}
$$

The equilibrium vector for this chain is

$$[a/1-\alpha, \qquad b/1-\beta, \qquad c/1-\gamma, \qquad d/1-\delta] \quad .$$

If ℓ_i (where i = A, B, C, D) is the average lifetime for a plant of species i, then, provided $\ell_i > 1$, the equilibrium vector takes the form:

$$[a\ell_A, \qquad b\ell_B, \qquad c\ell_C, \qquad d\ell_D] \quad .$$

(This follows from the fact that $\alpha = 1 - 1/\ell_A$, etc.)

As an illustration of the type of information that might be obtained from this approach, the probability parameters were estimated from the estimated transition matrix of Section 5. The parameter estimates were:

	Persistence (α, etc.)	Replacement (a, etc.)
F	.31	.29
A	.12	.15
E	.09	.11
G	O	.15
P	.02	.12
R	O	.18

7. CONCLUSIONS

By fitting a Markov chain model to annual values of the relative amounts of a number of species, I have been able to make a more stringent test of this type of model for plant succession than has previously been done. It is not surprising that such a simple model does not give a perfect fit. But the model is sufficiently successful to make it a good starting point for finding a better model. Moreover, the plant-by-plant replacement form of the model that I have used is a particularly attractive experimental tool in that it offers the possibility of relating the behaviour of individual plant species to the behaviour of the whole plant community.

8. ACKNOWLEDGEMENTS

I would like to thank Mr. J.N.R. Jeffers, Director of the Institute of Terrestrial Ecology, for suggesting this problem to

me. I would also like to thank Professor R.E. Hughes and
Dr. J. Dale, also of the Institute of Terrestial Ecology, for
making available their data to me.

9. REFERENCES

Bledsoe, L.J. and Van Dyne, G.M. (1971) A compartment model
simulation of secondary succession, *In* "Systems Analysis and
Simulation in Ecology", (B.C. Patten, ed.), Academic Press,
London.

Horn, H.S. (1975a) Forest succession, *Scientific American*, **232**,
pp. 90-98.

Horn, H.S. (1975b) Markovian properties of forest succession,
In "Ecology and Evolution of Communities", (M.L. Cody and J.M.
Diamond, eds), Belknap Press of Harvard University Press,
Cambridge, Mass.

Lee, T.C., Judge, G.G. and Zellner, A. (1970) Estimating the
Parameters of the Markov Probability Model from Aggregate Time
Series Data, North-Holland Publishing Company, Amsterdam.

Shugart, H.H., Crow, T.R. and Hett, J.M. (1973) Forest succession
models: a rationale and methodology for modelling forest
succession over large regions, *Forest Science*, **19**, pp. 203-212.

Theil, H. (1961) On the use of incomplete prior information in
regression analysis, *Journal of the American Statistical
Association*, **58**, pp. 401-414.

Van Hulst, R. (1979) On the dynamics of vegetation: Markov
chains as models of succession, *Vegetatio*, **40**, pp. 3-14.

Waggoner, P.E. and Stephens, G.R. (1970) Transition probabilities
for a forest, *Nature*, **225**, pp. 1160-1161.

Williams, W.T., Lance, G.N., Webb, L.J., Tracey, J.G. and Dale,
M.B. (1969) Studies in the numerical analysis of complex rain-
forest communities. III. The analysis of successional data,
Journal of Ecology, **57**, pp. 515-535.

POPULATION STRUCTURE AND GENE EXTINCTION

E.A. Thompson

*(Statistical Laboratory, University of Cambridge,
Cambridge, England)*

1. INTRODUCTION

1.1 Components of population structure

In interpreting data observed on natural populations, it is important to assess the possible effects of population structure. Conversely it is desirable to characterise the historical structure in terms of its effects on the genetic constitution of a population. Since the major effect is on the distribution of times of gene survival, and on the within-population variability, we shall assess structure in terms of its effect on the joint survival of ancestral genes.

By "structure" we shall mean any factor which causes a population to deviate from the population geneticists' ideal of an infinite pool of randomly uniting gametes. These include finiteness of population size, and the fact that in practice population sizes are often small, and not constant. Further, gametes are packaged in diploid organisms, and even for hermaphrodite species selfing is normally precluded. Finally, individuals do not mate at random; sex ratios may be distorted, populations are geographically subdivided, individuals arise in families having some family-size distribution, and in human populations there are prohibitions and preferences in marriage based upon genealogical relationships.

1.2 Haploid population models

The effects of a complex mating structure have been considered by Thompson (1979), and Thompson (1981) has analysed the effects of diploid monogamous family-size distributions. More fundamental than these are the aspects we shall consider in the present paper; structural effects within a haploid population. Even in this simple case there are effects of varying population size and differential reproduction, which must be assessed in order to provide a hierarchical partition of the structural

causes of within-population variability. Such haploid models
may be analysed within the framework of the conditioned-
branching-processes of Karlin (1968) and Felsenstein (1971).
We shall use this theory in considering population size effects.
Although it could also be used to illustrate effects of different offspring distributions, a simpler procedure is to introduce a multivariate Polya-urn model inducing symmetric correlations in the identity of parents.

The basis of the haploid conditioned-branching-process models
is a pool of N equivalent exchangeable genes. The next generation is formed by generating offspring independently from each
individual, according to the offspring generating function f(s),
but conditioning the total number produced to be N*. Thus the
probability that a particular set of k genes ($1 \leq k \leq N$) has j
replicates in the next generation is

$$P_{kj} = \frac{\text{coeff. of } s_1^j \, s_2^{(N*-j)} \text{ in } f^k(s_1) f^{N-k}(s_2)}{\text{coeff. of } s^{N*} \text{ in } (f(s))^N} \qquad (1.2.1)$$

Transition probabilities may similarly be given for a multiplicity of sets of genes, and may be extended to the bisexual case
(Karlin, 1968), but (1.2.1) will be sufficient for our purpose.
Selection may also be incorporated by allowing different offspring generating functions for genes of different types, but we
shall consider only the case of selectively equivalent alleles.
The only fundamental restriction of these models is that offspring number is independent of sibship size, and the classical
Wright model is a simple special case given by a Poisson distribution of progeny;

$$P_{kj} = \binom{N*}{j} \left(\frac{k}{N}\right)^j \left(1 - \frac{k}{N}\right)^{N*-j} \qquad (1.2.2)$$

In this case we may view the N_{t+1} offspring as being independently assigned to N_t parents, with equal probabilities for each.
For other progeny distributions, knowledge of identity of some
parent affects the probability that this same individual is the
parent of others.

2. GENE EXTINCTION

2.1 *Parental distributions and gene transitions*

Our aim is to view structure in terms of joint gene survival to a current observable population. In considering evolution over t generations we shall therefore consider the genes t generations ago to be, by definition, distinctly labelled. To compute the distribution of numbers of surviving genes   consider

$$G_{ij}^{(t)} = \text{Prob. } \{\text{sample of i genes descends from } j \text{ "originals", t generations ago}\} \qquad (2.1.1)$$

Then

$$x_j^{(t)} = G_{N_0 j}^{(t)} = \text{Prob. } \{\text{precisely j original genes survive in the current population}\}$$

$$(2.1.2)$$

where N_0 is the current population size, and

$$x_j^{(t)} = \Sigma_k \, x_k^{(t-1)} G_{kj} \qquad (2.1.3)$$

where G_{kj} is the one-generation transition appropriate to k genes in a population of size N_t. (Note N_t is the population size t generations <u>ago</u>). Thus by using the appropriate transition for the population sizes we may use (2.1.3) to analyse gene survival under variable size. Note that while Felsenstein (1971) used the G_{ij} to investigate asymptotic properties of loss of variability for constant population size, our form (2.1.3) differs slightly from his. A backwards recursion is more convenient for the present purpose. For the Wright model, the independent assignment of offspring to N parents gives

$$G_{kj} = \binom{N}{j} \sum_{r=0}^{j-1} (-1)^r \binom{j}{r} \left(\frac{j-r}{N}\right)^k \qquad (2.1.4)$$

(Feller, 1968.)

In addition to the matrices G we have also the transition matrices P with elements

$$P_{ij}^{(t)} = \text{Prob. } \{i \text{ originals } t \text{ generations ago have } j \text{ replicas currently}\}.$$

These latter are useful for computing the probability of extinction of (at least) a specified set of genes:

$$q_i^{(t)} = P_{iO}^{(t)} = \text{Prob. } \{i \text{ originals } t \text{ generations ago currently extinct}\}.$$

The analogue of (2.1.3) is

$$q_i^{(t)} = \Sigma_j \; P_{ij} \; q_j^{(t-1)}. \qquad (2.1.5)$$

Again, this is a backwards recursion, the matrix $\underline{\underline{P}}$ being that applicable to the transition t generations ago. There is, of course, a relationship between P and G; either provides a complete specification of the process. However this relation is not immediate since x refers to the extinction (or survival) of precisely a given number of genes, and q to the extinction of at least a specified set:

$$q_i^{(t)} = \Sigma_{j \geq i} \; \{ \binom{j}{i} x_{N_O - j}^{(t)} \bigg/ \binom{N}{j} \} \qquad (2.1.6)$$

It is simplest therefore to consider separately the equations (2.1.3) and (2.1.5).

2.2. *Measures of structure*

Previous analyses of conditioned-branching-processes and other population models have derived asymptotic results. For the Wright model (e.g. Littler (1975)), results on expected times to loss of alleles have been based on large-population approximations. The most widely-used practical measure of structure has been "effective population size", again an essentially asymptotic measure based on co-ancestry of pairs of genes. Here we wish to consider larger sets of genes, to consider variety of ancestors rather than identity, and to develop measures which display immediate short-term effects.

Within a population of specified history of sizes, or a specified genealogy or mating system, knowledge of survival of a given ancestral gene decreases the survival probability of others. Similarly knowledge of the extinction of any set of ancestors

decreases the extinction probability of any disjoint set; some
genes must survive. (Where knowledge of survival provides information on population size, this is not necessarily the case, but
we consider only models of evolution within a stochastically pre-
specified size framework.) These correlations of extinction and
survival provide useful indices of short-term structure
(Thompson, 1979). However, the magnitude of these correlations
is dominated by overall probabilities of gene extinction; we
therefore consider a normalised correlation.

$$\text{Let} \qquad E(A) = \begin{cases} 1 & \text{if all genes of set A are extinct} \\ 0 & \text{otherwise} \end{cases}$$

and $S(A) = 1 - E(A)$, survival of a set of genes thus
meaning survival of any gene in the set.

Let $p(A) = \text{Prob.} \{E(A) = 1\}$.

Then the correlation in extinction, or survival, between disjoint
sets of genes A and B is

$$\rho = \{p(A \cup B) - p(A)p(B)\}/\{p(A)(1 - p(A))p(B)(1 - p(B))\}^{\frac{1}{2}} \leq 0$$

and we define

$$\left. \begin{aligned} \alpha^{(E)} &= |\rho| \cdot \left\{ \frac{(1 - p(A))(1 - p(B))}{p(A)p(B)} \right\}^{\frac{1}{2}} = 1 - \frac{p(A \cup B)}{p(A)p(B)} \\[2em] \text{and} \\[1em] \alpha^{(S)} &= |\rho| \cdot \left\{ \frac{p(A) \cdot p(B)}{(1 - p(A))(1 - p(B))} \right\}^{\frac{1}{2}} = 1 - \frac{q(A \cup B)}{(1 - p(A))(1 - p(B))} \end{aligned} \right\}$$

$$(2.2.1)$$

where $q(A \cup B) = 1 - p(A) - p(B) + p(A \cup B)$ is the probability of
survival of at least one gene from each of sets A and B. The
quantity $\alpha^{(E)}$ is thus an index of association in extinction,
varying from 0 when extinction of the two gene sets are independent to 1 when extinction of one set of genes precludes that of

the other: $\alpha^{(S)}$ is an analogous index of association in gene
survival.

2.3 *Components of association*

Within a haploid population, restrictions in population size
are the major aspect reflected in associations in extinction or
survival. A severe bottleneck will increase extinction probabilities of larger sets of genes; extinction of one set will preclude that of another to a lesser degree than in a population
of constant size. Superposed on this is the effect of variation
in progeny number. The greater the variance in progeny distribution, the greater the stochastic identity of parents, and the
larger the set of genes which becomes extinct.

Diploidy and individual mating patterns create a new source
of association. At an autosomal locus an individual carries two
genes; only one is passed to each offspring. Thus if one survives the other is less likely to, to an extent dependent on the
number of his offspring. Further one gene of the pair is maternal, the other paternal. Thus if maternal genes survive, paternal are less likely to, to an extent dependent on the number of
offspring of the parent couple. For a given number of genes,
correlations are maximal within individuals, next largest for
spouses, and decrease with increasing distance from common des-
cendants (Thompson, 1979). Further, the magnitude of the association in extinction is determined mainly by the number of
Mendelian segregations in the first opportunity for interaction
between different ancestors - the number of primary common des-
cendants (Thompson, 1981). Thus Mendelian segregation imposes a
further hierarchy of interactions, and mating restrictions a
further level above this. The present aim of characterising
associations in haploid populations should be viewed as assessing the foundations of interactions observable in natural populations such as that of Tristan da Cunha (Thompson, 1979b).

Note that associations and interactions are primarily short
term effects. Unless a population contains complete isolates,
each surviving gene will become evenly spread over the population, and ultimately only one gene will survive. Associations
are then of no interest. The dominant component of any interaction arises at the first major event involving the joint descen-
dants of the original ancestors under consideration; the first
population bottleneck, or the first restriction in joint gene
survival due to progeny restriction or mating pattern. Thus any
characterisation of structure via associations in extinction and
survival should concentrate on effects over a few generations -
the number of generations over which genealogical or structural
information may be available for a natural population.

3. VARIATION IN POPULATION SIZE

3.1 *Size transitions*

For the Wright model of independent allocation of progeny to
parents, the extent to which extinction of one set of genes precludes that of another depends on the sequence of population
sizes and the proportion of genes in the populations that constitute the sets. For a qualitative analysis it is therefore
sufficient to consider only small populations; we shall consider
population cycles with an effective size of 8 haploid genes.
Systems of 4 diploid individuals are sufficient to illustrate
the full range of components of structure described in the Introduction. In particular, consider extinction associations

$$\alpha_{r,r}^{(E)} = 1 - P_{2r,0}^{(t)} / \{P_{r,0}^{(t)}\}^2, \quad r \leq \tfrac{1}{2}N, \qquad (3.1.1)$$

between disjoint sets of r genes over t generations.

Some results for a single transition are given in Table 1(a).
Extinction of one set can preclude that of another to a marked
degree, some associations approaching 1. Clearly associations
will always increase with the size of the sets considered; for
the range considered here the value depends on r and N_1 only via
r/N_1. (N_1 denotes the population size 1 generation ago, and N_0
denotes the current size.) Further all associations increase
with N_0 and decrease with increasing N_1. The larger the current
size, and the smaller the previous one, the more genes of the
previous generation must have replicates in the current one.

3.2 *Bottlenecks, cycles and oscillations*

Severe restrictions in population size decrease the number of
surviving genes, and hence decrease associations in gene extinction. Thus for given effective size, extinction associations
are maximal in a constant population. Table 1(b) shows the
effects of a variety of patterns of cycle and oscillation, all
providing the same harmonic mean size. Although over a single
cycle effects are not large, we see that sharp decreases in population size give smaller associations in extinction than do
sharp increases. Again this reflects the higher probabilities
that few original genes survive.

We may also consider the effect of slower cycles, and other
patterns. For greater comparability of results we consider
always a total set of eight original genes, and give also the

TABLE 1

Size variation, bottlenecks and cycles: $\alpha_{r,r}^{(E)}$

$N_0, N_1, N_2, \ldots$								r=1	r=2	r=3
(a) Single transitions										
4	4							0.37		
8	4							0.60		
16	4							0.99		
4	8							0.08	0.37	0.83
8	8							0.15	0.60	0.96
16	8							0.28	0.99	-
4	16							0.02	0.08	0.20
8	16							0.03	0.15	0.36
16	16							0.07	0.28	0.59
(b) Cycles and oscillations										
8	8	8	8					0.07	0.30	0.71
8	4	16	8					0.06	0.26	0.67
8	16	4	8					0.06	0.28	0.69
8	8	8	8	8				0.04	0.21	0.55
8	16	16	4	8				0.03	0.20	0.54
8	4	16	16	8				0.03	0.17	0.51
8	8	8	8	8	8	8	8	0.03	0.15	0.44
8	4	16	16	4	16	16	8	0.02	0.10	0.38
8	16	16	4	4	16	16	8	0.02	0.11	0.39
8	4	4	16	16	16	16	8	0.03	0.13	0.41
8	8	8	4	8	16	16	8	0.03	0.14	0.42

constant population result for the same number of generations.
The slower the cycles the higher the extinction associations;
the sharper the oscillations the lower the associations. Comparing these values for those in regular mating systems in populations of size 4 (Thompson, 1979), we see that mean associations
are more affected by population size than by mating structure,
and over many generations, this is the dominant factor. However,
mating systems provide a variety of associations, depending on
initial gene position, and over a few generations the largest
associations are much larger than those of Table 1(b) and the
smallest much smaller. Thus with regard to joint survival of
specified genes, such as those in spouses, the pattern of mating
is the dominant feature. Superposing mating structure on
bottlenecks in population size again demonstrates that overall
it is the size characteristics that dominate, but that with
regard to genes within small interbreeding subdivisions, the
pattern of inbreeding and outbreeding is more important.

4. EFFECT OF FAMILY STRUCTURE

4.1 *The Polya urn model*

Family structure is essentially an increased or decreased
identity of parents, over that given by independent assignments
of offspring to parents. In natural populations it is normally
an increase; the variance of family size is greater than that
given by a Poisson progeny distribution. This may be simply
modelled using a multivariate Poly-urn model. Consider an urn
which initially contains s balls of each of N colours, the different colours labelling the individuals of the parent generation.
Let N* balls be drawn in succession, identifying the parents of
each of the N* individuals of the offspring generation, with c
balls of the same colour as that drawn being added to the urn
between each draw, the ball drawn also being replaced.

Then let

$$X_{ij} = \begin{cases} 1 & \text{if jth individual of parental generation} \\ & \text{is the parent of ith in the offspring} \\ & \text{generation} \\ 0 & \text{otherwise} \end{cases}$$

Then
$$E(X_{ij}) = 1/N, \quad 1 \le i \le N^*, \quad 1 \le j \le N$$

and
$$\text{Var}(X_{ij}) = \frac{1}{N}(1 - \frac{1}{N});$$

all individuals of parent generation are equiprobably the parent
of any specified offspring.

Also

$E(X_{ij}X_{ij'}) = 0$; each individual has only one parent

$E(X_{ij}X_{i'j}) = \dfrac{1}{N^2}(1+\rho(N-1))$; identity of parents between different offspring

and

$E(X_{ij}X_{i'j'}) = \dfrac{1}{N^2}(1-\rho)$; non-identity of parents between different offspring

where   (4.1.1)

$\rho = c/(c + s)$.

Thus the Polya-urn model induces symmetric correlations ρ in the identity of parents: in our numerical examples we shall for convenience take $s = 1$.

If we require only the extinction probability of, at least, a specified set of r genes, we may group the genes in question and reduce the problem to that of the usual two-colour Polya-urn. The initial constitution may be assumed to be r red balls and $(N-r)$ black. The probability of immediate extinction of the genes is

$$\prod_{j=0}^{(N^*-1)} (1 - r/(N + jc)) \qquad (4.1.2)$$

while the probability of k replicates of the set at the next generation is   (Feller, 1968)

$$P_{rk} = \begin{pmatrix} N^*-k+(N-r)/c \\ k \end{pmatrix} \begin{pmatrix} k-1+r/c \\ N^*-k \end{pmatrix} \begin{pmatrix} N^*-1+N/c \\ N^* \end{pmatrix} \qquad (4.1.3)$$

The availability of these explicit transition probabilities makes the Polya-urn model more convenient for the analysis of variance in progeny distribution than the conditioned branching process transitions (1.2.1).

4.2   Extinction associations with family structure

As in (2.1.5) we have that the extinction probability of a set of r genes over the t generations to the present is given recursively by

$$q_r^{(t)} = \sum_k P_{rk}(N_t, N_{t-1})\, q_k^{(t-1)} \qquad (4.2.1)$$

TABLE 2

Effect of family structure; population of 8 genes

	c = 0	1	2	3	∞
	ρ = 0	0.5	0.67	0.75	1

(a) Extinction probabilities in single transition

$P_{r,0}$: r =					
1	.344	.467	.538	.586	.875
2	.100	.200	.273	.328	.750
3	.023	.077	.128	.172	.625
4	.004	.026	.054	.084	.500
5	.000	.007	.020	.036	.375
6	.000	.001	.006	.013	.250
7	.000	.000	.001	.003	.125

(b) Associations in extinction

$\alpha_{r,r}^{(E)}$: r =					
1	.15	.08	.06	.05	.02
2	.61	.36	.27	.22	.11
3	.91	.76	.63	.55	.36

where the arguments of P_{rk} denote that the relevant population sizes in this transition are those at t and (t-1) generations ago, respectively. Again we have a backwards formulation.

As the parameter c, and hence the parental correlation ρ, of the Polya-urn model increases, so also does the extinction probability of larger sets of genes. At c = 0 the probability that none of a set of six genes in a population of 8 is represented in the next generations is only 0.00002. For c = 3 it is $1\frac{1}{2}$%. For the limit c = ∞, all individuals are produced by a single parent; the probability that this is not one of the set of six genes is 25%. Further values are given in Table 2(a), while Table 2(b) gives the corresponding extinction associations.

We see that increasing correlation in parental identity, sharply decreases extinction association. Conversely survival associations would be increased. The correlation ρ gives the variance in progeny number:

$$\text{Var } \{ \sum_{i=1}^{N} X_{ij} \} = (1-\frac{1}{N}) + N(N-1).\frac{1}{N}\rho(1-\frac{1}{N}) \text{ from } (4.1.1)$$

$$= (1-\frac{1}{N})(1+\rho(N-1)) \tag{4.2.2}$$

The correlations presented in Table 2 thus lead to substantial increases in variance of progeny number. That for c = 1 (ρ = 0.5) is, however, not outside the range for natural populations, and even for c = 1 associations are decreased by 50% for small sets of genes (Table 2; r=1,2). For larger sets of genes, extinction still precludes extinction of an equivalent set to a substantial degree, but there will now be populations in which almost all genes become extinct within a very few generations.

5. CONCLUSIONS

The structure of a population has substantial effects on within-population variability, and numbers of surviving ancestral genes.

In order to characterise population structure it is necessary to identify its separate components and assess the effects of each.

In the current paper, we have analysed structural effects present within a haploid population, to provide a firmer foundation for previous analyses of diploid effects and complex mating structures.

Our interest is in joint survival of sets of ancestral genes, and in the effect of knowledge of extinction of some genes on the probability of that of others. These effects can be assessed via the negative correlations in extinction and survival events for disjoint sets of genes. To remove the effect on the interaction of overall levels of survival and extinction probabilities, we introduce normalised association indices which vary from 0 to 1 with the extent to which survival/extinction of one set of genes precludes that of another.

Haploid effects result from patterns of varying population size and progeny distributions. The effects of cycles in size and rapid expansions and decreases have been considered on the basis of the Wright model.

In natural populations, variance in progeny distribution is greater than given by the Wright model. To provide a simpler formulation than that of conditioned branching processes, a multivariate Polya urn model inducing symmetric correlations in parental identity has been considered. It is seen that variance in progeny distribution has substantial effects on the extinction probabilities of large sets of ancestral genes.

6. REFERENCES

Feller, W. (1968) An Introduction to Probability Theory and its Applications, **1**, (3rd edition), Wiley, New York.

Felsenstein, J. (1971) The rate of loss of multiple alleles in finite haploid populations, *Theor. Pop. Biol.*, **2**, pp. 391-403.

Karlin, S. (1968) Equilibrium behaviour of population genetic models with non-random mating, *J. Appl. Prob.*, **5**, pp. 487-566.

Littler, R.A. (1975) Loss of variability in finite populations, *Math. Biosciences*, **25**, pp. 151-163.

Thompson, E.A. (1979) Genealogical structure and correlations in gene extinction, *Theor. Pop. Biol.*, **16**, pp. 191-222.

Thompson, E.A. (1979b) Ancestral inference, III: the ancestral structure of the population of Tristan da Cunha, *Ann. Hum. Genet.*, **43**, pp. 167-176.

Thompson, E.A. (1981) Gene competition without selection, *In* "Current Problems in Sociobiology", King's College Sociobiology Group (ed.), Cambridge University Press.

HUMAN MIGRATION AND POPULATION STRUCTURE

R.W. Hiorns and G.A. Harrison

*(Departments of Biomathematics and Biological Anthropology,
University of Oxford, Oxford, England)*

1. INTRODUCTION

Movement is well recognized as one of the major determinants
of the genetic structure of populations. It has been particularly important in human evolution and, today, it is without
doubt the major factor changing the frequency of genes in
human populations. However, most of the treatments of the
effects of movement in theoretical population genetics have
grossly oversimplified the forms of movement which actually
occur, especially in modern societies. It is, for example,
frequently assumed that migrant groups immediately enter into
random mating with the sedentary groups they have joined, or if
not, that the two groups are clearly biologically recognizable.
This is often palpably not the case. In many places throughout
the world, particularly in cities, one finds widely differing
ethnic groups living side by side with little or no mating
between them, and frequently these groups are not very distinct
at the level of external appearance, though they may vary
considerably from one another in gene frequencies in some
genetic systems. The wide-spread ancestral geographical origin
of Europeans now living in Australia and the United States are
cases in point, and for cultural reasons entirely, the groups
often do not interbreed to any appreciable extent, at least for
a number of generations. Their existence can cause marked
heterogeneity of genetic structure in what might appear at first
sight to be a structurally homogeneous population. This can
particularly cause problems when biological data have been
collected with some other purpose than structural analysis in
mind e.g. blood group frequencies from blood transfusion
services.

Another assumption that is often entered into genetic models
of human movement is equal mobility of males and females. Again
this clearly often does not apply, particularly in long range
migration. Both in the past and at present there are many cases
where migrants, especially in the early phase of a migration

are almost exclusively men. Such a pattern obviously disturbs
the sex-ratio in the recipient population and in any generation
affects the capacity of the mixed group to mate at random.

A different set of issues arises when considering the genetic
system itself. Most migration models have concentrated on
effects at single loci, but consideration of two or more loci
can be anthropologically revealing. It is customary nowadays to
view linkage disequilibrium in a population as arising from
selective processes, and no doubt this is often the case.
However, as has been pointed out by Degos (1974) and Mourant
(1980) linkage disequilibrium can as well arise from the intermixture of populations and may well constitute a guide to the
ancestral origins of groups which have developed in this way.
A question of some importance in attempting to determine these
origins is the rate of decay of the linkage disequilibrium at
various levels of linkage, and the detection of the disequilibrium level. Even unlinked loci will not pass to an equilibrium
state following a single generation of random mating (Falconer,
1960) and again the passage to equilibrium may be illuminating
of ancestral composition for populations which have fairly
recently arisen by the intermixture of groups which differ in
gene frequency at a number of independent loci.

It is with the effects of the different migration processes
and with ancestral compositions to intermixed groups that this
paper is concerned. These are examined respectively in terms
of detecting disturbances of Hardy-Weinberg equilibria and in
detecting disequilibrium states in the passage to equilibrium.

2. THE IMPORTANCE OF POPULATION STRUCTURE

2.1 Single locus

In this section we examine the consequences of population
subdivision in the context of some simple situations. To begin
with, we may think of a single locus at which there are two
possible alleles, A and a, and the subgroups have frequencies
for the A allele of p_1 and p_2, and relative population sizes v
and (1-v). Since the probability distribution for the three
available phenotypes is a simple binomial in each subgroup, the
distribution for the population viewed as a whole is a mixture
of two binomials. We may compare this mixture with a single
binomial which has the same mean as the mean of the mixture,
viz., $vp_1 + (1-v)p_2$ and we notice that the variance of the
mixture exceeds that of the single binomial by an amount
$2v(1-v)(p_1^2 - p_2^2)$. This is an indication that the phenotype
frequencies are not in Hardy-Weinberg equilibrium. The reduced
heterozygosity in the whole population which results from the

subdivision depends upon the mixture parameter v and the sub-group gene frequencies p_1 and p_2. This reduction is sometimes expressed in standarized form by dividing by the product $\bar{p}\,\bar{q}$ where $\bar{p} = \frac{1}{2}(p_1 + p_2)$ and $\bar{q} = 1 - \bar{p}$, and it is then known as *Wahlund's variance of gene frequencies.*

Departures from Hardy-Weinberg equilibrium are usually tested using the x^2- statistic and we now investigate the change in the value of this statistic which we may expect from the results of subdivision alone. To illustrate the point, we simplify the situation to a population subdivided into unequal groups but with gene frequencies which have complementary values with $p_1 = p$ and $p_2 = 1 - p = q$. We introduce d for the difference $p - q$ and we tabulate the phenotype frequencies for the whole population ignoring the subdivision and also for the Hardy-Weinberg case with no subdivision:

Phenotype	Frequency in whole population ignoring subdivision	Hardy-Weinberg frequency if no subdivision
AA	$vp^2+(1-v)\,q^2 = q^2+vd$	$p_0^2= (q+vd)^2$
Aa	$2pq$	$2p_0q_0=2pq+2v(1-v)\,d^2$
aa	$vq^2+(1-v)\,p^2 = p^2-vd$	$q_0^2= (p-vd)^2$

If we take a sample of size n from the total population ignoring the subdivision, we can see from the tabulated values that the contribution to the x^2- statistic due to this cause is

$$x^2 = n\{v(1-v)\,d^2\}^2 \,/\, \{(q+vd)^2(p-vd)^2\} \qquad (2.1.1)$$

with one degree of freedom. By expressing the deviation from Hardy-Weinberg in this form we may consider the extent to which "significant" x^2- values produced in population sampling may be explained by population subdivision effects. For example, with equal-sized groups and a 5% significance level for the test, sample sizes exceeding $3.84/d^4$ will be required to detect the subdivision effects. (Here 3.84 is the x^2 critical value at the 5% significance level with 1 degree of freedom). Some other values are given in the table.

d, the difference between the subgroups gene frequencies	Sample size for detection at Significance level	
	5%	0.1%
0.5	62	174
0.4	150	423
0.3	475	1337
0.2	2400	6768
0.1	38400	108279

For a fixed sample of 1000, the critical value would be reached, at the 5% level, if p_1 exceeds 0.648 and p_2 is less than 0.352.

From the values in the table, we can see that if the subgroup frequencies are closer than 0.2, the detection of subdivision effects will be impossible in common practice where sample sizes are often less than 1000.

As well as providing the means of investigating subdivision effects for populations with known group sizes, the expression in equation 2.1.1 also allows for the determination of group sizes. The importance of this application may be that the demographic characteristics of groups may not be known even though genetic information is available from the groups or from their ancestral origins. The computation is straightforward using known gene frequency p and x^2- value calculated from a whole population sample of size n, recalling that $v=p-(1-p)=2p-1$ for symmetric gene frequencies in the subgroups. We find that

$$v = \tfrac{1}{2} + \tfrac{1}{2} \sqrt{\{1 - 4pq / [(\sqrt{(n/x^2)}-1)\ d^2]\}} \qquad (2.1.2)$$

which with $1-v$ comprise the solutions of the quadratic equation derived from equation 2.1.1. A sample of 1000 which produces a x^2- value of 10 with known subgroup gene frequencies p = 0.3 and q = 0.7 leads to relative subgroup sizes of 0.178 and 0.822 respectively. An alternative method, not using the calculated x^2- value but instead the gene frequencies determined from the whole population sample, may be preferred as it provides simple confidence limits for v. We recall that $p = vp_1 + (1-v)p_2$ in which p_1 and p_2 are the known gene frequencies in the subgroups and p is determined by gene counting from the sample. Thus,

$$v = (p - p_2)/(p_1 - p_2)$$

is the estimator of the relative size v, and its standard error is

$$s.e.(v) = \sqrt{(pq)/(nd)}$$

where $d = p_1 - p_2$ and $q = 1 - p$.   Confidence limits for v may
be constructed from the estimator and its standard error when
p is not close to 0 or 1 and when this is violated by solving
for v, the quadratic equation for exact limits:

$$v^2(1 + z^2 d/n) - (2v_c + z^2(1 - 2p_2)/n) + v_c^2 - z^2 p_2(1-p_2)/nd = 0$$

where z is the normal deviate with probability corresponding to
the confidence required (e.g. for 95% limits, z = 1.96) and v_c
is the estimate of v calculated from the sample as described
above. This procedure makes straighforward the testing for the
existence of a subdivision and the test is much more sensitive
than the method using x^2. This is due to the fact that known
frequencies are being used for the subgroups as well as the
deficiency of x^2 in this situation. The sample sizes required,
tabulated below, indicate clearly the worthwhileness of using
known frequencies and the improved procedure:

d, the difference between the subgroups gene frequencies	Sample size for detection at Significance level	
	5%	1%
0.5	16	39
0.4	25	60
0.3	43	107
0.2	97	239
0.1	385	955

We note that a similar improvement was commented upon by
Haber (1980) in his discussion of the detection of inbreeding
using a x^2- statistic with unknown gene frequencies as compared
with direct estimation by maximum likelihood where the frequencies are known.

2.2. *Several independent loci*

The extension of methods from the previous section will be
straightforward and we expect to find the effects of subdivision
at any locus or at all loci taken together. Where the loci considered are independent of each other the x^2- values for testing
the departures from equilibrium may be summed over all loci.
In the general case of k independent loci, with two alleles at

each locus,

$$\chi^2 = n\Sigma[\{v(1-v)d_i^2\}^2 / \{(q_i + vd_i)^2(p_i - vd_i)^2\}]$$

(2.2.1)

with k degrees of freedom, where d_i is the difference in

frequency of an allele at the ith locus between the two groups
of the subdivision and v is the relative size of the first group
so the 1-v is the relative size of the second group. We point
out that there is no suffix on v because the subdivision affects
all loci equally. In view of the aggregation of the effects
over all loci which takes place in calculating this statistic,
the presence of subdivision becomes easier to detect when all
loci are considered together.

For comparison with the single locus situation, we may
imagine that the frequencies p_i are the same for all loci and

that the groups are of equal size. The following table shows
the effect of additional loci upon the sample size required to
detect the subdivision.

d, the difference between the subgroups gene frequencies	Sample size for detection (at 5% significance level) Number of loci					
	1	2	3	5	10	20
0.5	62	48	42	36	30	26
0.4	150	117	102	87	72	62
0.3	475	370	322	274	227	194
0.2	2400	1872	1628	1384	1145	982
0.1	38400	29950	26034	22140	18307	15705

We notice that it is beneficial to use information from several
loci but that the reduction in sample size is not sufficiently
dramatic to warrant the collection of data on many systems for
this purpose and no other. Furthermore, we realise that the
statistic used here is not particularly sensitive, and dis-
regards the fact that departures from equilibrium caused by
population subdivision will all be in the same direction. A
non-parametric test using 5 loci at each of which there was
evidence of reduced heterozygosity would be significant (at the
level used above) whatever the magnitudes of the departures.
(This result is for the simple sign test, more powerful non-
parametric tests could require fewer loci for the same significance.) Nevertheless, the test is so commonly applied to data
of this kind that we think that it is important to demonstrate
its power to detect population structure in the way outlined
above.

We proceed to examine the more sensitive procedure introduced
in the last section. The extension of that procedure presents
no analytical problems in the case of independent loci and it
will suffice for us to consider the much reduced sample sizes
required in order to detect the subdivision effect ('+' denotes
a sample of less than 10):

d, the difference between the subgroups gene frequencies	Sample size for detection (at 5% significance level) Number of loci					
	1	2	3	5	10	20
0.5	16	+	+	+	+	+
0.4	25	13	+	+	+	+
0.3	43	22	15	+	+	+
0.2	97	49	33	20	10	+
0.1	385	193	129	77	39	20

This simple analysis shows that using existing procedures a
great deal of heterogeneity of structure arising from population
subdivision will go undetected in most anthropological studies;
these very rarely sample more than a few hundred individuals.
And, as already indicated, the problem is most acute practically
where groups of different origin are not easily distinguishable
on physical appearance. In these situations no genetic locus
is likely to differentiate the groups very much.

2.3 Two linked loci

In this section we consider the possibility of linkage
between two loci where a population is subdivided into two equal
sized groups and the gene frequencies differ in the two groups.
For the purpose of our illustration, we further assume that the
frequencies of one gene, A, at one locus are q and $p(= 1 - q)$
in the two groups and conversely, those of a gene B at the other
locus being considered are p and q. The simplicity of this
symmetrical arrangement of the gene frequencies in the groups
allows us to investigate the linkage disequilibrium and to
illustrate the difficulties in interpreting this measure in
subdivided populations.

The customary definition of linkage disequilibrium is in
terms of the gamete frequencies for the four gametotypes AB,
Ab, aB and ab:

$$D = (AB)(ab) - (Ab)(aB) \qquad (2.3.1)$$

where brackets are used to denote the frequencies of the
enclosed gametes. In the first group, with frequency q for A

and p for B, these gamete frequencies are then

$(AB) = q(1 - q)$, $(Ab) = q^2$, $(aB) = (1 - q)^2$ and $(ab) = q(1 - q)$.

Substituting into (2.1.5), D thus becomes

$$D = q^2(1 - q)^2 - q^2(1 - q)^2 = 0$$

suggesting that there is no evidence of linkage in that group. Similarly, for the second group we have

$(AB) = q(1 - q)$, $(Ab) = (1 - q)^2$, $(aB) = q^2$ and $(ab) = q(1 - q)$.

The linkage disequilibrium is again zero.

If the subdivided population is viewed as a whole, however, the gamete frequencies become, averaging over the above values for the two groups,

$(AB) = q(1-q)$, $(Ab) = \frac{1}{2}\{q^2 + (1-q)^2\}$, $(aB) = \frac{1}{2}\{q^2 + (1-q)^2\}$ and

$$(ab) = q(1-q)$$

and then

$$D = q^2(1 - q)^2 - \tfrac{1}{4}\{q^2 + (1 - q)^2\}^2$$
$$= -\tfrac{1}{2}(2q - 1)^2 \qquad\qquad (2.3.2)$$

which is only zero if $q = \frac{1}{2}$. In general, therefore, where a population consists of subdivisions which have genes at two independent loci with different frequencies, linkage disequilibrium will be deemed to exist even in the absence of linkage!

3. THE DYNAMIC EFFECTS OF MIGRATION

3.1 Single locus model

We restrict our attention for most of what follows to a study of the effects of single shot migration. By this we mean that migration takes place at one instant and thereafter populations remain closed. Later on, we turn briefly to the case of continuous migration with migrants moving between populations in each generation through time.

3.1.1 Migrants not selected by sex

Where the proportion m of the individuals in a population migrate to another population to be replaced reciprocally by individuals from that population, the disturbance to the genotype distribution will depend upon the difference in gene frequencies between populations and m. In this illustration we suppose that the population frequencies are p_1 and p_2 for a particular gene so that the phenotype frequencies in the first population immediately following the migration are

$$mp_1^2 + (1-m)p_2^2, \quad 2m(p_1 \; q_1 + p_2 \; q_2) \text{ and } mq_1^2 + (1-m)q_2^2.$$

Following the procedure of the earlier sections, we obtain the χ^2 value to be expected because of the structural effects of migration, this is

$$\chi^2 = nm(1 - m)(p_1 - p_2)^2 .$$

The sample sizes required for this quantity to reach significance at the 5% level are shown in Fig. 1. and it is apparent that for differences between p_1 and p_2 of 0.2 or greater, the sample sizes are well below 1000 for reasonable migration rates in the ranges 0.15 to 0.85. These results indicate that the structural explanation can be confirmed in many practical situations but not where differences in gene frequencies between populations are small.

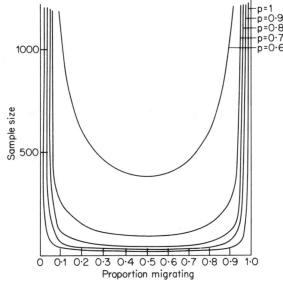

Fig. 1 The relationship between sample size and proportion migrating for different gene frequencies in two populations experiencing single shot migration which is not sex-selected. The population frequencies for this illustration are taken to be p_1 (=p) and p_2 (=1-p).

TABLE 1

Single sex migration: males only moving

		Males			Females		
		AA	Aa	aa	AA	Aa	aa
INITIALLY:							
Population I		1	0	0	1	0	0
Population II		0	0	1	0	0	1
AFTER MIGRATION:							
Parents							
	I	$1-m$	0	m	1	0	0
	II	m	0	$1-m$	0	0	1
Offspring							
	I	$1-m$	m	0	$1-m$	m	0
	II	0	m	$1-m$	0	m	$1-m$
Total							
	I	$1-m$	$\frac{1}{2}m$	$\frac{1}{2}m$	$1-\frac{1}{2}m$	$\frac{1}{2}m$	0
	II	$\frac{1}{2}m$	$\frac{1}{2}m$	$1-m$	0	$\frac{1}{2}m$	$1-\frac{1}{2}m$
NEXT GENERATION:							
Offspring							
	I	$(1-\frac{1}{2})m^2$	$m(1-\frac{1}{2}m)$	$\frac{1}{4}m^2$	same as males		
	II	$\frac{1}{4}m^2$	$m(1-\frac{1}{2}m)$	$(1-\frac{1}{2}m)^2$	"	"	"
Total							
	I	$1-m-\frac{1}{4}m^2$	$\frac{1}{2}m(3-m)$	$\frac{1}{4}m^2$	"	"	"
	II	$\frac{1}{4}m^2$	$\frac{1}{2}m(3-m)$	$1-m-\frac{1}{4}m^2$	"	"	"

3.1.2 Sex-selected migrants

Where an initial mixing of populations, in single shot
fashion, consists of males only moving, this is an extreme
form of sex-selected migration. The consequences of this type
of mixture upon the phenotype frequencies of the offspring are
particularly severe when the gene frequencies of the populations
differ widely. For example, in an extreme case, the two mixing
populations may be completely homozygous but for different
genes so that one population consists of only AA individuals
and the other of only aa individuals. If the migrants are male
only then the offspring of matings involving migrants will all
be heterozygous. If all of the males migrate or equivalently
if non-migrant males are not involved in mating then the next
generation will comprise only heterozygotes. As we noted in
the previous section, the phenotype distribution is not
disturbed in this way when the migrants are not sexually
differentiated.

In Table 1 we give the phenotype frequencies in two populations affected by the migration described in this section.
Where the migration is single shot, the second generation of
offspring are in Hardy-Weinberg equilibrium. However, population samples do not always have different generations
separately identified and problems of interpretation will then
arise. From the "total population" frequencies in the first
and second generations shown in the table it is clear that these
frequencies are very different from their equilibrium values.

In Fig. 2 the consequences of migration upon a male sample
taken from the parents and offspring in the generation following
the migration are considered. Only small samples are required
to detect the effects of this migration. One surprising
feature of this situation is the equilibrium which results from
a particular migration rate close to 0.9. This has little
practical value and results from a singularity of the sample
size function.

Fig. 3 shows the position in the succeeding generation and
contrasts a combined sample of parents and offspring with a
sample of offspring only. The benefit of identifying the offspring separately is clear in that smaller samples are required.
Furthermore, we can see that for a wide range of migration
rates, a sample of 1000 will ensure that the departure from
Hardy-Weinberg equilibrium caused by this type of migration and
population mixture will be detected.

Where migration is repeated each generation through time,
the detection of structural effects becomes more and more
difficult. Fig. 4 illustrates this difficulty which arises from

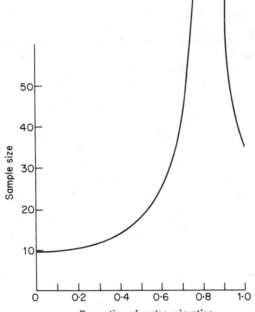

Fig. 2 The relationship between sample size and proportion
        migrating for males-only single shot migration where
        parent and offspring males are sampled in the first
        generation following the migration. The initial
        population gene frequencies for this illustration are
        taken to be $p_1 = 1$ and $p_2 = 0$.

the fact that, for high rates of migration, the populations
become similar more rapidly than in the single shot case. This
means that for practical purposes the mechanism considered here
can only be ascertained for a short while after migration
commences or, alternatively, if the rate is very low.

3.2 *Two linked loci*

In this section we turn to the effects of intermixture upon
two linked loci. As in the case of the subdivided population,
we introduce two alleles at each of the two linked loci, so that
the gametes are again represented by

$$AB \qquad Ab \qquad aB \qquad ab$$

and we denote the frequencies in the first population by

$$p_1 \qquad p_2 \qquad p_3 \qquad p_4$$

and those in the second population by

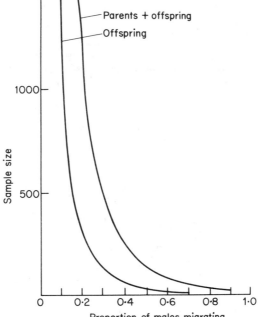

Fig. 3 As for Fig. 2 but where the parent offspring males are sampled in the second generation following the migration. In addition, the offspring only sample size curve is shown.

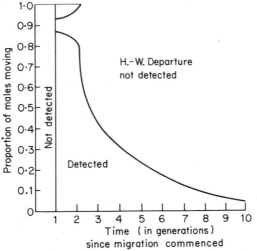

Fig. 4 For the case of continuous migration through time, the time from first migration to the time when Hardy-Weinberg departure not detectable is shown for different proportions of males migrating. The initial gene frequencies in the two populations are taken to be 1 and 0 and a fixed sample size of 1000 is assumed for this illustration.

$$p_1' \qquad p_2' \qquad p_3' \qquad p_4' \ .$$

For a migration rate m, the resulting frequencies of the gametes after migration and random mating become, in the first population:

$$(1-m)p_1 + mp_1' \qquad \text{etc.,}$$

and in the second:

$$mp_1 + (1-m)p_1' \ .$$

We recall that the linkage disequilibrium

$$D = p_1 p_4 - p_2 p_3$$

and in terms of D the offspring gamete frequencies become

$$p_1 - rD \qquad p_2 + rD \qquad p_3 + rD \qquad p_4 - rD$$

where r is the recombination fraction (which is ½ for no linkage and 0 for complete linkage). Substitution of these values into the expression for D gives D_1 (after 1 generation)

$$D_1 = (p_1 - rD)(p_4 - rD) - (p_2 + rD)(p_3 + rD) = (1 - r)D \ .$$

Similarly, we may express the linkage disequilibrium after t generations in terms of the initial value D_0:

$$D_t = (1 - r)^t D_0 \ . \qquad\qquad (3.2.1)$$

But we replace the initial gamete frequencies by those after the single shot migration, using D' to represent the initial disequilibrium in the second population,

$$D_0 = (1-m)^2 D + m^2 D' + m(1-m)\{p_1'p_4 + p_4'p_1) - (p_2'p_3 + p_3'p_2)\}$$

$$(3.2.2)$$

If we proceed to substitute D_0 from eqn. (3.2.2) into eqn. (3.2.1) we are then able to

a) calculate the linkage disequilibrium over time from a speci-

fied amount of migration and initial gamete frequencies in the
two populations; and

b) estimate m from the aggregated disequilibrium value after a
specified time and from the initial gamete frequencies together
with the knowledge of the linkage operating expressed as r.

Figs. 5 and 6 depict for two amounts of linkage, corresponding to r = 0.01 and 0.05, the sample sizes required for the
detection of linkage disequilibrium through time following
single shot migration with m = 0.5. We note that for close
linkage the effects persist through many generations and quite
small samples are sufficient to detect them. For unlinked loci,
migration produces a disequilibrium effect and this may be
detected in the first few generations only and then if the
frequencies of the gametes differ markedly between the populations. The sample sizes required in this case are illustrated
in Fig. 7, again with single shot migration, m = 0.5.

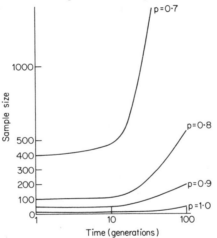

Fig. 5   The sample size required to detect linkage disequilibrium after single shot migration (m = 0.5) with linkage
determined by r = 0.01 and initial gene frequencies
at both loci in the first population p_1 (= p) and in the
second population p_2 (= 1-p). Curves for four values
of p are shown p= 0.7, 0.8, 0.9 and 1.

This analysis confirms that linkage disequilibrium between
closely linked genes may well be a very useful anthropological
indicator of ancestry and distant intermixture, but it also
demonstrates that after recent intermixture unlinked genes will
often be in such a disequilibrium state as to cause potential
difficulties in other analyses, e.g., when examining selection
for gene arrays.

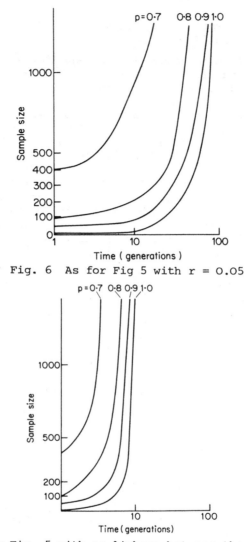

Fig. 6   As for Fig 5 with r = 0.05

Fig. 7   As for Fig. 5 with no linkage between the two loci
         (r=0.5)

4.   CONCLUSIONS

    We have considered the effects of population structure and
migration upon the genetic composition of populations together
with the ability of population samples to detect these effects.
This analysis shows that genetic heterogeneity deriving from
migration will go undetected using conventional methods in most
anthropological studies because of inadequate sample size.

However, when the heterogeneity is detected it can easily be ascribed to some other cause than migration, unless historical information about a population's origin is available.

5. REFERENCES

Degos, L. (1974) Migrations des peuples primitifs: la résponse des génèticiens, *La Recherche*, **5**, No. 47, pp. 683-685.

Falconer, D.S. (1960) Introduction to Quantitative Genetics. Edinburgh: Oliver and Boyd.

Haber, M (1980) Detection of inbreeding effects by the χ^2-test on genotypic and phenotypic frequencies, *Am.J.Hum.Genet.*, **32**, pp. 754-760.

Mourant, A.E. (1980) Linkage equilibrium and disequilibrium in human population studies, *Ann.Hum.Biol.*, **7**, pp. 109-114.

MEASURING CIRCADIAN RHYTHMS IN CELL POPULATIONS

P.D.M. Macdonald

*(Department of Mathematical Sciences,
McMaster University, Hamilton, Ontario, Canada)*

1. INTRODUCTION

There is ample experimental evidence that in many different
biological tissues the rate of cell proliferation varies with
the time of day. This paper considers models for cell population growth under periodically varying laws. A series of
examples show how rhythms in different phases of the cell cycle
will reveal themselves in the usual experiments of cell kinetics.

Mathematical modelling is inescapable in the study of cell
proliferation kinetics. While many experimental techniques have
been devised which permit the experimenter to observe and measure
a cell population at a given time, the processes of development,
growth and differentiation cannot be observed directly. A mathematical model interprets the observable features of the population in terms of the underlying processes which govern its evolution. The simplest analyses assume a population structure
which is constant in time. More complicated, and generally more
informative, techniques involve the response to some perturbation, for example, the approach to an induced synchrony or the
decay of synchrony. The objective may be simply to describe the
population kinetics, or it may be to predict the response to an
intervention such as chemotherapy. Most of the different
approaches to modelling can be found in Valleron and Macdonald
(1978).

Because binary fission underlies cell proliferation, branch-
ing-process models have been applied for many years with considerable success (Harris, 1963; Jagers, 1975). The most widely
used class of models (Steel, 1977) assumes that the proliferative characteristics do not vary with time and that the population has reached a steady state of exponential growth; that is,
the population is growing exponentially but it is very large and
the age, phase and type structure of the population is stable.
The success of these models derives from a fortunate correspondence between the unknown parameters (typically few in number) and

the information available from the usual experimental data.
Hence it has been possible to estimate such kinetic parameters
as mean cycle duration, mean durations of phases within the
cycle, and the relative fractions of quiescent and proliferating
cells (Macdonald, 1970, 1973; Steel, 1977).

At the same time, many examples have been found of tissues
which, in vivo, show different rates of cell division at different times of day. Mrs. Droogleever Fortuyn - van Leijden (1917)
was the first to recognize the significance of periodic division
rates for cell kinetics. She noted that this effect was already
well-known in several plant tissues, rootlets of hyacinth and
onion, for example, and demonstrated the existence of rhythms in
mammalian tissues; specifically, the mesentery the outer stra-
tified epithelium of the cornea, and the epithelial cells of
Lieberkühn's crypts in newborn cats. More recent studies have
also focused on epithelial tissues. They include various epithelial tissues in the mouse (Bullough, 1948, 1952; Pilgrim et al.,
1963; Clausen et al., 1979); various tissues in the rat (R.M.
Klein, 1980); and the hamster cheek pouch (Brown and Berry, 1968;
Izquierdo and Gibbs, 1972, 1974; Møller et al., 1974). Numerous
other studies are cited in the foregoing papers.

The analysis of kinetic data in these tissues is complicated
in two ways. Firstly, the mathematical model must allow for
periodically varying rates and probabilities, and so the usual
theory of branching processes must be modified in a non-trivial
manner. Secondly, we will now be estimating periodic functions
instead of constants for the rates and probabilities. This makes
the estimation problem considerably more difficult and may nece-
ssitate that a given experiment be repeated at many different
times of day in order to define the whole rate function
adequately.

A potential application of periodic variation is to chemotherapy. For example, using a cytostatic drug such as arabinosyl cytosine which specifically kills cells in the S, or DNA-
synthetic, phase of the cell cycle, the first dose could be
timed to have effect when the proportion of tumour cells in S
phase is highest. The mathematical model could then be used to
predict future S-phase peaks and hence the timing of subsequent
doses. Halberg et al. (1978, Fig. 4) have shown that the effectiveness of arabinosyl cytosine in treating leukaemic mice can
be enhanced by administering the drug in sinusoidally-varying,
rather than level, doses, and that the phase of the schedule
relative to the 24-hour clock is critical. However, their work
is inconclusive from a cell kinetics viewpoint because it has
not been ascertained whether the internal rhythms are in the
proliferation kinetics of leukaemic cells, in the proliferation

kinetics of normal cells, in the ability of the animal to meta-
bolize the drug, or a combination of these.

Following Halberg's definitions (Halberg et al., 1978, for
example), I will refer to a rhythm with a period of exactly 24
hours as "circadian", even though circadian refers to a period
of "about a day". This, however, is preferable to the adjective
"diurnal" which, being the antonym of "nocturnal", could imply
either a 12-hour or a 24-hour period.

In Section 2, I will describe the most common types of cell
kinetics experiments, in order to show what aspects of a cell
population can be observed and hence what aspects should be predicted by a model.

Section 3 outlines the different mathematical methods that
various authors have used to model cell kinetics with circadian
rhythms. This will be of interest to anyone applying branching-
process models to natural populations with rhythms imposed by
the environment, be they circadian, annual, or otherwise.
Section 4 shows how the Klein and Valleron (1977) model can be
applied, with some discussion of the problems arising when computing the model and fitting it to data. Finally, in Section 5,
a series of examples is presented, computed by the Klein and
Valleron model, which shows how circadian variation will show up
in the usual cell kinetics experiments.

2. WHAT IS OBSERVABLE IN CELL KINETICS EXPERIMENTS

Steel (1977) describes the standard experimental methods of
cell kinetics. As instrumentation advances, the field continues
to develop and any current issue of Cell and Tissue Kinetics,
for instance, will present new variants of the standard methods.
The techniques described in this section have been chosen because
they are sufficiently fundamental to represent most types of
experiments in current use.

From this methodology has emerged a model of the cell cycle
as a sequence of four phases, and it is in terms of this model
that these experiments are interpreted. The phases are called
G_1, S, G_2 and M, respectively. M is the period of visible mitotic activity preceding cell division, S is a period of DNA
synthesis, and G_1 and G_2 are "gaps" during which no DNA is syn-
thesized. The model is, of course, an idealization. In particular, it may be unreasonable to assume sharply-defined bounda-
ries between the phases, but the effect of ill-defined bounda-
ries will be confounded with any natural variation there might
be in phase durations.

The <u>mitotic index</u>, or MI, is defined as the ratio of the number of cells in M to the total number of cells. Since M (mitotic) cells can be distinguished from other cells under an ordinary light microscope by the visible configuration of chromosomes in the nucleus, this is the oldest of cell kinetics measurements. Periodic variation in the mitotic index was the first indication of circadian rhythms in cell proliferation (Droogleever Fortuyn - van Leijden, 1917). For more recent data, see Clausen et al. (1979).

The <u>labelling index</u>, or LI, is used to measure what proportion of the population is in the S phase at a given time. A radioactive DNA precursor such as tritiated thymidine is made available to the cells and those which incorporate it are thereby identified as being in S (the DNA-synthetic phase).

Those cells, and, for a reasonable number of generations, their daughter cells, will be radioactive and can be identified by autoradiography: after a sample of cells has been fixed on a microscope slide and coated with photographic emulsion, clusters of silver grains will appear over radioactive cells when the emulsion is developed. The labelling index is the ratio of the number of cells in S phase to the total number of cells.

The <u>fraction labelled mitoses curve</u>, or flm, combines the two previous ideas. The population is given the label as a short "pulse". At successive times afterwards, the fraction of M phase cells which are labelled is recorded. When plotted against time, there is an initial delay while the labelled cells pass through G_2. The fraction then rises and falls as they pass through M, and the width of that peak is, roughly speaking, the duration of S. Finally, their daughter cells arrive once more in M, forming a second peak, and the time between peaks indicates the total cycle duration. There will be subsequent waves, but variation in phase and cycle durations has a damping effect and for this reason, among others, only the first two peaks are normally observed. For a more precise description of the flm curve, see Macdonald (1970). Hartmann et al. (1975) compare different models and numerical methods for fitting flm curves to data and Guiguet et al. show the danger of fitting one of these models to data from a population with circadian rhythms.

The experimental procedure is a demanding one, as cells must be sampled and fixed for later counting every hour or two for at least 36 hours after the initial pulse. The counting cannot be automated, and involves examining thousands of cells on dozens of slides under a light microscope. There are also problems of interpretation. The main difficulty comes from cells that are synthesizing DNA at a slow rate, as they may or may not show up as labelled cells depending on the intensity of the radioactive label, the emulsion exposure time, the grain-count threshold used to distinguish labelled from unlabelled cells, and other experimental conditions (Shackney, 1974). This implies that S phase, as determined by thymidine labelling, is not well defined: the flm curve might be useful for measuring the average total cycle duration but the estimate of S phase duration that it gives may depend too much on the experimental conditions. In vivo systems present special problems, as the labelled thymidine may collect in thymidine pools after injection, to be utilized and re-utilized later, and a true "pulse" of label is impossible. Also, the successive time points on the curve will require either the sacrifice of replicate animals or serial biopsies. In section 5, however, it is seen that, among all the experimental methods considered, a set of flm curves started at different times of day is by far the most informative way to determine periodically-varying cell kinetic parameters.

The DNA distribution in a cell population was first available only through microdensitometry. In that technique, cells are stained with a DNA-specific dye and the amount of DNA in each cell is determined by measuring the absorption of a specific wavelength of light by individual nuclei seen under a light microscope. The procedure is tedious. Macdonald (1975) illustrates a statistical analysis of microdensitometry DNA histograms.

Completely automated DNA histograms can now be obtained by flow microfluorometry. The only limitation is that the cells must be prepared in a suspension. (This precludes most botanical tissues and opens the possibility of experimental artifacts in other tissues where the cells can be separated with difficulty.) The cells are stained with a DNA-specific fluorescent dye. A sample of the suspension, containing tens of thousands of cells, is then passed through an aperture wide enough for one cell and the fluorescence of individual cells is compiled into a histogram on an automatic recorder.

In principle, the DNA histogram obtained by either method will give the proportion of cells in G_1, S and G_2 plus M, since all G_1 cells will have the same DNA content, all G_2 and M cells will have double that amount, and S cells, which are in the process of duplicating each chromosome, will be somewhere in between. The true DNA distribution will thus consist of two discrete probabilities with a density in between, as shown in Fig. 1. The observed distribution, however, will incorporate variation in staining and measurement error, broadening the discrete peaks, and giving a distribution which is usually bimodal (Fig. 2D) but which may be unimodal or multi-modal in a perturbed population. The analysis of observed DNA histograms has become a hotly-

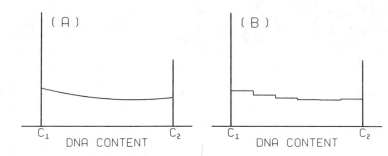

Fig. 1 The true distribution of nuclear DNA in a cell population. All G_1 cells have content c_1, all G_2 and M cells
have content c_2, and S cells are in between. The shape
of (A) is typical in steady-state populations. In (B)
the S-phase portion has been approximated by a density
uniform over intervals.

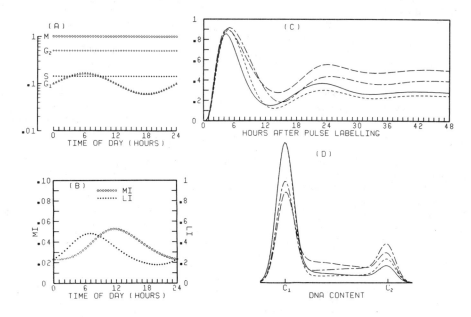

Fig. 2 Circadian variation in G_1 only (section 5.2)

(A) Total rates of passage through the four cytological phases.
(B) Mitotic index and labelling index. (C) Fraction labelled
mitoses curves obtained after pulse labelling at 0 hr. (———),
6 hr.(— — —), 12 hr.(—·—), 18 hr.(-----). (D) Observed DNA
distributions at 0 hr., 6 hr., 12 hr., 18 hr.; the solid and
dashed lines have the same meaning as in (C).

argued area of cell kinetics, especially when the population
structure or the DNA synthesis rates are not known a priori.
See Dean (1980) and White (1980) for recent work and references
to previous authors.

Flow microfluorometry is just one example of flow cytometry,
which has revolutionized cell kinetics in the last few years
(see Zietz and Nicolini (1978), for example), and flow systems
are now available which can measure DNA and RNA simultaneously,
and even physically sort the cells according to their DNA contents. In this paper, it will be enough to examine the effect
of circadian variation on the DNA distribution. Møller and
Larsen (1978) have analyzed DNA distributions from tissues with
circadian variation.

3. MODELS FOR CELL KINETICS WITH CIRCADIAN RHYTHMS

3.1 The age-dependent branching process with time-varying kinetics

The following results are summarized from Macdonald (1978).
As noted there, other authors have found similar results for the
general time-varying case but no-one has yet succeeded in speci-
alizing them to periodically-varying kinetics, except as described in Section 3.2.

Let $\phi(u|t)$ be the probability density function, $\Phi(u|t)$ the
cumulative distribution function, for cycle duration of a cell
born at time t. Let $\alpha(t)$ be the mean number of proliferative
daughter cells to remain in the population after a mitosis at
time t. In the time-invariant case $\phi(u|t) = \phi(u), \alpha(t) = \alpha$, and
the following results are well known. The population will
approach a steady state of exponential growth, provided that
$\alpha > 1$. The Malthusian parameter k, which is the asymptotic
average rate of production of additional cells by mitosis, per
cell in the population, per unit time, is the positive real
solution of

$$\alpha \int_O^\infty e^{-ku} \phi(u) \, du = 1 \qquad (3.1.1)$$

and the asymptotic age distribution is

$$g(u) = \{\alpha/(\alpha-1)\} \, ke^{-ku} \{1 - \Phi(u)\}. \qquad (3.1.2)$$

With time-varying kinetics, the Malthusian parameter is no
longer a constant but is a time-varying function k(t) which

satisfies the integral equation

$$\alpha(t) \int_0^\infty \frac{\alpha(t-u)/\{\alpha(t-u) - 1\}}{\alpha(t)/\{\alpha(t) - 1\}} \frac{k(t-u)}{k(t)} e^{-\int_{t-u}^t k(x)dx} \phi(u|t-u)du = 1, \tag{3.1.3}$$

which is a generalization of (3.1.1). In principle, it should
be possible to find a function $k(\cdot)$ which satisfies a given
boundary condition, such as an initial age distribution. When
$\phi(u|t)$ and $\alpha(t)$ are periodic in t with the same period, it
should be possible to find a periodic solution to (3.1.3).
Once $k(\cdot)$ is known, the age distribution at time t is easily
shown to be

$$g(u|t) = \frac{\alpha(t-u)}{\alpha(t-u)-1} k(t-u) e^{-\int_{t-u}^t k(x)dx} \{1 - \phi(u|t-u)\}, \tag{3.1.4}$$

a generalization of (3.1.2). Furthermore, since $k(\cdot)$ does not
depend in any way on the phases within the cycle, the various
distributions of age-in-phase can be found using the same approach as in Macdonald (1973, 1978).

This approach is attractive because it generalizes the well-
known steady state of exponential growth. The asymptotic periodically varying Malthusian function $k(\cdot)$ will be a necessary con-
sequence of a given $\phi(u|t)$ and $\alpha(t)$. If a population can be
assumed to have the asymptotic periodically varying age and phase
structure, this structure can be deduced entirely in terms of
$\phi(u|t)$, $\alpha(t)$ and the distributions of phase duration.

A paper by Yakovlev et al. (1978) should also be cited here.
They considered the differences between flm curves initiated at
different times of day and concluded that they must be explained
in terms of time-varying kinetics and not just in terms of the
transient unstable behaviour of a perturbed population. The two
explanations do not appear to be as mutually exclusive as they
imply, however. It is the time-varying kinetics themselves
which keep the population in a continually perturbed state.
The asymptotic periodically varying structure results when the
cumulative effect of waves from many past periods approaches a
stable wave form.

3.2   Direct measurement of time-varying fluxes

By measuring directly the time-varying rate at which cells
are entering certain phases, it is possible to use age distributions of the form (3.1.4) without having to solve (3.1.3). Even
more important, it is not necessary to assume that an asymptotic
periodically varying age and phase structure applies, so such an
analysis will have a much wider validity. Examples are given by
Clausen et al. (1979), Hartmann et al. (1977), and Hartmann and
Møller (1978). The flux of cells into M at a given time can be

determined by observing the mitotic index before and after a
short period of exposure to colchicine, which arrests mitoses.
The increase in the mitotic index will indicate the number of
cells which entered mitoses during the interval. Similarly, the
flux of cells into S can be measured by double pulse labelling
in the presence of colchicine: cells which entered S during the
interval between the pulses will be labelled by the second pulse
only, assuming that the interval is too short for any cells to
enter and leave S during the interval. The colchicine ensures
that the total number of cells remains constant. In this manner
a detailed picture of the time-varying age distribution can be
built up.

3.3 The Klein and Valleron model

Kendall (1948) showed that an age-dependent branching process
can be approximated by a multitype Markov branching process
where each cell is required to traverse a series of "types",
thought of as a sequence of subphases, during its cycle. In
the simplest case of time-constant kinetics and a constant
average rate of passage through each subphase, the duration of
each subphase will be exponentially distributed and the combined
duration of a series of subphases will follow a gamma distribution with coefficient of variation equal to the reciprocal of
the square root of the number of subphases. Allowing the subphases to have different rate parameters increases the flexibi-
lity of the model but also complicates it by introducing more
parameters. Mendelsohn and Takahashi (1971) have used this
model extensively to interpret cell kinetics data, assuming that
each cytological phase of the cell cycle is divided into a number of subphases with rate parameters specific to the cytological phase. The difficulty with this model is that it may become
unwieldy if too many subphases are used (as will be required
when coefficients of variation are small). Furthermore, the
subphases have no biological meaning.

Klein and Valleron (1977) recognized that this model remained
theoretically and computationally tractable when the transition
rates (rates of passage through the subphases) are periodic
functions of time. Applications to cell kinetics with circadian
rhythms were further elaborated by Guiguet et al. (1978) and by
Klein and Guiguet (1978). Klein and Macdonald (1980) have
worked out in detail the asymptotic properties of the multitype
Markov branching process in a periodically-varying environment.
Certain of these results are summarized in section 4. Section
5 of this paper, in the spirit of Guiguet et al. (1978), uses
the Klein and Valleron model to simulate the results of different cell kinetics experiments under various assumptions about
the circadian rhythms, making use of the theoretical and computational results of Klein and Macdonald (1980).

3.4 The Hopper and Brockwell model

Hopper and Brockwell (1978a, 1978b) developed a "random walk" model for the cell cycle in discrete time. The cycle is modelled as a sequence of steps to maturity. In any time step a cell can either remain where it is or pass on to the next maturation level. This is just the Klein and Valleron model in discrete time, described by a system of matrix operations instead of by a system of differential equations, and results parallel to those of Klein and Macdonald (1980) have been found. Their model has been fitted to Møller's hamster cheek-pouch data, including time-varying mitotic index and labelling index curves, and fraction labelled mitoses curves initiated at different times of day.

3.5 Direct computer simulation models

This category includes computer simulation systems which keep direct track of individual cells in the population as it evolves according to prescribed laws. Tibaux and Firket (1978) describe such a system. By simulating circadian variation in various cell cycle parameters and adjusting them to the data they found a very convincing fit to the time-varying LI and MI curves of Izquierdo and Gibbs (1974).

4. APPLYING THE KLEIN AND VALLERON MODEL

4.1 Some general results

The experiments of section 2 are invariably applied to large populations. If several time points are required, independently replicated populations are sampled. Hence only the expected large-population age and phase structure is required for the analysis of these data. Klein and Macdonald (1980) give the asymptotic theory of the multitype Markov branching process but only the properties of $M(\tau, t)$, the matrix of conditional means, are required here. The matrix element $m_{ij}(\tau,t)$ is the expected number of type j individuals at time t, given that there was a single type i at time τ. $M(\tau,t)$ satisfies the boundary condition $M(\tau,\tau) = I$ and the equation

$$\partial M(\tau,t)/\partial t = M(\tau,t)\, A\,(t),\qquad\qquad (4.1.1)$$

where the elements of $A(t)$ are $a_{ij}(t) = a_i(t)\,\{L_{ij}(t) - \delta_{ij}\}$, $a_i(t)$ being the mean transition rate of a type i individual at time t and $L_{ij}(t)$ being the expected number of type-j offspring to ensue if it does then transform. When $A(t)$ is periodic with period T the solution to (4.1.1) can be written in the rather elegant form

$$M(\tau,t) = P_0^{-1}(\tau) \; e^{(t-\tau)R_0} \; P_0(t) \qquad (4.1.2)$$

where R_0 is a constant matrix defined by

$$e^{TR_0} = M(0,T) \qquad (4.1.3)$$

and $P_0(t)$ is a periodic matrix defined by

$$P_0(t) = e^{-tR_0} \; M(0,t). \qquad (4.1.4)$$

Because $P_0(t)$ is periodic, it is only necessary in principle to integrate (4.1.1) numerically from $M(0,0) = I$ to $M(0,T)$ in order to compute the general solution (4.1.2).

For computation, however, it is more convenient to assume, without loss of generality, that $0 \le \tau < T$ and to replace (4.1.2) by either

$$M(\tau,t) = M^{-1}(0,\tau) \; M^m(0,T) \; M(0,t \bmod T) \qquad (4.1.5)$$

or

$$M(\tau,t) = M(\tau,T) \; M^{m-1}(0,T) \; M(0,t \bmod T), \qquad (4.1.6)$$

where m is the number of complete periods in the interval $(0,t)$. While (4.1.6) has the disadvantage that $M(\tau,T)$ must be computed for various initial times τ, it avoids the problem with (4.1.5) that $M(0,\tau)$ will often be too ill-conditioned to invert unless τ is very close to 0. The ill conditioning is not surprising, in that $M^{-1}(0,\tau) \equiv M(\tau,0)$; matrix inversion is being used, in effect, to integrate (4.1.1) backwards in time and this cannot, in general, be done uniquely over a long time interval.

The asymptotic properties depend on the largest characteristic root $\rho > 0$ of $M(0,T)$ which will exist if $M(0,T)$ is primitive. Let $v_0(u_0)$ be the corresponding left (right) characteristic vector and define

$$v(t) = v_0 P_0(t), \qquad (4.1.7)$$

$$u(\tau) = P_0^{-1}(\tau) u_0. \qquad (4.1.8)$$

Then, by the Perron-Frobenius theory,

$$\lim_{n\to\infty} M^n(O,T)\ \rho^{-\dot n} = u_O v_O$$

and hence, for large t,

$$M(\tau,t)\ \rho^{-(t-\tau)/T} \sim u(\tau)\ v(t). \qquad (4.1.9)$$

Also, it was shown that the vector of type proportions converges in probability to $v(t)/(v(t)1)$, where $1 = (1, \ldots, 1)'$. The easiest way to compute $v(t)$ is found by substituting (4.1.4) into (4.1.7) and noting that v_O is also a characteristic vector of e^{-tR_O}, giving

$$v(t) = \rho^{-t/T}\ v_O M(O,t). \qquad (4.1.10)$$

4.2 Application to cell kinetics

To specialize the multitype branching process to the Kendall (1948) multiphase cell cycle model with a total of k subphases, it is easily seen that $L(t)$ must have the form

$$L(t) = \begin{bmatrix} O & 1 & & & \\ & O & 1 & & \\ & & \ddots & & \\ & & & O & 1 \\ \alpha(t) & O & \cdots & O & O \end{bmatrix} \qquad (4.2.1)$$

where $\alpha(t)$ is the mean number of proliferative daughter cells to remain after a mitosis, as in section 3.1. Hence $A(t)$ has a very simple form. The ith row of $M(O,t)$, call it $y(t)$, is found by integrating the system

$$\dot y_1 = -y_1\ a_1(t) + y_k\ \alpha(t)\ a_k(t)$$

$$\dot y_j = y_{j-1}a_{j-1}(t) - y_j\ a_j(t) \quad (j=2,\ \ldots,\ k)\ (4.2.2)$$

from the initial condition $y_j(O) = \delta_{ij}$ $(j=1, \ldots, k)$. Similarly the ith row of $M(\tau,T)$, required in (4.1.6), is found by integrating (4.2.1) from the initial condition $y_j(\tau) = \delta_{ij}$ $(j=1, \ldots, k)$.

To model the conventional four phases G_1, S, G_2, M, let the first n_{G1} of the k "types" or subphases be the subphases of G_1, let the next n_S of them be the subphases of S, the next n_{G2} the subphases of G2, and the last n_M the subphases of M, so that $n_{G1} + n_S + n_{G2} + n_M = k$. The numbers of subphases will have to be selected for any given application. Next, let 1_M denote a column vector with 1's in the final n_M positions and 0's elsewhere. Similarly, let 1_S denote a column vector with 1's in positions $n_{G1} + 1$ to $n_{G1} + n_S$ and 0's elsewhere. When the population is in the asymptotic periodically varying state, the proportions of cells in the different subphases at time t will be given by $v(t)/(v(t)1)$. Hence the time-varying mitotic index and labelling index curves are given by

$$MI(t) = \frac{v(t) \, 1_M}{v(t) \, 1} \qquad (4.2.3)$$

and

$$LI(t) = \frac{v(t) \, 1_S}{v(t) \, 1} \qquad (4.2.4)$$

To derive the fraction labelled mitoses curve under asymptotic periodically varying kinetics, assume that the pulse labelling occurs at time τ. Since we only require expected numbers of cells, it will suffice to assume that $v(\tau)$ gives the initial number of cells in each subphase. The pulse will label the/ cells that are initially in S. Hence the initial number of labelled cells in each subphase is given by $v^*(\tau)$, which is defined by

$$v_i^* (\tau) = \begin{cases} v_i(\tau) & (i = n_{G1} + 1, \ldots, n_S), \\ 0 & \text{otherwise.} \end{cases} \qquad (4.2.5)$$

At a later time t, the expected total number of mitotic cells will equal $v(\tau) \, M(\tau,t) \, 1_M = \rho^{(t-\tau)/T} \, v(t) \, 1_M$ and the expected total number of labelled mitotic cells will equal $v^*(\tau) \, M(\tau,t) \, 1_M$. Hence

$$flm(t|\tau) = \frac{v^*(\tau) \, M(\tau,t) \, 1_M}{\rho^{(t-\tau)/T} \, v(t) \, 1_M}. \qquad (4.2.6)$$

The actual DNA distribution at time t, as shown in Fig. 1, assuming that the population is in the asymptotic periodically varying state, has probability $(v(t)\, l_{G1})/(v(t)\, 1)$ at the G_1 DNA content and probability $(v(t)\, l_{G2+M})/(v(t)\, 1)$ at the G_2 + M DNA content, where l_{G1} and l_{G2+M} are defined similarly to l_S and l_M. Following White (1980), I have assumed that each subphase of S corresponds to a constant increment in DNA content, so the probability density for S-phase DNA content is obtained by dividing the interval between the G_1 and the G_2+M levels into n_S equal parts. The distribution within each interval is then taken to be uniform, an approximation which will be adequate when n_S is large. The proportion of all cells in the populating having DNA content in the ith S-phase interval is just $v_{n_{G1}+i}(t)/(v(t)\, 1)$, $i = 1, \ldots, n_S$. The resulting distribution of DNA content will have the appearance of Fig. 1B.

To derive the observed DNA distribution at time t, I have chosen the simplest assumption, that the observed DNA content of a cell is normally distributed about the true DNA content with a standard deviation σ which does not depend on DNA content. This assumption allows the convolution of a normal density with a uniform density to be expressed as a difference of two normal cumulative distribution functions. Thus, if c_1 denotes the true G_1 DNA content and c_2 denotes the true G_2 + M DNA content, and if P(z) denotes the standard normal probability integral, the following expression is the probability density for the observed DNA distribution at time t:

$$\beta(x\,|\,t) = \frac{v(t)\, l_{G1}}{v(t)\, 1}\; \frac{1}{\sqrt{(2\pi)}\,\sigma}\; e^{-\frac{1}{2}\left(\frac{x-c_1}{\sigma}\right)^2}$$

$$+ \sum_{i=1}^{n_S} \frac{n_S}{c_2 - c_1}\; \frac{v_{n_{G1}+i}(t)}{v(t)\, 1}\; \left\{ P\left(\frac{b_i - x}{\sigma}\right) - P\left(\frac{b_{i-1} - x}{\sigma}\right) \right\}$$

$$+ \frac{v(t)\, l_{G2 + M}}{v(t)\, 1}\; \frac{1}{\sqrt{(2\pi)}\,\sigma}\; e^{-\frac{1}{2}\left(\frac{x-c_2}{\sigma}\right)^2}, \qquad (4.2.7)$$

where $b_i = c_1 + \dfrac{i}{n_S}(c_2 - c_1)$ is the right end-point of the ith S-phase interval, $i=1, \ldots, n_S$. The examples in section 5 assume

$\sigma = 0.08 (c_2 - c_1)$ to give realistic-looking distributions. Because n_S and σ are both sufficiently large, the central part of the density appears smooth despite the approximation of the true DNA distribution in S phase by a distribution uniform over intervals.

4.3 Parameterizing the time-varying transition rates and fitting the model to data

Following all authors since Kendall (1948) who have used the multiphase Markov model of the cell cycle, I have assumed that one transition rate function applies to each subphase of G_1, another applies to each subphase of S, and so on, so that four periodic rate functions must be specified. In addition, of course, it will be necessary to specify the numbers of subphases n_{G1}, n_S, n_{G2}, n_M and the daughter factor $\alpha(t)$.

Hopper and Brockwell (1978a) specified the time-varying rates in discrete 1-hour steps over the 24-hour period. This is clearly unsatisfactory for routine application, as it introduces 24 parameters to be estimated for each periodic rate function. Their fitting involved some trial and error.

Guiguet et al. (1978) used periodic rates of the form $b_0 + b_1 \sin(2\pi t/T)$. This is useful for simulating examples, but is not convenient for fitting to data because the shape is not flexible enough and because negative rates are possible with inappropriate choices of b_0 and b_1.

The examples in section 5 use rate functions of the form

$$a(t) = \exp \left\{ \psi_0 + \sum_{n=1}^{r} \psi_n \sin \left(2n\pi \frac{t-\theta_n}{T} \right) \right\}. \qquad (4.3.1)$$

Use of a Fourier series allows moderately complicated functions to be expressed with as few as 5 or 7 parameters, while the exponential avoids negative rates. For small b_1, (4.3.1) will approximate the rate function used by Guiguet et al. if we take $r=1$, $\psi_0 = \ln b_0$, $\psi_1 = b_1/b_0$ and $\theta_1 = 0$. However, even with $r=5$, for a total of 11 parameters per rate function, (4.3.1) is not able to reproduce the abruptly-changing rates used by Hopper and Brockwell (1978a).

At this stage, it does not appear that the Klein and Valleron model is suitable for routine fitting to data. The best that can be done is to choose in advance the number of sub-phases and the number of terms in the Fourier series of (4.3.1), and to assume that some of the cytological phases G_1, S, G_2 and M have constant rather than periodic rates of passage. Even then, there remain at least 20 parameters to be adjusted and that will require an inordinate amount of calculation when using direct-search optimization. Klein and Valleron (1977) suggest an alternative scheme, based on gradients, to estimate the rate functions from experimental LI and MI curves, but the practical computational details remain to be worked out.

The critical step for efficient computation of the model is the numerical integration of (4.2.2). The system is not stiff, and should not pose any numerical difficulties. When enough memory is available in the computer the amount of numerical integration can be reduced by storing arrays $M(0,t)$ for various values of t, $0 < t < T$. This was used for the example in section 5 but was only feasible there because the number of subphases was restricted to 16.

5. SOME EXAMPLES

5.1 *The choice of examples*

The first five cases are designed to show how circadian rhythms in different phases of the cell cycle will show up in different cell kinetics experiments. The theoretical curves were computed by the Klein and Valleron model, as explained in sections 4.2 and 4.3. The rate functions were kept as simple as possible, to facilitate interpretation of the results. To be compatible with a similar study by Guiguet et al. (1978), I have chosen $n_{G1} = n_S = n_{G2} = n_M = 4$, for a total of $k = 16$ subphases, and $\alpha(t) = 2$. The rate function (4.3.1) for each subphase of cytological phase $\nu \in \{G_1, S, G_2, M\}$ is computed as

$$a_i(t) = \frac{n_\nu}{\mu_\nu} \exp\{\psi_\nu \sin(2\pi t/T)\}, \qquad (5.1.1)$$

where i indexes a subphase of cytological phase ν, $T = 24$ hours, and $\psi_\nu = 0.5$ or $\psi_\nu = 0$ according to whether phase ν does, or does not, have circadian variation. Choosing $\psi_\nu = 0.25$ would make the simulations more nearly compatible with those of Guiguet et al. (1978) but the larger amplitude implied by $\psi_\nu = 0.5$ makes the periodic effects easier to see. When there is no periodic variation, μ_ν is just the expected transit time for phase ν and the choices $\mu_{G1} = 10$, $\mu_S = 7$, $\mu_{G2} = 2$, $\mu_M = 1$, for a total average cycle duration (in the absence of circadian rhythms) of 20 hours, are the same as have been used by Guiguet et al. (1978), Hartmann et al. (1975), and Mendelsohn and Takahashi (1971).

The sixth case illustrates more complicated rate functions, obtained by fitting (4.3.1) to the rate functions that Hopper and Brockwell (1978a, 1978b) got by fitting their model to experimental data.

5.2 Variation in G_1 only

The results are shown in Fig. 2. The rate of transit into S is greatest around 6 hours (Fig. 2A). This causes a peak in the labelling index around 6.5 hours which reappears as a peak in the mitotic index about $\frac{1}{2}\mu_S + \mu_{G2} = 5.5$ hours later (Fig. 2B). Since a pulse of label will label more cells at around 6 hours than at any other time, the highest of the four fraction labelled mitoses curves in Fig. 2C is the one from the pulse at 6 hours.

The initial rise of the curve is relatively independent of the time of labelling, indicating that a reliable estimate of the (nonperiodic) mean G_2 duration is possible. Fig. 2D shows a relatively high proportion of cells in early S at 6 hours, moving to late S by 12 hours; by 18 hours the fraction in S is low again.

5.3 Variation in all phases

This example (Fig. 3) is artificial in that the periodic variations are matched in amplitude and phase, so that just as the flow of cells into S, say, increases, it is matched by a corresponding increased flow out of S and the fraction in S remains the same. Only the flm curve (Fig. 3C) gives any evidence of circadian variation. It does so because it records the transient behaviour of a partially synchronized group of cells, those that were in S when the pulse was given. When the transient behaviour dies out, the differences disappear.

The flm curves can give a rough direct estimate of the time-varying rate of passage through G_2, in the following way. The usual graphical estimate of mean G_2 duration in the time-constant case is the delay between the pulse and the flm curve first reaching 50%. Each time of labelling will give a different estimate of "mean G_2" in the periodic case, but it can be verified empirically that the reciprocal of this "mean G_2" is close to the total rate of passage through G_2 (that is, n_{G2}^{-1} times the

rate of passage through a subphase, here given by (5.1.1) that
was in effect at the time of labelling.

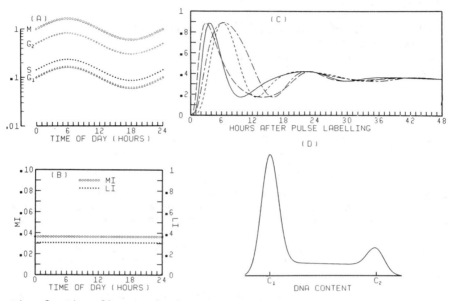

Fig. 3   Circadian variation in all cytological phases with
         matched phase and amplitude (section 5.3).
(A) Total rates of passage through the four cytological phases.
(B) Mitotic index and labelling index. (C) Fraction labelled
mitoses curves obtained after pulse labelling at O hr. (——),
6 hr. (— — —), 12 hr. (— - —), 18 hr. (-----). (D) Observed
DNA distributions at O hr., 6 hr., 12 hr., 18 hr.; the solid
and dashed lines have the same meaning as in (C).

5.4   Variation in G_1 and S only

Fig. 4 shows the case where variation in G_1 and S has the
same amplitude and phase, so that changes in influx and efflux
are nearly balanced in S and the labelling index remains relatively constant. However, the varying efflux from S maintains
variation in the mitotic index (Fig. 4B) and in the proportion
of G_2 cells (Fig. 4D). The flm curves indicate that mean G_2
duration is constant (Fig. 4C).

Fig. 5 shows what happens when the rate of passage through
S is slowed down just at those times when the rate of passage
through G_1 is highest. This was done by inserting a phase shift
θ_S = 12 hr. in (5.1.1) when computing the rate of passage
through S. The result is virtually the same as that obtained
when periodic variation is in G_1 only. If there is any

indication that S is varying in this example, it is the variation in the widths of the first peaks of the flm curves. In
fact, in this case, the reciprocal of the width of the first
peak at the 50% level gives a rough direct estimate of the total
rate of passage through S at the time of labelling.

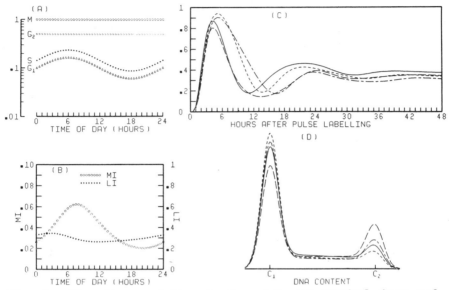

Fig. 4. Circadian variation in G_1 and S with matched phase and
        amplitude (section 5.4).
(A) Total rates of passage through the four cytological phases.
(B) Mitotic index and labelling index. (C) Fraction labelled
mitoses curves obtained after pulse labelling at O hr. (———),
6 hr. (— — —), 12 hr. (— - —), 18 hr. (-----). (D) Observed
DNA distributions at O hr., 6 hr., 12 hr., 18 hr.; the solid and
dashed lines have the same meaning as in (C).

5.5 Variation in G_2 only

Periodic variation in G_2 induces variation in the mitotic
index (Fig. 6B) but that variation is damped out by random variation in the durations of M and G_1, with the result that the
labelling index is nearly constant. The S-phase portion of the
DNA histogram is relatively constant (Fig. 6D), as is the width
of the first peak of the flm curves (Fig. 6C). The delay
between the pulse and the first peak varies more or less according to the rate of passage through G_2 at the time of labelling.

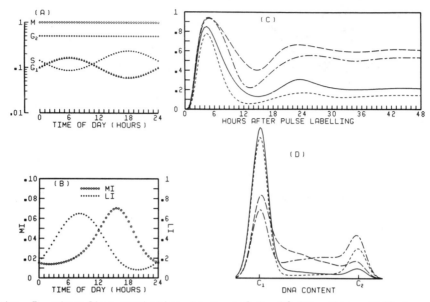

Fig. 5   Circadian variation in G_1 and S, 12 hr. phase difference
(section 5.4).
(A) Total rates of passage through the four cytological phases.
(B) Mitotic index and labelling index. (C) Fraction labelled
mitoses curves obtained after pulse labelling at 0 hr. (————),
6 hr. (— — —), 12 hr. (— - —), 18 hr. (-----). (D) Observed
DNA distributions at 0 hr., 6 hr., 12 hr., 18 hr.; the solid and
dashed lines have the same meaning as in (C).

5.6   Hopper and Brockwell's example

The Fourier series in the exponent of (4.3.1) was fitted to
the logarithm of the rate functions published by Hopper and
Brockwell (1978a) (Fig. 7A). The results will not be entirely
comparable as the present simulation uses $n_{G1} = n_S = n_{G2} = n_M = 4$
whereas Hopper and Brockwell used $n_{G1} = 5$, $n_S = 88$ and assumed
that G_2 and M have no random variation. One consequence is that
the double peak in their mitotic index curve is here lost in the
random variation (Fig. 7B). Because of the very long G_1, the
flm curves (Fig. 7C) do not reach second peaks. The widths of
the first peaks are comparable to those obtained by Hopper and
Brockwell. As in section 5.4, the reciprocal of peak width
gives, at least roughly, the rate of passage through S at the
time of labelling. Hence a possible explanation for why Hopper
and Brockwell (1978a) were unable to fit the experimental flm
curves satisfactorily is that there is not, in fact, any circadian variation in S. It should be noted that Hopper and

Brockwell also adjusted their fit for a shortening of G_2 induced by the injection of tritiated thymidine. This will only serve to reduce the delay until the first rise by about 1 or 2 hours, however, and will not substantially change the preceeding argument, which is based on peak width. It would be worthwhile to re-analyze Møller's data, possibly fitting the labelling and mitotic indices and the flm curves simultaneously and allowing for the shortening of the initial G_2.

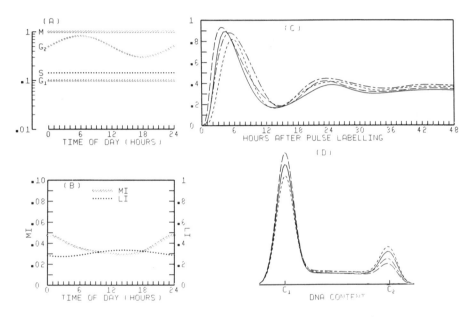

Fig. 6 Circadian variation in G_2 only (section 5.5).

(A) Total rates of passage through the four cytological phases. (B) Mitotic index and labelling index. (C) Fraction labelled mitoses curves obtained after pulse labelling at 0 hr. (———), 6 hr. (— — —), 12 hr. (— - —), 18 hr. (-----). (D) Observed DNA distributions at 0 hr., 6 hr., 12 hr., 18 hr.; the solid and dashed lines have the same meaning as in (C).

6. CONCLUSIONS

There is adequate theory available to study time-varying and periodic cell kinetics in cases where the flow of cells through the cycle can be measured directly. In other cases, the asymptotic periodically varying age and phase structure might be assumed, but it is knownexplicitly only for discrete-time and continuous-time multiphase (or multicompartment) Markov branching processes and these appear to be too unwieldy for routine fitting to data.

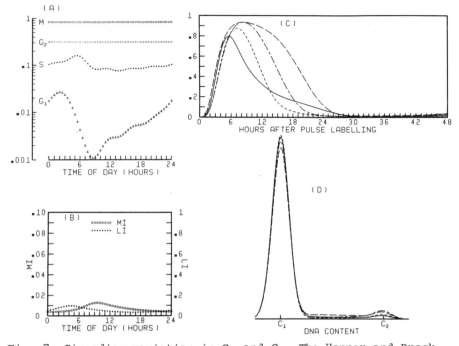

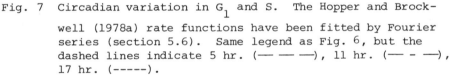

Fig. 7   Circadian variation in G_1 and S. The Hopper and Brockwell (1978a) rate functions have been fitted by Fourier
series (section 5.6). Same legend as Fig. 6, but the
dashed lines indicate 5 hr. (— — —), 11 hr. (— · —),
17 hr. (-----).

The multiphase Markov branching process is convenient for
simulating examples, nonetheless. The examples given indicate
that labelling index and mitotic index are not really informative about circadian variation in the cell cycle. The phase
fractions from the DNA histogram cannot tell the entire story
either. By far the most informative experiment is a set of
fraction labelled mitoses curves initiated at different times of
day, because the initial, transient behaviour of the labelled
cells is indicative of the cell kinetics at the time of
labelling.

7.   ACKNOWLEDGEMENTS

    I thank N.R. Hartmann and N. Keiding for very helpful dis-
cussions during the preparation of this work, and M.B. Pyshnov
for help with translation from Russian. This research is
supported by the Natural Sciences and Engineering Research
Council, Canada.

8. REFERENCES

Brown, J.M. and Berry, R.J. (1968) The relationships between diurnal variation of the number of cells in mitosis and of the number of cells synthesizing DNA in the epithelium of the hamster cheek pouch, *Cell Tissue Kinet.*, **1**, pp. 23-33.

Bullough, W.S. (1948) Mitotic activity in the adult male mouse, Mus musculus L., The diurnal cycles and their relation to waking and sleeping, *Proc. R. Soc.* **B135**, pp. 212-242.

Bullough, W.S. (1952) Stress and epidermal mitotic activity, I, The effects of the adrenal hormones, *J. Endocr.* **8**, pp. 265-274.

Clausen, O.P.F., Thorud, E., Bjerkness, R., and Elgjo, K. (1979) Circadian rhythms in mouse epidermal basal cell proliferation, Variations in compartment size, flux and phase duration, *Cell Tissue Kinet.*, **12**, pp. 319-337.

Dean, P.N. (1980) A simplified method of DNA distribution analysis, *Cell Tissue Kinet.*, **13**, pp. 299-308.

Droogleever Fortuyn-Van Leijden, C.E. (1917) Some observations on periodic nuclear division in the cat, *Proc. K. Ned. Acad. Wet.* **19**, pp. 38-44.

Guiguet, M., Klein, B. and Valleron, A-J. (1978) Diurnal variation and the analysis of percent labelled mitoses curves, *In* "Biomathematics and Cell Kinetics", (A-J. Valleron and P.D.M. Macdonald eds), North-Holland, Amsterdam, pp. 191-198.

Halberg, F., Haus, E. and Scheving, L.E. (1978) Sampling of biologic rhythms, chronocytokinetics and experimental oncology, *In* "Biomathematics and Cell Kinetics", (A-J. Valleron and P.D.M. Macdonald eds), North-Holland, Amsterdam, pp. 175-190.

Harris, T.E. (1963) The Theory of Branching Processes, Springer-Verlag, Berlin.

Hartmann, N.R., Gilbert, C.W., Jansson, B., Macdonald, P.D.M., Steel, G.G., and Valleron, A-J. (1975) A comparison of computer methods for the analysis of fraction labelled mitoses curves, *Cell Tissue Kinet.*, **8**, pp. 119-124.

Hartmann, N.R., Møller, U. and Lebeda, J. (1977) Analysis of cell kinetic data on the basis of mathematical models, *In* "Growth Kinetics and Biochemical Regulation of Normal and Malignant Cells", (B. Drewinko and R.M. Humphrey eds), Williams and Wilkins, Baltimore, pp. 471-480.

Hartmann, N.R. and Møller, U. (1978) A compartment theory in the cell kinetics including considerations on circadian variations, *In* "Biomathematics and Cell Kinetics", (A-J. Valleron and P.D.M. Macdonald eds), North-Holland, Amsterdam, pp. 223-251.

Hopper, J.L. and Brockwell, P.J. (1978a) A stochastic model for cell populations with circadian rhythms, *Cell Tissue Kinet* 11, pp. 205-225.

Hopper, J.L. and Brockwell, P.J. (1978b) Analysis of data from cell populations with circadian rhythm, *In* "Biomathematics and Cell Kinetics", (A-J. Valleron and P.D.M. Macdonald eds), North-Holland, Amsterdam, pp. 211-221.

Izquierdo, J.N. and Gibbs, S.J. (1972) Circadian rhythms of DNA synthesis and mitotic activity in hamster cheek pouch epithelium, *Exp. Cell Res.* 71, pp. 402-408.

Izquierdo, J.N. and Gibbs, S.J. (1974) Turnover of cell-renewing populations undergoing circadian rhythms in cell proliferation, *Cell Tissue Kinet.*, 7, pp. 99-111.

Jagers, P. (1975) Branching Processes with Biological Applications, Wiley, London.

Kendall, D.G. (1948) On the role of variable generation time in the development of a stochastic birth process, *Biometrika* 35, pp. 316-330.

Klein, B. and Guiguet, M. (1978) Relative importance of the phases of the cell cycle for explaining diurnal rhythms in cell proliferation in the tissues with a long G_1 duration, *In* "Biomathematics and Cell Kinetics", (A-J. Valleron and P.D.M. Macdonald eds), North-Holland, Amsterdam, pp. 199-210.

Klein, B. and Macdonald, P.D.M. (1980) The multitype continuous-time Markov branching process in a periodic environment, *Adv. Appl. Prob.* 12, pp. 81-93.

Klein, B. and Valleron, A-J. (1977) A compartmental model for the study of diurnal rhythms in cell proliferation, *J. Theoret. Biol.* 64, pp. 27-42.

Klein, R.M. (1980) Analysis of intestinal cell proliferation after guanethidine-induced sympathectomy, III, Effects of chemical sympathectomy on circadian variation in mitotic activity, *Cell Tissue Kinet.*, 13, pp. 153-162.

Macdonald, P.D.M. (1970) Statistical inference from the fraction labelled mitoses curve, *Biometrika* 57, pp. 489-503.

Macdonald, P.D.M. (1973) On the statistics of cell proliferation, *In* "The Mathematical Theory of the Dynamics of Biological Populations", (M.S. Bartlett and R.W. Hiorns eds), Academic Press, London, pp. 303-314.

Macdonald, P.D.M. (1975) The distribution of DNA in exponentially growing cell populations, *In* "Perspectives in Probability and Statistics: apers in Honour of M.S. Bartlett on the Occasion of his Sixtyfifth Birthday" (J. Gani, ed.), Academic Press, London, pp. 387-401.

Macdonald, P.D.M. (1978) Age distributions in the general cell kinetic model, *In* "Biomathematics and Cell Kinetics", (A-J. Valleron and P.D.M. Macdonald eds), North-Holland, Amsterdam, pp. 3-20.

Mendelsohn, M.L. and Takahashi, M. (1971) A critical evaluation of the fraction of labelled mitoses method as applied to the analysis of tumor and other cell cycles, *In* "The Cell Cycle and Cancer", (R. Baserga ed.), Marcel Dekker, New York, pp. 55-95.

Møller, U., Larsen, J.K. and Faber, M. (1974) The influence of injected tritiated thymidine on the mitotic circadian rhythm in the epithelium of the hamster cheek pouch, *Cell Tissue Kinet.*, **7**, pp. 231-239.

Møller, U. and Larsen, J.K. (1978) The circadian variations in the epithelial growth of the hamster cheek pouch: quantitative analysis of DNA distributions, *Cell Tissue Kinet.*, **11**, pp. 405-413.

Pilgrim, C., Erb, W. and Maurer, W. (1963) Diurnal fluctuations in the numbers of DNA synthesizing nuclei in various mouse tissues, *Nature (Lond.)* **199**, p. 863.

Shackney, S. (1974) A cytokinetic model for heterogeneous mammalian cell populations, II, Tritiated thymidine studies: the per cent labelled mitoses (PLM) curve, *J. Theoret. Biol.* **44**, pp. 49-90.

Steel, G.G. (1977) Growth Kinetics of Tumours, Oxford, Oxford.

Tibaux, G. and Firket, H. (1978) Computer simulation model for cell kinetics in various conditions, *In* "Biomathematics and Cell Kinetics", (A-J. Valleron and P.D.M. Macdonald eds), North-Holland, Amsterdam, pp. 31-42.

Valleron, A-J. and Macdonald, P.D.M. (eds) (1978) Biomathematics and Cell Kinetics, North-Holland, Amsterdam.

White, R.A. (1980) A theory for the estimation of DNA synthesis rates by flow cytometry, *J. Theoret. Biol.* **85**, pp. 53-73.

Yakovlev, A.Y., Lepekhin, A.F. and Malinin, A.M. (1978) The labelled mitoses curve in different states of cell proliferation kinetics, V, The influence of diurnal rhythm of cell proliferation on the shape of the labelled mitoses curve, *Cytologia* **6**, pp. 630-635.

Zietz, S. and Nicolini, C. (1978) Flow microfluorometry and cell kinetics: a review, *In* "Biomathematics and Cell Kinetics" (A-J. Valleron and P.D.M. Macdonald eds), North-Holland, Amsterdam, pp. 357-394.

SOME PROBLEMS IN MODELLING CELLULAR GROWTH

P. Clifford

(University of Oxford, Oxford, England)

1. INTRODUCTION

Most cells growing under natural conditions are members of a community. The size of the community is controlled, either crudely by constraints on the supply of nutrient as with bacteria, or in more subtle ways which depend on intercellular communication within a complex organism as with mammalian cells. Even with the simplest cells the spatial organisation of the community plays an important role in the control process; cells in the centre of a proliferating mass are relatively deprived of nourishment and therefore divide slowly, if at all. In complex organisms spatial information determines the process of differentiation and the control of replication.

In order to grow cells in an environment in which they can be observed, it is necessary to break down these control mechanisms. If this can be done, cells divide rapidly and the population doubles in size at a constant rate. In its infancy the mathematical theory of branching processes was able to provide an explanation of this very tangible phenomenon. The theory has subsequently been generalised to accommodate every foreseeable development in the biological understanding of unconstrained population growth. Thus, in principle the multi-type process described by Arthreya and Ney (1970) could be used to model not only the detailed biochemistry of cellular growth and division of individual cells, but also the correlations between these growth processes in closely related cells. This state of affairs is not as satisfactory as it may seem. It is rather like saying that any observed temporal process can be adequately modelled by a Markov process, since the state space can be made large enough to accommodate all relevant aspects of history. Unfortunately, as the state space expands, our ability to understand the phenomenon decreases, and at the same time we encounter formidable problems of estimation, owing to the multiplicity of parameters involved and the attendant problems of identifiability. The establishment of a general framework is only the beginning of

the problem of modelling. The next stage is to provide an econo-
mical description of the phenomenon under study. The description
should incorporate a minimum of parameters as constituents of a
plausible mechanism for which there is some hope of validation
by direct or indirect observation. The purpose of this paper is
to see how far this programme of economisation has been carried
in the theory of branching processes, and to discuss alternative
methods in the light of new experimental techniques.

2. AGE-DEPENDENT AND COMPARTMENTAL MODELS

Under conditions of unconstrained growth, cells devote themselves wholeheartedly to the task of converting the nutrient
supply into the chemical components required for reproduction.
It is unrealistic to model the lifespan of a cell by an exponential distribution since the cell cannot divide until it has manu-
factured certain minimum quantities of the vital components, i.e.
until it is ready. It is tempting to let the age of the cell
stand as a proxy for its degree of development, arguing that the
older the cell is the more developed it is. Thus, although one
would wish to say that what determines when a cell will divide
is its physiological state, it may be expedient to make do with
its age. This leads to the age-dependent model of division.
The fallacy of this argument is brought out by what one might
call the Rip Van Winkle effect. Imagine that a bacterial population is frozen for a week. At the end of the week the cells are
thawed out and they continue to grow very much as if they had
not been frozen. However, each cell is over one week old. What
is preserved during the period of freezing is the physiological
state of each bacterium. Evidently, if means can be found to
measure this state, it will provide a more reliable predictor of
the future behaviour of the cell than the amount of time that
the cell has existed. Of course, freezing is just one example,
albeit an extreme one, of the kinds of environmental factors
which affect the association between age and the division process. It might be argued that the process is age-dependent under
particular fixed conditions but this would be a worthless model
since it would provide no prediction of the age-dependence under
different conditions.

It seems therefore that the state of the cell must be considered. But if we are to economise, we should perhaps restrict
the number of states. A familiar example of this is the 4-type
or 4-compartment model of the mammalian cell cycle. The 4 categories of cell are usually denoted by G_1, S, G_2 and M, where S
category cells are synthesising DNA, M category cells are visibly
dividing, and G_1 and G_2 category cells are at intermediate stages
of development, before and after DNA synthesis respectively.
The simplest model assumes that the times spent by each cell in

each of the 4 categories are independent and exponentially distributed. This model is a priori implausible but it does provide
an adequate fit of the observed proportions in the various categories at any fixed time. It will fail, however, to explain the
dynamic behaviour in a series of observations.

To provide a more realistic distribution for the time spent
in a particular category, the model may be expanded to split the
category into a number of sub-categories through which the cell
must pass successively, each taking an exponential time. The
objection to this would be that the existence of these sub-categories is not susceptible to scientific testing. They are merely
artefacts used to shape the distribution of the time spent in
the category. This approach is therefore equivalent to the more
straightforward one of allocating independent sojourn times to
each category. Such an "age" dependent model will evidently be
vulnerable to the Rip Van Winkle effect. Furthermore, certain
known phenomena such as correlations between lifetimes of closely
related cells would not be explained.

3. SIZE-DEPENDENT MODELS

Since the aim of model building is to explain certain observ-
ables and to make predictions about observations which are to be
made at some future time, it is important to bear in mind which
characteristics of a cell can be readily observed. In practice
it is extremely difficult to observe all the ages of a large
population of cells. Recent research has led to the development
of differential staining techniques for characterising the degree
of maturity of the cell. This is in addition to the use of
radioactively labelled compounds which can be used to determine
the number of cells capable of taking up the compound at any
particular time. For the future we can envisage that automated
analyses will yield, for each cell in a population, a vector of
observations providing information about the quantity of various
chemical components present in the cell. We shall refer to this
vector as the size of the cell. Denoting the value of this
vector at time t by $S(t)$, we shall assume that the probability
of division in the interval $(t, t+\tau)$, given that the cell has not
already divided, is given by $\lambda\{S(t)\}\tau + o(\tau)$, where $\lambda\{\cdot\}$ is a
positive function. Division at a fixed threshold is included as
a special case. Size will be assumed to change either deterministically or stochastically according to the equation

$$dS(t) = p\{S(t), A(t)\}dt + dB(t) \qquad (3.1)$$

where $A(t)$ represents environmental conditions, $B(t)$ is a process
of random fluctuations and $p\{\cdot, \cdot\}$ is a real valued function. An
immediate consequence of the introduction of size-dependence is
that cells no longer develop independently. That is, if (as

seems reasonable) size is conserved on division, each of the
daughters will receive a portion of the size of the mother.
Obviously, daughters of large mothers, i.e. mothers for whom all
the elements of S are large, will tend to be larger than
daughters of smaller mothers, thus introducing a positive correlation between the size of sisters. If a large size at birth
leads to rapid division and a small size leads to a protracted
division cycle then a negative correlation between the lifetimes
of mothers and daughters will be produced.

To see a concrete application of this type of argument, it is
necessary to turn to the bacterial literature. For bacteria the
simplest measurement is cell-volume. In 1932 Bayne-Jones and
Adolph suggested that the time of division was determined primarily by the volume of the organism. The hypothesis was first
made quantitative by Koch and Schaechter (1962) and has been
studied subsequently by Powell (1955, 1964), Bell and Anderson
(1967), Clifford and Sudbury (1972, 1973) and Grimmett (1980).
Bell and Anderson consider a very general case in which division
depends not only on volume, but also on age, and in which there
is the joint possibility of age and volume dependent death.
Their approach is to assume an infinite population model and thus
avoid the questions of stochastic convergence for populations
evolving from a finite number of individuals. Clifford and
Sudbury adopt a stochastic approach but do not allow for the
possibility of death. Their main concern is to obtain estimates
of the correlations between the lifespans of closely related
cells. Grimmett considers a special case of one of the models
discussed by Clifford and Sudbury in which size is incremented
by a Poisson process. He is able to show that when the function
λ is linear the process is equivalent to a 2-type process, thus
obtaining strong convergence results. The papers by Powell have
importance not only for their pioneering role but also in introducing a simplifying hypothesis: that the division volume must
lie in the range V to 2V. This restriction is apparently borne
out by some experimental evidence (Powell (1964) and Bell and
Anderson (1967)). Clifford (1977) exploited this hypothesis to
deduce strong convergence results for quite general growth rates
by identifying an underlying age-dependent structure which acts
as a skeleton for the size-dependent process.

A number of problems remain to be solved in this area. In
particular, complications are introduced by the length-biasing
of lifetimes in sampling from a population. This produces, in
consequence, a biasing of volumes which in turn leads to distor-
tions in the observed correlations between closely related cells.
It can be shown that, in some cases, the correlation between the
lifetimes of mothers and daughters which would be negative when
sampled by generation is transformed into a positive correlation
when the population is sampled contemporaneously. For mammalian

cells there is the further possibility of an association between cell-volume and the time at which the cell starts to synthesise DNA. This will introduce, in a very natural way, correlations between the times spent in G_1 and G_2, not only cell by cell, but also between mothers and daughters and between sisters.

The idea of using a single measure of size such as volume to characterise the stage of development of a cell whilst quite acceptable for bacteria seems less so for mammalian cells. Despite this there have been various attempts to apply the theory to mammalian cells. Bell and Anderson, for example, consider the volume distribution of murine fibroblasts, but this may well have been purely for illustrative purposes. For mammalian cells, however, it seems more reasonable to use two measures of size: the cytoplasmic volume and the nuclear volume. Although the volume of any part of the cell does not measure the quantity of any particular chemical, it does have the advantage of being relatively easy to obtain and may be determined by automated equipment. The next section contains a discussion of an example of the use of such measurements.

4. MEASURING THE PERCENTAGE OF GROWING CELLS

A fundamental problem in cell-biology is that of predicting whether or not a cell will live, using only those characteristics of the cell which are immediately observable. For example, both in cancer therapy and in immunosuppressive therapy following organ transplantation it is of vital interest to determine the viability of the white blood-cell population. Blood samples can be taken to provide a sample of the lymphocyte population but in its appearance there is nothing to distinguish a viable cell from a non-viable one. In normal blood most of the lymphocytes are in an inactive phase sometimes called the G_0 phase. To determine if they are viable it is necessary to stimulate them. If the stimulation is successful the cells will enter the usual division cycle. One possible way of determining the percentage of viable cells is to incubate them after stimulation in a medium containing radioactively labelled precursors of DNA. After a few days the number of labelled cells is then counted. The problem with this approach is that it is time consuming and in any case the assessment of viability is relative to cells cultured for a number of days rather than cells taken from fresh blood. The approach of Gibbs, Brown, Robertson and Swanson Beck (1979) is to measure the volume distribution of the cells 24 hours after stimulation and compare it with the volume distribution of unstimulated cells. They argue that there is good evidence that changes in volume are associated with the transition from G_0 to G_1, so that the method provides a quick way of estimating the percentage of viable cells. A similar approach is

that of Chandra, Chanana, Sipe and Cronkite (1978) who consider
instead the volume of the nucleus. Not suprisingly it takes
rather longer before changes in nuclear volume are apparent.
Before discussing their methods of estimating the proportion of
viable cells, it is as well to note that the definitions of viability are not the same. To determine the degree to which an
increase in cell-volume in G_1 is associated with a subsequent

increase in nuclear volume and the degree to which either of
these measures is associated with the ability to divide requires
a longitudinal study in which all these factors are recorded.
Since we do not have a quantitative assessment of these associations we shall take growth during G_1 as our endpoint and restrict

our comments to the statistical methods of Gibbs et al. These
authors note that the volume distribution of unstimulated cells
is unchanged over a 24 hour period. We shall assume throughout
that sample sizes are large enough that sampling fluctuations
can be ignored. Let us denote the probability density function
(p.d.f.) of this distribution by f_0. After stimulation a certain

proportion, π, of cells starts to increase in volume. Following
Gibbs et al.we shall assume that cells grow deterministically
and that to every value x of the volume after 24 hours there corresponds a unique starting volume $\phi(x)$. We denote the set of
positive functions with strictly positive derivatives by A.
Unlike Gibbs et al we do not assume a specific form for the
unknown function ϕ. Denoting the p.d.f. of the distribution of
volumes after 24 hours by f_1 we have

$$f_1 = (1-\pi)f_0 + \pi\phi' f_0(\phi) \qquad (4.1)$$

We shall say that f_1 is generated from f_0 by π and ϕ, and to
avoid trivial cases we assume that f_0 and f_1 are strictly positive. Since f_0 and f_1 are known, the problem is to estimate π
with the function ϕ as a nuisance parameter. Our concern will
be with the existence of other pairs π^*, ϕ^* such that

$$f_1 = (1-\pi^*)f_0 + \pi^*\phi^{*'} f_0(\phi^*) \qquad (4.2)$$

We shall call the set of values of π^* such that there exists a
$\phi^* \in A$ for which the equality (4.2) holds, the set of values
indistinguishable from π. Then, the following theorem holds.

Theorem

If f_1 is generated from f_0 by π and ϕ then the set of values indistinguishable from π is an interval of the form $(\pi_0, 1)$ where

$$\pi_0 = 1 - \min_x \frac{f_1(x)}{f_0(x)}$$

The consequence of this theorem is that the parameter π is non-identifiable without prior information about ϕ. Gibbs et al. assume a mathematically convenient form for ϕ, but from the theorem it follows that other slightly less convenient functions with differing values of π will fit the data equally well. As it stands, the experiment does not provide a great deal of information about π. However, if the cells in the initial population are sorted by size into two even crudely differing subpopulations the ambiguity is removed. This proposal raises a number of interesting problems which will be investigated elsewhere.

Proof of Theorem

First note that $\pi^*=1$, $\phi^*=F_1^{-1}(F_0)$ is always in the indistinguishable set, where F_i is the distribution function corresponding to f_i, $i=0,1$. Now consider equations (4.1) and (4.2) together so that

$$(1-\pi)f_0 + \pi\phi' f_0(\phi) = (1-\pi^*)f_0 + \pi^*\phi^{*'} f_0(\phi^*) \qquad (4.3)$$

or

$$(1-\pi)F_0 + \pi F_0(\phi) = (1-\pi^*)F_0 + \pi^*F_0(\phi^*) \qquad (4.4)$$

or

$$\left(1 - \frac{\pi}{\pi^*}\right)F_0 + \frac{\pi}{\pi^*}F_0(\phi) = F_0(\phi^*) \qquad (4.5)$$

Since the left-hand side of (4.5) has a positive derivative for $\pi^* \geq \pi$, it follows that the solution for ϕ^* is in A. There remains the problem of determining the minimum value of π^* for a given f_0 and f_1. Returning to (4.2) we have

$$F_1 = (1-\pi^*)F_0 + \pi^*F_0(\phi^*). \qquad (4.6)$$

But in order for this equation to have a solution for ϕ^*, which is in A, it is necessary and sufficient that

$$f_1(x) - (1-\pi^*)f_0(x) > 0 \text{ for all } x, \text{ or } \pi^* \geq 1 - \min_x \frac{f_1(x)}{f_0(x)} \text{ , which}$$

concludes the proof.

5. CONCLUSIONS

Size-dependence has been shown to provide a natural framework for the description of unconstrained cell growth. It seems likely that it plays an even greater role when growth is controlled and that advances in biology in this area will reveal a variety of intriguing mathematical problems.

6. REFERENCES

Athreya, K.B. and Ney, P.E. (1970) Branching processes, Berlin: Springer.

Bayne-Jones, A. and Adolph, E.F. (1932) Growth in size of microorganisms measured from motion pictures III, Bacterium Coli., *J. Cell. Physiol.*, **2**, pp. 329-348.

Bell, G.I. and Anderson, G.I. (1967) Cell growth and division I, *Biophys. J.*, **7**, pp. 329-351.

Chandra, P., Chanana, A.D., Sipe, C.R. and Cronkite, E.P. (1978) Proliferation of human lymphocytes in culture, *Nouv. Rev. Franc. Hem.*, **20**, pp. 545-555.

Clifford, P. (1977) On the age structure of the cell-size-dependent branching process, Trans. Seventh Prague Conf. on Information Theory and Statistical Decision Functions, pp. 97-101.

Clifford, P. and Sudbury, A.W. (1972) The linear cell-size-dependent branching process, *J. Appl. Prob.*, **9**, pp. 687-696.

Gibbs, J.H., Brown, R.A., Robertson, A.J., Potts, R.C. and Swanson Beck, J. (1979) A new method of testing mitogen-induced lymphocyte stimulation, *J. Immun. Meth.*, **25**, pp. 147-158.

Grimmett, G.R. (1980) A linear cell-size-dependent branching process, *Stoch. Proc. and their Appl.*, **10**, pp. 105-113.

Koch, A.L. and Schaechter, M. (1962) A model for statistics of the cell division process, *J. Gen. Microbiol.*, **29**, pp. 435-454.

Powell, E.O. (1955) Some features of the generation times of individual bacteria, *Biometrika*, **42**, pp. 16-44.

Powell, E.O. (1964) A note on Koch's and Schaechter's hypothesis about growth and fission of bacteria, *J. Gen. Microbiol.*, **37**, pp. 231-249.

Sudbury, A.W. and Clifford, P. (1973) Some results for the general cell-size-dependent branching process, *J. Appl. Prob.*, **10**, pp. 289-298.

AUTHOR INDEX

The numbers underlined refer to the Reference pages where the references are listed in full.